DOWN
THE ROAD

DOWN THE ROAD

Genuine Mileage on Classic Motorcycles

Steve Wilson

Drawings by Nicholas Ward

Haynes Publishing

Text © Steve Wilson 2000
Illustrations © Nicholas Ward 2000

Steve Wilson has asserted his right to be
identified as the author of this work.

First published September 2000

A catalogue record for this book is available from the British Library

ISBN 1 85960 651 2

Published by Haynes Publishing,
Sparkford, Nr Yeovil, Somerset BA22 7JJ, UK

Tel: 01963 442030 Fax: 01963 440001
Int. tel: + 44 1963 442030 Fax: + 44 1963 440001
E-mail: sales@haynes-manuals.co.uk
Web site: www.haynes.co.uk

Library of Congress catalog card no. 00-131900

Haynes North America, Inc.
861 Lawrence Drive, Newbury Park, California 91320, USA

Designed and typeset by G&M, Raunds, Northamptonshire
Printed and bound in Great Britain by J.H. Haynes & Co. Ltd., Sparkford

Contents

Dedication

I should like to dedicate this book to my editor at *Classic Bike Guide*, Frank Westworth, a large character in every sense. Frank was generous enough to give my words completely free rein in the magazine (or enough rope for me to hang myself) – no dictating of subject matter, and no cutting, for length or any other reason. For a writer, this freedom has been a gift beyond price.

Also, once again, more thanks than I can express to my wife Molly, without whose patience and techno-wizardry the book would never have been delivered on time and in good order.

And finally, to Nick Ward, my very talented colleague who has also become a good friend.

Acknowledgements

The majority of the articles which, in edited form, make up the bulk of this book appeared in *Classic Bike Guide* between 1990 and 1999. The exceptions are: Chapter 2, Conan Doyle, which first appeared in *British Bike Mechanics* issue 6 in March 1988; Chapter 2, Hugh Leach, which appeared in *The Classic Motor Cycle* volume 26, number 5, in May 1999; Chapter 4, Harry the Wheel, which appeared in *Silver Machine* issue 1 in May 1989; and Chapter 6, Made in Plumstead, which first appeared in *Motor Cycle Sport* volume 30, number 4, in May 1989.

I should like to sincerely thank the real subjects of these articles – the many individuals who freely gave up hours of their time to share their stories and memories with me. It has been a privilege to know them.

A short glossary

AMC   Associated Motor Cycles, based in Plumstead and
                   incorporating AJS, Matchless, Francis-Barnett, James, and
                   eventually Norton.
BSA   Birmingham Small Arms.
CBG   *Classic Bike Guide* magazine.
cc   Cubic centimetres.
dohc   Double overhead camshaft.
desert sled   Versions of motorcycles designed primarily for use in US
                   desert racing.
ISDT   International Six Days Trial.
MCN   *Motor Cycle News*, weekly motorbike paper.
MCS   *Motor Cycle Sport* magazine.
NVT   Norton Villiers Triumph.
ohv   Overhead valve.
pre-unit   Engine with separate gearbox.
SLS   Single leading shoe.
TLS   Twin leading shoe.
unit   Engine and gearbox manufactured as a single unit.
VMCC   Vintage Motor Cycle Club.
WD   War Department.

Introduction

There is one real question which people who ride old motorcycles are sometimes asked by others, and which they not infrequently ask themselves: Why?

There was once a man who called himself Mavis. Mavis of Stoke Newington. Back in the 1970s, Mavis wrote a letter to *Bike* magazine describing a disastrous trip to the seaside with a girlfriend, aboard his asthmatic Triumph-engined 650 twin. ('The breather has laid a fine oil mist on the right buttock of the lady's jeans. Decide not to tell her.') At the end of a difficult day, he wrote: 'The tragic truth has begun to dawn in a skull numbed by vibration, frustration, smoke and dirt and expense. It's a vicious circle: the beasts damage your brain, and in the end you get too stupid to ride anything else.'

Well, yes. It's a point of view, one from the far end of a spectrum which stretches all the way to the place where the strains of *Land of Hope and Glory* begin to swell in the background as the discourse turns to Our Industrial Heritage. (The truth, as usual, probably lies somewhere in the middle, and that middle ground comprises the rich and varied culture of manufacture, maintenance, work and play which this book seeks to celebrate.)

However, both extremes of argument regarding 'Why?' may be valid, but my money is with Mavis, since he grasped an essential truth: we can't help it. The great designer and industrialist Bert Hopwood concluded in his memoirs at the end of a long life in the British motorcycle industry that 'motorcycles are bought, not sold', and by people 'who know exactly what they like and ... are rarely weaned from fixations by the salesman.' There you have it. *Fixations*.

These are fixations as durable, in some cases, as the machines which are their subjects. The traditional industry had essentially collapsed by 1975, but today, 25 years on, there is probably a hard core of around 100,000

'Where motorcycles are concerned ...

… there's always a tearaway element.'

people in the UK, and many others abroad, who are still obsessed and involved with old, mainly British, motorcycles.

This obsession and involvement can take many forms, from the painstaking restoration of a machine back to its original specification, to the fiercely contested classic classes in road racing, scrambles, and trials. My own involvement, and that of the kindred spirits who make up most of the readership of the magazine I write for, *Classic Bike Guide*, can be summed up in the phrase 'ridden not hidden'. (And our artist Nick Ward is emphatically just such a kindred spirit.) The object of the exercise is to do whatever you have to do to get and keep the old dears running, and when they are, to ride them out on the road as often as possible; looking for the old good feeling.

In my case, I like it to be as long a road as possible. The American writer and former heroin user Ann Marlowe tells us: 'The chemistry of the drug is ruthless – it is designed to disappoint you. Yes, once in a while you get exactly where you're trying to go. Magic. Then you chase that memory for a month … The first few highs … feel better than the drug will ever make you feel again.' For me, the two-wheeled equivalent of what that first fix must feel like was a transfiguring journey I took at the age of 17, down through Europe to Greece. The only embarrassing fact about it, for this chronicler on the joys of British four-stroke motorcycles, was that I made the journey on an Italian two-stroke scooter.

The trip had as many highs, lows, and doldrums as they always do, but overall it took me straight out of beastly boarding school into a world of colour and light, wine and food, companionship and movement; an experience – yes, it has to be the F-word – a *freedom*, which I've been attempting to recapture ever since; as you will gather from the four descriptions of longish runs on my BSAs which intersperse this book. Only relatively long runs, because, stacked up against a trip to India or around the world, of course, these European jaunts are small beer. In the same issue of *Bike* in which Mavis wrote, another correspondent said: 'Sorry, I'm not impressed. The two blokes on Norton come-and-goes [ie Commandos] who rode down through the American continent. Well, OK, but I know two fellows who are doing the same thing on a pair of clapped-out Panthers'. And so on. There's always one. But the European trips are still an awfully big adventure for me.

Probably the ideal conjunction of man and machine came personally in the period before the one covered by this book. In the late seventies and early eighties I ran a fairly reliable black 750 Norton Commando. This was a model which, while relatively heavy and with a less than ideal riding position, was arguably the distillation of the whole British twin cylinder motorbike tradition, and an excellent all-rounder on the open road. The shadow of that Commando may sometimes rather hang over this book. I had started motorcycling on a succession of Norton twins, and I did some good long distance hauling on that one, before a time of change saw it go in favour of a succession of BSAs, between six and twenty years older than the come-and-go. Two steps backward, or what?

The BSAs have been mostly strong and satisfying mounts, but did this going for older machinery represent a deepening of nostalgia (which at least one dictionary defines as 'a sick longing for the past')? Ann Moore would agree, calling addiction 'a form of mourning for the irrecoverable glories of the first time. This means that addiction is essentially nostalgic, and as such, can show us what is deeply suspect about nostalgia. That drive to return to the past isn't an innocent one. It's about stopping your passage to the future. It's a symptom of the fear of death, and this phenomenon is clogging our society with art, music, design and ideas that are embraced mainly because they aren't new. The love of predictable experience ...'

Before we get into a really good guilty wallow on this one, let's also consider that although the classic mind-set values familiar things, looked at another way this can be construed as a reasonable desire for continuity, at a time when the pace of change, both technological and economic, make simple familiarity something to be cherished. Not because we cannot adapt, but because we were designed to look backward as well as forward, and, if we don't, we are the lesser for it. The very best of classic days can approach that state where, in the words of the poet, we 'arrive where we started, And know the place for the first time.'

At a less exalted level, another reason 'Why?' is that classic motorcycling is cheap motorcycling (again, relatively). The period of post-war affluence has seen the motorcycle in our society change from a primarily utilitarian (ride-to-work) machine, to a mainly leisure-orientated one (big boys' toys). So, mostly for fun, a couple of years ago I bought a 'modern' (ish) motorcycle. Immediately I had to pay £250 more insurance. The tyres had looked OK, but after just 3,000 miles since the last change, apparently they weren't, and new ones cost around £90 each. I loved the effortlessly powerful engine, but the seat made long distance travel agony. That would have been remediable, but the bills weren't, so it had to go. Motorcycling has always been basically democratic (the rain falls on everyone), and classic riding is an enclave where, unlike the 'born again' biking fraternity, an £8,000 entry level plus £1,000 for riding gear are not yet the norm.

Not that you won't spend money (oh yes), and time, as well as squandering accumulated brownie points with your partner because of the time and money spent. But there's a hidden benefit. Classic bikes can be better today than they were when they were new! Progress, in the form of reliable electronic ignition, stickier modern tyre compounds, and braking upgrades, plus some dedicated and knowledgeable rebuilders (though there are the other kind too), means that all the effort can actually produce something capable of doing what it was intended to do, as well as triggering people's memories (so many people!) while giving you a damn good time into the bargain.

Look at Nick's lovingly detailed drawings, read a few of the pieces, and in a little while perhaps you'll approach the question 'Why?' in a different light. I do hope so, because this fixation, these British iron horses, have been a large part of my life. Final guilty secrets: I am not mechanically adept; I have never been much of a speed merchant; and I have no real interest in motorcycle sport. But I have had a lifelong love of post-war British bikes, and of long roads. In the end, I think these have been positive things. I am lucky enough now to live again where I grew up, beneath the Uffington White Horse, and as they used to say in these parts: 'If you have a care, tell it to your horse. And ride on singing.'

Fawler, Oxon, August 2000

CHAPTER ONE

My journeys I: Portugal and back

This was one of the earliest 'Down The Road Apiece' columns which I wrote for Classic Bike Guide (CBG). *So far there has been one in every issue, since the first.*

The magazine's founder and editor, Frank Westworth, had introduced himself to me a couple of years previously at the Bristol Classic show, saying he'd read my stuff, fiction, non-fiction, and journalism. He said he was a fan. This was flattering, but surveying Frank's 20-ish stone figure, his goggle eyes behind thick glasses, and his long, greying, straggling hair and beard, I had to tell him that I'd always hoped for fans of a different shape and gender.

Frank's appearance, however, effectively camouflaged both a pretty mean rider, and an editor intelligent enough to let experienced writers on the CBG *team – such as myself, Jim Reynolds, and Dave Minton – get on with it, with only the gentlest of editorial direction, and almost no cutting or tampering at all. (This was in contrast to one previous lady editor, with feminist principles so fierce that she cut all my references to girls on the pillion, and when a co-columnist was knocked off his bike by a little old lady in a Morris Minor, altered the reference to read 'a little old man'!)* Classic Bike *was then overwhelmingly and deservedly the market leader in its field, but we felt that there was room for a less impersonal approach to our ... sport? Pastime? Obsession? Room, in fact, for a bit of 'New Journalism' (well, it had been new in the early seventies), where the personality of the writer became part of the story itself, and where feelings would be given the same weight as technical matters.*

As evidenced by the following piece. It was written in 1990, after I had returned from a three-month stay in Portugal. The effort of completing a big, six-volume, half-a-million word book on British bikes, plus a codicil work on two-strokes, meant that I had really needed a long break. I rented a small house in a Portuguese village a mile or two inland from the Algarve coast, and decided to go down there on my bike, a 1962 BSA 650 Star Twin. My friend, the actor Richard Howard, had been given (yes, given) this machine by a yuppie mate of his, but had never used it. He sold it on to me for just the cost of the SRM engine rebuild which I had encouraged him to splash out on.

That sounds simple enough. But though I had plugged away at the bike's many cycle part problems for the previous couple of years, often assisted by future world traveller Sean Hawker (see Chapter 5), fresh ones kept cropping up. The bike's most worrying aspect was the front fork; the A65 and its previous owner had once been in an accident, and the front end never felt quite right. Though Sean tightened down the steering head bearings, at the last minute before leaving I panicked and asked a local British bike shop to check them and look the bike over.

The result was an expensively rebuilt clutch, which within 30 miles was slipping so badly that the bike had to be RAC-ed back to the shop, delaying my departure for a week. Then, on the way down, the ride was marred by a terrifying intermittent castoring action of the stiff front end – until Portugal's extremely rough roads had shocked it into submission!

Later in the year, after I had ridden back as recounted here, I spent out on a full front-end rebuild by Tony at Miller Motorcycles in St Leonards-on-Sea, who really knew his stuff. This revealed that no fewer than four of the steering head ball bearings had escaped from their cup-and-cones, and were trapped down the side of the yoke ... Tony said that the A65's solid BSA build quality meant that there had been no damage to the yoke; he had once seen a Triumph twin with a similar problem which had left its lighter, less substantial yoke worn clean through.

As the piece says, 'I love my bike/ I hate my bike' – and never more so than with this particular troublesome twin. It went on to do some decent journeys, however, including the one described in Chapter 3, before ending up, just when it finally seemed sorted, as a competition prize in the magazine. It now lives in Norway.

'Where have I been? Oh, just down to Portugal for a bit, with the old BSA,' I say airily. 'No, no real problems. Did about 3,000 miles altogether on the old A65, no worries ...'

Behind this calm dinner party pose lies a different reality, which has very little to do with either calm or reason. This is the dreaded BBC – the British Bike Complex, which runs deep and devious in those who suffer from it. Like many neuroses it's marked by an inability to learn from experience, and is characterised by a violent oscillation between two mental poles. And the first of these is

I HATE MY BIKE! I've been on the Algarve with the bloody thing for three months, and apart from the business when I overtightened the back

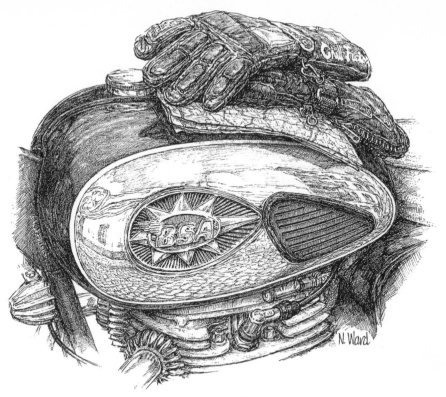

Reflections – Portugal

brake, and the trouble I had adjusting the clutch, and the way the front end horrors I had on the way down felt as if they were coming back whenever it was windy on the coast road (ie quite often), and the punishment I got from the Portuguese roads via rebuilt Girlings and forks with seals so knackered that enough oil pumped out of them to blow back on the plug caps – apart from that, it's been *fine*.

Until now, the morning before I am leaving to ride up through Portugal, over the western border to Spain, across the Picos de Europa mountains and down to the ferry at Santander. This last morning the carburettor, for no reason, chooses to jam wide open when I twist the throttle once before starting, so that when I fire up all hell breaks loose from a standing start and I have to switch off quickly before the valves bend. Oiling the cable, and taking off the tank and the top of the carb and spraying in WD 40 does nowt; my confidence is limited, so I'm reduced to pushing and freewheeling the dead bike, its suspension creaking and clicking in the silence, through the town, past the neighbours (shaken heads), past the local English who I'd already said goodbye to (expressions of concern, sly grins), down to the local Rent-a-Ride moped hire shop. The owners are English so I can at least explain the problem and beg the immediate attentions of the Portuguese mechanic. Three hours later

I LOVE MY BIKE! For a fiver, the mechanic, though with a lot of head shaking about 'How had I got this far?' and 'Had the carb had a bash?', has patiently eased off the internals where the (fairly new) slide had been sticking at the top. This shows how often I run at anything like full throttle, but it also transforms the incident from highly inconvenient to positively providential – I mean, supposing it had happened somewhere remote? Or the throttle had jammed wide open at speed on the road? No, the A65 has looked after me. And I bet that mechanic, good as he was, couldn't have fixed a bank of Kamiwaki carbs like he did a single Amal Concentric. Good old Brit bike simplicity etc etc.

But, that night, lying awake before an early departure, I HATE MY BIKE again for the hard times I suspect it's about to subject me to. The front end is still an uncertain factor, especially loaded up as I will be with a pair of Craven hard panniers, a Swagman tote bag and a tank bag full of spares. As usual I am riding alone; the RAC Eurocover ran out months ago, and all sorts of disaster scenarios are unreeling themselves behind my eyeballs. Why do I do this to myself, at my age? This is *definitely* the last time (but we've heard that once or twice before …).

Deeper than this nervousness, though, the relationship with the A65 is still genuinely problematic. Without getting too fanciful, after several thousand miles I don't yet feel I can trust it. The sometimes ineffectual cable-operated rear brake and the TLS front one that makes the forks judder alarmingly when it's applied hard, plus the occasional jumping out of third gear when under load – these are negotiable (change gear carefully, and use the excellent engine braking) till they can be fixed. But do I really like the unit twin BSA motor? I love the acceleration from 40 to 60, but leaving the vibration aside, it seems to run out of puff in top gear on steep climbs in a most un-British way, and I don't finally know whether this is due to a certain inherent reviness in the short-stroke engine, or to a fundamental lack of grunt. So assuming we get that far, how will it handle the Picos mountains?

With a certain amount of fear and trembling, then, but also with the battery topped up, oils changed and the rear chain tightened, and notes made of useful phrases like '*Preciso de assistencia*' ('I need help'), I wheel out the loaded bike early next morning. Then we're off (the BSA always starts well, thanks to the new three-phase alternator and Boyer ignition), and within an hour I LOVE MY BIKE! Partly it's the weather this May morning, just perfect for riding, bright and mild, with blue sky and a few white clouds, not too hot even in the middle of the day. But mainly, once the first ten miles of bumpy back road have been negotiated, the bike had nosed north on the good surfaces of the N264 and settled down to a steady droning 55, soon the ride ceases to be a mental and physical assault course and gradually becomes a pleasure. There's rarely much traffic, even on a Saturday, and running between tree-lined fields we're over half-way to Lisbon before the first stop for petrol and

I HATE MY BIKE! again, as the GALP pump attendant, agitated, points out the broad swathe of oil splashed back over the right-hand side panel and pannier. This figures, since there's now a black hole where the oil tank's filler cap used to be. The caps on the early A65s are screw-on items (and since then my most reliable ex-rocker source has told me that the trick to retaining them, as with Triumph rocker-box caps, is to use a rubber O-ring in place of their washer). The oil cap falls off, even the petrol cap leaks, every bloody thing about the A65 is a problem, etc etc.

But quickly I LOVE MY BIKE once more, as under the frowning gaze of one of the intense, obscurely discontented boys who seem to hang around every Portuguese petrol station, I rummage through the tank bag and come up with – a spare oil tank cap. What a clever fellow, eh? And also the hard luggage, though heavy, rules OK, with the pannier wiped clean easily and no oil penetrating its seal. I celebrate by breakfasting at the station's cafeteria on *café con leche* supplemented by a brown, pastry looking thing from under a glass case, which I obtain by pointing. It turns out to be a cold fish finger.

But neither this, nor the slight bish shot navigationally while bypassing Lisbon, can take away the pleasure of the day. A host of support vehicles and colourful bicycle racers, some of them English, whirr by in the opposite direction while I'm taking a rest in a lay-by in the shade of a cork and eucalyptus forest. Some of them urge me graphically to abandon the internal combustion engine in favour of pedal power, but at that stage I'm not remotely interested.

By three in the afternoon we've covered over 350 miles and are rolling down the hill and over the broad bridge into the old university town of Coimbra, and only at this point does the front end begin to feel funny, with the bars wagging perceptibly at lower speeds. After the day in the saddle I can't be bothered, and put it down to the town's tram lines. I find a hotel by the river and go off to my first movie in three months, and a last bowl of strawberries and white port.

Next morning I HATE MY BIKE again. It's another early start, it's been raining a bit, and wobbling out through the town's slippery, rutted suburbs, the front end is unmistakably iffy and unstable. Before the climb inland, through the mountains leading east to the Spanish frontier, I pull in for petrol, wondering if redistributing the luggage might help; and at the last moment spot an air hose and reluctantly decide to check the tyres, which are the one … little … detail that haven't been covered in the pre-departure work. The back Roadrunner is short 3lb, and the front 6. With a final tighten of the new oil tank cap we're off again, and both bike and rider feel so dramatically more stable that

I LOVE MY BIKE again, mostly, as we run along a lonely, almost Alpine valley and then climb up and down some twisting, narrow road through pine forests and over narrow stone bridges, with the rain left behind and scarcely any traffic. The brakes are a little pushed on some of the down-slopes – because I'm chary of overtightening the cable of the rear one, operating it involves pointing my toe like a ballet dancer and stabbing all the way down.

After about 40 miles like that, the terrain becomes rock-strewn plateau and the road, with one of those abrupt Continental changes, at the bottom of a long incline turns into a spanking new contoured dual carriageway. As usual the A65 soon begins to run out of breath in top, but changing down and grabbing an exploratory handful produces gratifying results; despite its full load the BSA roars powerfully up the long, quite steep curves at a steady 50 in third with plenty more in hand. All *right*.

The border is the same perfunctory formality it had been on the way in, but about a mile beyond I'm flagged down by a pair of bad-looking Spanish motorcycle cops. They make it very clear that the days of running on sidelights, as I'd been doing all the time in Portugal, are definitely over. I act (?) dumb and get away without a fine. Luckily the new electrics let you keep full beam on all day with no problems.

After that the road runs due east and mostly straight for nearly a hundred miles to Salamanca. Early on, skirting a rugged fortress town off to the right, with a shallow near-dry riverbed curling round in front of it, a black horse dashes out of the water raising splashes with its hooves. Then come the long slightly undulating straights, with the bike settling down to a steady drone. Soon I spot a really big bird on the road ahead pecking at something recently dead; beep the horn and it lumbers into the air. At the time I think 'kite', but with the huge dark blunt wings marked white beneath from front to back, the bird book says 'eagle'. Another slides overhead, awesomely large – we are talking eight foot wingspan here – its shadow alone, dark on the road, looking to be as long as a car.

Something is happening without me realising it. Things are harmonising, the mild sun overhead and the bike droning along satisfyingly mile after mile, with not enough time in the saddle for any aches and pains to be bad yet. Now there are ranches on each side of the road, and behind fences young short-horned bulls, black, or mottled grey and white, prance about or run hobbyhorse fashion over the wide grass pastures. The roadside is often lined with purple and yellow wild flowers, and poppies; once there is a strand of bent-over trees hung with moss, and once a stork, looking as large as the eagles, beats its way overhead. Through this mildly exotic landscape the bike never falters, and somewhere along these arrow-straight roads, an understanding is reached, and I think that whatever strokes the A65 may pull from now on, I know that at base, beyond love and hate, I like it.

The rest of the day is anti-climax, really. I turn north at Salamanca, forced by an incomplete bypass through the city whose road surface has an attitude problem, and then press on north for another hundred flat, not very interesting miles and more, through Zamora, round to the east of Leon and into the southern foothills of the Picos, where I draw to a knackered, claw-handed and bum-sore halt in the aptly named tourist town of Cisterna, where fairground dodgems with an ear-blasting sound system have been thoughtfully set up on waste ground directly behind the hotel I unwittingly select.

The long haul has served the purpose of leaving me time the following day for a leisurely run up and over the Picos. But next morning, still fairly fagged and sore from the previous two hard days, when I push the BSA out into nasty misty rain, when one of the tank bag's rubber straps – no doubt corroded by leaking petrol – promptly parts as I fix on the bag, I HATE MY BIKE again. Here I am fully laden and about to tackle mountains where even the passes are 4,000 feet up, with forks empty of oil, an engine that won't climb in top and now a tank bag jury-rigged with a spare webbing strap. I change the plugs, but as we chug off down the narrow valley roads through the ring of hills, the A65 echoes my own not very good heart, feeling as if it lacks power for the final hurdle. Altitude? The new plugs? Or just *knackered*?

The actual rain stops but the first phase is grim. The road runs through bleak mountain landscape and crosses the top of a couple of dams. I stop beside a rather menacing Highland-style barren reservoir, in front of a tunnel, to rearrange the strap, which has worked loose. As I bend by the stationary bike, a traffic police Land Rover rolls by, without slackening pace to see if I'm in trouble. Their indifference is a little chilling, but in the silence with the engine off, as the day grows warmer there's a lot of birdsong to compensate.

Setting out again, immediately I HATE MY BIKE anew because the dank, wet, unlit tunnel through the mountain ahead is very scary, since in this situation my headlamp turns out to be useless, with no beam as such, just a feeble ectoplasm-type illumination dancing somewhere weakly off to one side. After that and another lake, the narrow road goes beside swift-running streams, through tiny five or six-house villages, and then we're going for it, up a gradually and then dramatically steepening hill with long straights: the main pass. The bike seems to be pulling better, though it jumps out of gear a couple of times. There is the familiar loss of power in top on the shallower climbs, and then we're droning up flatly in the lower gears, and am I imagining a suggestion of lack of power towards the very top? – if so it's the altitude affecting the carburation (my ears are popping too), as with the summit approaching, that's the last of the trouble.

At that point, about a hundred yards from the top of the pass, thick mist envelopes us, and as we go up and over it stays that way for many miles; the descent is far longer than the climb, with endless steep hairpin bends, one after another. The ride down, despite the tip-toe rear and juddering front brake, is exciting rather than scary, because using the gears and engine braking works well, and though the road needs complete concentration there's virtually no other traffic, and nothing coming from behind. We pass big herdsman's dogs with wooden sticks dangling from their thick collars, see the men themselves in capes by the roadside, and above the motor's low drone, hear cowbells in the mist. The bike handles well at low speeds, and despite some clanking from the engine (I later discover that the face strip of the primary chain tensioner is coming loose from the blade) I LOVE MY BIKE for the way it holds the road and can be waltzed gently and surely down the steep curves. Eventually the mist falls away and we ride down the valley.

From there on it is literally all downhill. I stop to nibble a Mars bar I've been carrying since Portugal, and note that the landscape in these high valleys is not Scottish but magnificently Chinese, very tall steep-sided mountains with mist wreathing their crags and stark falls of scree around the precarious trees clinging to their slopes. There's more traffic now, some buses and a few lorries carrying stone, so the narrow curves need caution, but there's also a feeling of mounting exhilaration – it looks as though we've done it. And then finally the valley opens up, the air gets warmer, and the road runs across gentler slopes down to the pretty coastal town of Santillana del Mar, and the sea.

The last leg is very good, 50 miles of excellent road inland of the coast; the bike really flies, and early in the afternoon we've done it, and are ensconced in the fleshpots of the ferry port, Santander. This is a pleasant city which the Spanish government used to retreat to in the heat of the summer, which with a little time to explore it proves remarkably large and elegant, and provides the best Spanish grub I've ever had in my life. As the boat slides away next morning and the *'Preciso de assistencia'* notes are ceremonially shredded, it's 'Worries? What worries?' They're so hard to remember as soon as a trip is done.

I Love My Bike, I Hate My Bike. In my country this song can go on for *years …*

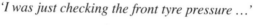

'I was just checking the front tyre pressure …'

CHAPTER TWO

Our past

The 20th century has been the century of the motorcycle. Historic figures with two wheel connections, like Conan Doyle and Lawrence of Arabia, come alive today for enthusiasts who share their passion.

Motorcycles had always appealed to loners and mavericks like Lawrence. But it was in the fifties, when the teenager with his rock'n'roll soundtrack was born and the author began to ride, that motorbikes and rebellion became irrevocably linked.

I have never been a student of the pioneer days of motorcycling, but I was particularly heartened to find that Sir Arthur Conan Doyle had had a hand in those adventurous times. As a child, my real introduction to story-telling and literature had come as I sat on the sofa in my grandfather's study and listened to Sherlock Holmes stories read aloud to me from his bound copies of The Strand Magazine, *in which the tales had first appeared. My other grandfather, the sportsman and journalist Freddie Wilson, apparently once sat with Conan Doyle on a bench on the platform of a railway station and argued the toss about spiritualism, which Sir Arthur passionately believed in and Freddie, after three years in the trenches during World War One, did not. Their discussion was said to have been so intense that they missed two trains.*

This piece was written in 1989, the year before Hinckley Triumph kick-started the British motorcycle industry once more with competent, relatively conventional designs. Meanwhile at Shenstone, Nortons with their revolutionary rotary engines were in limited production for a while, and the article as a whole sought, as the pioneer motorcyclists had had to do, to find some principle 'to identify the few really fruitful new designs from the many notions that end up littering the roadside of history.' My conclusion was that well-rounded individuals like Doyle were the best men for that difficult job.

Conan Doyle

You may have noticed recently a good deal of media noise about the centenary of Sherlock Holmes. There was not a lot of mention of the fact that his creator, Sir Arthur Conan Doyle, was a pioneer motorist and motorcyclist.

Conan Doyle was a real all-rounder. In addition to creating characters who have entered the long gallery of the world's archetypes, he was a practising doctor of medicine, once bowled out W.G. Grace, saved countless lives by introducing life-jackets and rubber rafts for the navy, and was not only riding a ROC (Ride of Comfort) motorcycle as early as 1904, but from his literary earnings provided financial backing for the ROC's designer, the great pioneer A.W. Wall.

By 1912 Doyle was chugging around his estate on one of Wall's Auto Wheels, a motor-wheel attached to the rear wheel of a bicycle. The Auto Wheel proved a sound enough design to be still in production, on scooters like the Silva, well into the 1920s.

Conan Doyle was a visionary, like his contemporary H.G. Wells. He often saw the broad shape of the future (tanks, modern body armour, etc) without necessarily discerning the details, as revealed by his tactics with a motor car when it went wrong. 'Making no pretence to a mechanical mind, he would simply open the bonnet and jab with his umbrella at the engine until something happened.'

Like most early motorists, he had many accidents. Interviewed by *The Motor Cycle* in 1905, he explained that he found his vee-twin ROC machine very simple – despite its mysterious tendencies to fly up a bank and turn a somersault.

Reporters then as now were known for a tendency to ask dumb questions, and Sir Arthur was subjected to the following: 'May I ask whether we can expect to hear of the famous detective hunting down his quarry, accompanied by the faithful Watson, both mounted on the newest and finest type of motorcycle?' 'No!' said his host with some vehemence. 'In Holmes' early days motor bicycles were unthought of!'

Conan Doyle really was a remarkable man, because 'Holmes' early days', the late Victorian era, were the author's own – he had taken up motorcycling in his mid-40s. Such energy and breadth of vision leads one inexorably to the problem of the progressive, of Futureshock, of beastly change.

What we need, I believe, for the way forward, are whole persons, a modern equivalent of Conan Doyle. Anyone who can bowl out Dr Grace *and* write *The Speckled Band* deserves a good looking at.

T.E. Lawrence

T.E. Lawrence (or 't.e.' as CBG, with its sometimes erratic production standards, managed to call him) was the most famous motorcycling casualty of them all. Yet as in life, so in his death, the facts about his fatal accident remain tinged with mystery.

He suffered the crash that would kill him on 13 May 1935. He had been riding from Bovington Camp village in Dorset towards his rented cottage, Cloud's Hill. He was thought to have lost control after swerving to try and avoid two delivery boys, Frank Fletcher and a friend, who were bicycling in the same direction as himself. The second boy, Albert Hargreaves, was knocked from his bicycle and ended up unconscious in hospital.

However, at the inquest one witness, a Corporal Catchpole, also spoke of a black car approaching Lawrence from the opposite direction and apparently passing him head on, a few seconds before the crash. But the dip in the road at that point prevented this witness seeing whether the car was involved in the accident. The boys, confused, had no recollection of it, and the driver never came forward. Conspiracy theorists have made hay with this one, particularly since Lawrence's last errand had been to send a telegram to the increasingly eccentric writer Henry Williamson, author of Tarka the Otter *but at that time also a vocal supporter of the rising tide of European fascism.*

Whatever the circumstances, Lawrence swerved clear across the road and left it on the right side. He flew over the handlebars and landed with sufficient force to crack his skull, dying in a coma six days later in the hospital at Bovington Camp. The accident had happened just 300 yards from his home. So a man who had meticulously recorded extremely high annual mileages on his succession of seven Brough Superiors, had finally gone down after a short trip to the Post Office and the Red Garage in Bovington.

In 1984 I rode my Norton Commando to the spot, where a spindly tree had just been planted to commemorate the crash. (With the tree now more substantial, Nick Ward wonders how long it will be before some crazed T.E.L. wannabe rides into it at speed.) Looking around, I found it hard to visualise the crash. Unlike the version of events in the film Lawrence of Arabia, *this was no twisting lane. The road, though narrower then, ran almost dead straight for several hundred yards, though there was that undulation in the direction of Bovington.*

Riding around, I realised that this was a different Dorset from the part I knew, the beautiful ridge of hills and winding lanes a little way north. This was heathland, with long straight lanes and apparently reasonable visibility, goading the right hand to crack on – the witness estimated Lawrence had been travelling at a possible 60mph – and then bending to reveal unexpected hazards. Once, indeed, I swerved round a gaggle of cyclists from a nearby works, but more often it was sweating groups of jogging squaddies from Bovington Camp and its nearby armoured vehicle testing ground. At those points you were reminded rapidly that these were lanes, and not always as wide as you had thought.

Probably no-one will ever know now what actually happened that day, although fresh facts about the enigmatic hero do keep emerging. His most famous motorcycle-related episode was the race with the Bristol Fighter biplane recounted in his book The Mint, *but as recently as 1985, C.C. Jackson from Australia wrote to* The Classic Motor Cycle *to say that in the early thirties he had been an apprentice motorcycle engineer at Bridlington, Humberside, and had become acquainted with Lawrence while the latter, as Aircraftman Shaw, had been stationed at a Marine Unit there. Not only, wrote Mr Jackson, was Lawrence at that time designing and building a steam engine which he intended to fit into a Brough Superior frame, but also 'while he was at Bridlington he was challenged by the crew of a Handley Page bomber, to race his Brough against their aircraft from Catfoss airfield (just west of Hornsea) to the priory church in Bridlington and back. Lawrence won.'*

Lawrence of Arabia was Britain's most famous motorcycling hero, as well as a martyr to the road. 'His drug was speed,' as one friend observed, 'and it cost him his life'.

Too fast to live, maybe, but perhaps not too young to die. When the fatal accident came on 13 May 1935, Lawrence was 46 years old and had just left his haven in the RAF as Aircraftman 338171 Shaw. Explaining his retreat into relative anonymity in the other ranks of the Service to his friend the playwright George Bernard Shaw, he had written: 'You see I'm all smash inside, and I don't want to look prosperous or be prosperous, while I know that.' Perhaps with the crash it was time for the inside and the outside to cohere.

Like most of my generation I was introduced to the Lawrence legend by David Lean's epic film. Irreverently referred to by us as 'Florence of Belgravia', the actual first screenings at Leicester Square in the depths of the famously harsh winter of '61 had their comic moments, with the cinema management perceptibly turning up the heating before the interval so that a combination of shimmering desert visuals and sweltering auditorium meant record sales of ice cream and Kia-Ora.

But we had all been riveted by the impressionistic opening sequence of the fatal crash, with the final shot of goggles dangling on a thorn bush. Never mind that the Brough Superior used in the sequence was incorrectly registered UL 656, which had been the number of Lawrence's previous SS

'Getting ready for the road' (Brough Superior SS80, etching and aquatint).

100, the one given to him by Bernard Shaw. In 1961 his actual final mount, GW 2275, had just been discovered under a tarpaulin in a back garden at Fareham and purchased for £1, prior to loving restoration.

What drove Lawrence, both on the roads and into the ranks? Straight society had lifted its skirts to him early on, both personally in its reaction to the stigma of his illegitimacy (his father was a titled Anglo-Irishman); and politically, in the post-war perfidy of the European states towards his friends the Arabs, whose cause he had wholeheartedly espoused, to the point of unwisdom. Stir in the fact that a combination of nature and nurture (severe beatings as a child) appear to have left him a deeply unhappy, mostly repressed homosexual masochist with a profound dislike of women. With all that, plus the impossibly high ideals and standards he set for himself, so that he was constantly disappointed, of course he was a rebel and a tortured soul – one who would write 'In speed we hurl ourselves beyond the body.'

He was also, however, a paradox, possibly because at a fundamental level his personality failed to cohere: he wrote to his friend the distinguished military man B.H. Liddell Hart: 'At an OTC field day I was once told to disguise myself as a battalion in close order; and have done so ever since!' Despite this (and suitably paradoxically), as Liddell Hart wrote, 'to the force [of his personality] all who came in close contact with him have borne testimony'. David Stirling, a founder of the SAS, attributed this to 'a power to probe behind [any group of men's] minds and to uncover the well-springs of their actions'. Yet, as Liddell Hart concluded: 'He knew others, himself he did not know. Perhaps because he saw too many facets.' Or perhaps, as his younger brother A.W. Lawrence wrote, it was due to his 'diffident weak core, so controlled by his colossal will-power that its underlying presence was rarely suspected.'

All of these contradictions applied to his motorcycling. While the conventional view had him in the early wartime days in Egypt 'scorching about between Cairo and Bulaq on a Triumph motorcycle, an offence to the eyes of his senior officers', in fact a friend of his from those times, Ernest Dowson, would write of Lawrence at Giza 'riding out on his motorcycle Boanerges with a care which was remarkable both there and also later when he visited the Government Press at Bulaq'. (Interesting to note that Lawrence was evidently already referring to his two-wheeled steeds by the classical tag Boanerges, 'son of thunder', over a decade before the famous Brough example of that name on which he would race a Bristol Fighter biplane.)

Post-war there was nothing so crude and unequivocal as a death wish about Lawrence, because if there had been, the roads of the day and his exceptionally high mileages (an average of 27,000 miles a year for four years!) afforded him plenty of opportunity to satisfy it. Yet he was clearly no cautious charlie either. The American soldier Ralph H. Islam, who knew him post-war, overturned another accepted truth, for Lawrence was usually known and presented himself as a teetotaller. 'When we dined together he drank wine of various sorts freely,' wrote Islam, and (possibly as a result?), 'it gave him pleasure to ride his motorbike through the tram tunnel under Kingsway or down the Duke of York's steps'!

Lawrence was an expert mechanic with a feeling for fine machinery which led him to George Brough's creations. He was as aware as anyone of the pose value of a big vee-twin with a stainless steel tank, and wrote to a friend's young son at school: 'Expect a loud roaring outside the school gates. That will be my motor bike. The schoolmasters will not let you talk to ordinary men in uniform: but when they hear the roaring of my bike they will say "That is not an ordinary airman: that is an extraordinary machine." So it will be alright.'

But he most definitely saw deeper than the Brough's charismatic surface. Commenting disparagingly on the avant-garde plastician theory of art, he wrote 'when a man starts talking to me of impastos I say epicyclic gears at him, and a slow fog of misunderstanding creeps between us. So many plasticians seem to admit to their notice the outside of machinery, and to exclude its purposefulness, which is to put the skin before the will.'

As well as these theoretical considerations, however, his Broughs did also provide Lawrence with a superficial sense of identity plus a means of release, when he entered the 'other ranks' of the Forces in 1922. After a fiasco when the Press discovered the identity of 'Aircraftman Ross' and he was thereafter discharged from the RAF, he promptly enlisted in the Tank Corps as Private Shaw. Alec Dixon, a comrade in 1923 at Bovington Camp, later wrote that 'Lawrence's Brough motorcycle was the only machine of its kind in the district, and it was a luxury which represented about two years' pay to his fellow recruits ... Even when his identity became generally known at Bovington the troops were not unduly impressed by "the Lawrence legend"; it was "Broughie" Shaw who claimed their admiration and respect. At that time he had a sidecar attached'. In June 1923 Lawrence would write of something being 'as irrational as what happened on our coming here, when I swerved Snowy Wallis and myself at 60mph on the grass by the roadside, trying vainly to save a bird which dashed out its life against my sidecar.'

Earlier in the year, with the bike evidently solo, there had been epic runs to London and back. '126 miles each way, and I was in place to answer my name for both noon and evening roll calls. A good ride, or race, rather. Everyone thought it was impossible for me to get up and down in the afternoon.' (He had averaged 44.5mph, not bad on side roads today but astonishing on the often unmade roads of the twenties.) And again, 'at 10am. I leapt on my bike, and raced her madly up the London road: Wimborne, Findwood, Romsey, Winchester, Basingstoke, Bagshot, Staines, Hounslow by 1.20pm (three hours less five minutes). Good for 125 miles: return journey took 10 minutes *less*!' But he was honest enough to add later: 'I should have said that I bust the bike just outside camp. Ran over a broken glass bottle, burst the front tyre, ran up a bank and turned over. Damage to self nil; to bike somewhat.'

The high-speed runs were a necessity for Private Shaw in the harsh Army life, which he found less congenial than the RAF. 'My motor-bike is called into use when I find myself on parade facing an unconscious Sergeant with my fists clenched. A hundred fast miles seem to make camp feel less confined afterwards.' And again, in bleaker form: 'When my mood gets too hot and I find myself wandering beyond control I pull out my motor-bike and hurl it at top speed through these unfit roads for hour after hour. My nerves are jaded and gone near dead, so that nothing less than voluntary danger will prick them into life; and the "life" then is a melancholy joy at risking something worth exactly 2/9d a day.'

Sadly even this pleasure was temporarily ripped away from him at the end of 1923 when 'my noble cycle, the poor beast who allayed my "shrinking nerves" was taken out secretly by a beast who left her broken, in a ditch; and she is too ruined to mend, even if I could like her again.' But he soon had another Brough; he would own five between 1922 and late 1926, when he was posted to India by the RAF, which he had transferred to during 1925. There was some talk of moderating his riding; in December 1924 he wrote that 'the bike is a glorious one, but I indulge it only when the weather is not misty, and the roads not wet ... Also even in fine weather my advanced age [he was 36] sometimes feels too advanced for a hard ride.'

To a young friend thinking of beginning, he wrote encouragingly: 'Matchlesses are not dear, and *good*. Second hand is better than new, so long as it is last year's model, and not a crash, rebuilt'; and later: 'I hope the Matchless is going as it should; it sounded right. Just run in, and nippy in type. When you are my age you will be sighing for heavier things which are less acrobatic to ride, and suggest ease to their decaying owners. The point of glory in a Brough was that lazy touring speed, maintained, you felt, without effort on the engine's part, for all day.' And elsewhere: 'It's usually my pleasure to purr along at 60mph, drinking in the air.'

But early in 1925 he wrote excitedly that 'Brough has brought out a new and most wonderful 'bike, which will do 112mph so long as the tyres will stand it. I'm going to blow £200 of Cape's [his publishers] on that. Yes, I know what you will say: – but I like the lovely things, and it's money well lost.' And that August he wrote to author John Buchan that 'the bike (Boanerges is his name) did 108 miles an hour … I think the news of my transfer [to the RAF] had gone to its heads (cylinder heads of course)'. Even this was not the ultimate; soon afterwards he wrote that 'I will go over to Nottingham on Saturday week and try to see Brough, who has a 1926 SS 110 waiting for me.' That was RK 4907, the one with which he raced the plane.

As is well known, Lawrence was in close touch with George Brough. While all owners of the luxury bolides got personal service from Brough and the Nottingham factory, George, no slowcoach himself, clearly recognised Lawrence's incisive technical mind and unusual enthusiasm, and there is some evidence that as well as customising Lawrence's machines with touches like the smaller (19-inch) wheels to suit his 5 ft 2 in stature, the high-mileage conveyances were sometimes used as mobile testbeds for new components. The tone between the two riders is indicated in a 1935 letter from Lawrence in answer to a query by the innovative Brough concerning propeller shapes for an engine cooling fan – Lawrence in the RAF had made valuable contributions to both the Schneider Trophy seaplanes and to the development of high-speed launches.

'Our props are so different an intention. The water is so solid an element. Have you considered Ethylene glycol for cooling? Or is the engine getting too hot for its oil? In the desert I ran a tiny condenser for our old Fords, and so boiled all day without using a pint of water, and with thermal advantage'. He continued: 'I have wondered of late how the new engine is shaping. You were going to make a new angle of inlet for the mixture. Now you are working on the timing gears! Please tell Mr J.A.P. [Brough's engines then derived from J.A. Prestwich] that if I had his sized firm and couldn't get an air-cooled twin right in 18 months, I'd eat my test-bench and wash it down with my flow-meter!' In 1926 Lawrence provided an unsolicited testimony for Broughs which concluded that 'your present machines are as fast and reliable as express trains, and the greatest fun to ride … the jolliest things on wheels.'

There was one drawback to the transfer to the RAF: 'Airmen are not allowed to carry pillion riders, or ride pillion.' 'Airmen are the only people in England forbidden [pillion riding]: not soldiers, not sailors. It's rather an insult to what we fondly hope is the most dangerous service.' A log of Lawrence's exploits gives a slight clue why. He was still an all-weather rider, and in the winter of 1925 'crashed off the Brough last Monday: knee; ankle; elbow; being repaired. Tunic and breeches are being replaced. Front mudguard, name plate, handlebars, foot-rest renewed. Skid on ice at 55mph. Dark: wet: most miserable. Hobble like a cripple now.'

Clothing and equipment, of course, were rudimentary. 'Will you,' he asked a friend, 'dig out ... my black helmet (motorcycling). There is a brown one but I want the black one with the fur edging to the forehead.' The helmets in question were simple leather flying-type jobs against the wind and cold; and it was a nine-inch fracture of the skull that would eventually do for Lawrence. 'I have no fear of mud and rain,' he wrote a fortnight after the crash described above, 'but ice-ruts, with a blizzard continuing on top – No, that's not motorbiking weather.'

There were, unfortunately, other winter hazards in those days. In December 1926, shortly before he left for India, he took a last ride on RK 4907. 'I started about 7.30am but Islington streets were greasy (I had to see GBS on the way) and I got into a trough in the wood paving, and fell heavily, doing in the off footrest, kick-start, brake levers, $\frac{1}{2}$ handlebar and oil pump. Also my experienced knee-cap learned another little trick. Alb. Bennett took the wreck for £100. I limp rather picturesquely.'

It wasn't enough to put him off motorcycling, despite the two year lay-off in India, where he often worried how he would finance a new Brough. On his return Bernard Shaw's gift of the SS 100, reg UL656, took care of that. 'Some anonymous person or persons bought and sent me a very large and new apolaustic Brough ... yet there's a fly in the jam. So large a present (valued at three years of my pay) pauperises me a bit, in my own sight, for accepting it,' he wrote to author E.M. Forster. (As will be evident, for a humble Aircraftman, Lawrence kept some pretty fancy company, among them Noel Coward – 'Dear 338171 (May I call you 338)' – and Winston Churchill, who believed that Lawrence's 'renunciation of all power in great affairs' might have been reversed had he survived until the coming of World War Two.)

Four months later he was writing that the new bike was 'a peach. 4,000 miles, only, on it: but all good,' then adding in a mood we may all occasionally be familiar with, 'Alas how tired I am of bikes and books and music'. He kept UL 656 for three years, but perhaps the very hard riding days were waning as he got into his forties. 'There is the Brough in stable: used for transport, not for sport. I go to places on it. The Devon roads are vile'. 'Yes, a Brough does eat up the miles; but I seldom go out of camp, for one reason and another, often financial.'

It didn't stop him getting his seventh and last Brough early in 1932. After collecting GW 2275, he wrote to George Brough: 'It is the silkiest thing I have ever ridden. Partly because of the Spring Sprocket I suppose. The gear is not too high, I can get down to 16mph; and she pulls fairly at 30mph and at 50 she is a dream. Just popples along so mildly that I can count the revs. It was very cold but a beautiful ride. The back plug lasted until Welwyn.' (Broughs tended to oil up their rear plugs at lower speeds, and the man who would take over the rebuilt GW 2275 after the fatal crash wrote that 'the introduction of the 30mph speed limit in built-up areas was its death-knell to me.')

'The second plug,' Lawrence continued, 'is still running ... I think this is going to be a very excellent bike. The crowds that gape at her will stop looking after she gets dirty and that may be soon. If only the RAF gave me enough spare time to use the poor thing. I am very grateful to you and everybody for the care taken to make her perfect.'

By 1935 and his discharge from the RAF, GW 2275 had been ridden only twice that year, and though 'it goes like a shell, and seems as good as new,' Lawrence was thinking about a push-bike, though another Brough was ordered, and reflecting that 'the loss of my RAF job halves my income, so that my motor-cycling would have been much reduced for the future, even without this 30mph idea.' However, he got out the Brough on 13 May, rode from his cottage, Cloud's Hill, to Bovington Camp village to send a telegram, and on the way back, 300 yards from home, became motorcycling's most famous casualty. But while he lived, riding had provided his often unhappy existence with something at which he excelled, and which undoubtedly gave him deep satisfaction.

'Don't worry – it's colour coded ...'

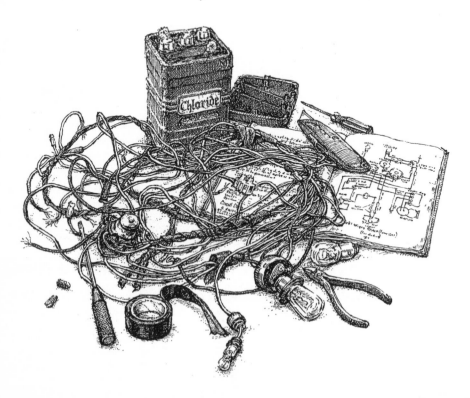

Hugh Leach

'Intrepid' is not too strong a word to use in describing Hugh Leach. I was lucky enough to meet him while wearing another journalistic hat, as he had just won Land Rover's 'Search for a Legend' competition.

Together he and 'Martha', his Series IIA, had survived wars, coups d'états, Central Asian expeditions and drunken Libyans. They had often driven along the old Hedjaz railway, which the subject of our previous piece, T.E. Lawrence, had comprehensively wrecked. Indeed, Martha's dashboard carried a brass '1906' dating plate from one of the trains that Lawrence had blown up.

Hugh, who did all his own maintenance and had never, ever let another man behind Martha's wheel (and she drove like a dream), typically had little time for the competition's modern prize vehicle. So perhaps it should have come as no surprise that, as well as Martha and a vintage sports car, his vehicles had always included a British motorcycle. I only hope that what follows conveys the quality of this eccentric gentleman's memories, as well as his elegant way with both the written and the spoken word.

Hugh Leach OBE, soldier, diplomat, explorer and winner of Land Rover's 'Search for a Legend' competition, has always had a proper motorcycle in his stable. When Land Rover celebrated their 50th birthday last year with the competition to find a man and machine which exemplified the marque, they might have had Hugh and 'Martha', his 1967 Series IIA, in mind.

After 250,000 miles together exploring and adventuring in the Middle East and Central Asia, both are now retired in rural Somerset. But at the age of 64 Hugh still sallies forth on expeditions for the Royal Society of Asian Affairs (last year's was to Kyrghystan). And he still keeps a vintage sports car and a 500 single cylinder motorbike garaged beside 'Martha'. Disciplined as the professional soldier he once was – all his vehicles are in good order – yet profoundly eccentric as only a lone English traveller can be, Hugh Leach told me the story of his motorcycling life.

'I think I always had a sort of atavistic urge to have a motorbike, but the family business, Thomas Leach Ltd, were printers to the Church, and my father, a Methodist lay preacher, didn't approve of the things. My mother had died in childbirth, and I was sent to Abingdon School, first as a boarder and later as a day boy.

'It was there in the early fifties that I spotted an old 98cc Cyc-Auto under a dustsheet in a garage by the school armoury. It belonged to a master, J.B. 'Piggy' Alston, and I persuaded him to sell it to me for £4 – for use in the holidays only, of course.

'I was 16 or nearly so, and I have a feeling that you didn't need a licence for a 98cc autocycle then. You had to pedal to start it, and I remember that this one had no clutch, so that if you stopped, it stopped. I would guess maximum speed was 12mph, but it started my days of taking things to bits.

'I hungered for more power though, so I sold it at a profit and bought an early thirties 150cc hand-change Excelsior two-stroke. This one had a very bad headlamp, as the reflector had been painted over with silver paint. One night I was coming back from Oxford with the wind behind and going well, when I saw a motorbike light behind. I gave it full throttle up Hinksey Hill through Bagley Wood, and as far as I was concerned we were racing. Eventually I had to pull in to let the engine cool down, and the other rider did too. I thought he was going to say "My God, you've got a whopper there!", but he dismounted from a 500cc Matchless and said "You've got a bloody awful headlamp, I was only staying behind to help you out!" It left me totally deflated, I can tell you.

'The Cyc-Auto had started a craze for bikes at school. As boarders it was completely illegal for us to have them – you were liable to be beaten or expelled, or both, and I don't know how we got away with it. We used to swap bikes, so I got to know them all fairly well. John Westall had a Bantam, with performance like the Excelsior, but by then I despised two-strokes – I thought they were rather unmanly sort of machines that didn't make the right sort of noise. My friend John Hullett had a hand-change 250 side-valve BSA with a square red tank. At the end of term he was spotted by a master trying to smuggle the bike onto the Abingdon Bunk, a steam train running between Abingdon and Radley. By the time he got home, the school had rung up his parents and he was forced to get rid of it. John Furby had a Sunbeam, and then a hand-change Rudge. But the best of all was Brian Leech, who had a 600 sloper Panther. It was held together with wire and it leaked oil like billy-o, but it didn't half go!

'Some of our illegal motorcycle gang kept their bikes on a nearby estate with the day hogs (day boys, who were considered not quite the thing). Believe it or not, the rest of us put them in a ditch by the perimeter fence round Abingdon's Shippon aerodrome. We never chained them up, and they were never touched. I can't think where we got the money for them, when our pocket money was five shillings (25p) a week at most. Perhaps I cashed in a National Saving Certificate my Aunt had given me? And we all had Post Office jobs at Christmas. Tax? Insurance? I can't remember. None of us wore helmets, but there was very little traffic on the roads.

'Next for me came a Royal Enfield 250 side-valve. It was my first proper motorcycle, with footchange, but I didn't like it at all. In fact I vowed never to buy another Enfield, rather ironically in view of what I ride now. I sold it to an airman from Abingdon, half now and half later, but I never got the other half, which reversed my gradual accumulation of wealth up till then.

'Next I bought the motorcycle I have the most fond memories of, a 250 OK Supreme with an ohv JAP engine. They say you only fall in love once, and I don't really know why but I think I loved that model more than any other before or since. I also dismantled it more than any other! It had total loss oiling, or 'dead loss' as we rather rudely called it; a red tank with a rather rakish badge on it; and an upswept exhaust so that the pillion passenger always burnt their trouser legs.

'But love or not, I sold it after six months, probably because I wanted something bigger. I really admired a 350 Velocette KTT which another boy at school had, but all I could find was a 1934 KSS, also a 350. It was a well-made bike but low-slung, and I was already becoming lanky. It also wet-sumped within a week, so I put an on/off tap in the oil line. I put something round the tank to remind me and mercifully always remembered, but even now I wake up in a sweat about not turning on that tap!

'Having had five machines in about two years, by then I was a dab hand at strip-downs. I have memories of splayed-out Whitworth spanners, a wonderful thing called an Easi-Out, of annealing copper gaskets and relining the little wedge-shaped pieces of cork used in a Burman clutch. There were trips to Pride and Clarke in South London for spares, and I could replace my own big ends, and dismantle a bike by the side of the road, though we quite often ended up towing each other home.

'Some of the beaks had bikes too. Royd Barker the music master had a 350 ex-WD Ariel, still in khaki. George Duxbury, a dear man, the Mr Chips of the school, had a 150cc hand-change BSA from around 1935, on which he chugged in daily from Frilford Heath, getting overtaken by schoolboys on bicycles. I volunteered to improve it for him, and removed the head and ground in the valves, all during a school break. I think it only made things worse, but he was a kindly man, and never complained …

'In chapel, when there were hymns with lines relating to motorcycles, the illegal fraternity would catch each others' eyes and sing with great gusto. Hymn No 431 in the Ancient and Modern, for instance – "Disposer Supreme and judge …", or "scorching Sunbeams day by day"; or from "For All The Saints" – "steals on the ear the distant Triumph song". On the last day of one term, we smuggled the OK Supreme up the stairs at night, and rode it from the common room to the chapel. The Head, Sir James Cobban, a great man who was knighted for looking after horrid little boys like us, later told me that he'd known all about it, but that by then we were all too big to beat! I visited him 40 years later, riding my present Enfield with its staccato engine note, in my black leathers, and he took one look and said "You're still at it!"'

Hugh went from school to the Royal Military Academy at Sandhurst to train as a professional Army officer. 'We were taught to ride bicycles, horses and motorcycles, all with their own drill. I bought a maroon 350 3T Triumph twin, with teles and a dual seat, the most modern bike I'd ever had. But a lot of the fun was taken away, I realised, because the wretched thing never broke down!'

There followed years of active service abroad. After commanding one of the first tanks to storm ashore at the Suez landings, in 1957 Hugh's regiment was posted to Libya, where he ran the regimental motorcycle team, riding Matchless G3s. 'We practised in the desert, usually with the regimental despatch riders. But once I was out alone instructing an inexperienced corporal, who hit a pothole and broke a leg badly, with the bone protruding. I had to leave him there and find my way back to our base at Homs, the old Roman camp of Leptus Magna, and then lead the regimental ambulance back and find the corporal again.'

Home on leave for a while, Hugh spotted an advert in the *Evening Standard* for a Series C Vincent, for £92. It had belonged to a policeman, and Hugh bought it and kept it for nearly 25 years. He only used it on leave, while his distinguished career as a soldier and then a diplomat took him all over the Middle East, and beyond.

For most of us the Vincent, which Hugh had had rebuilt at Conway Motors in the early seventies, would be an ultimate, but Hugh had reservations. 'It was certainly fast, but for me, at six foot four, it was uncomfortable. The frame was too small, my knees came above the tank and I never felt safe on it. The performance was fine, but a lot of the mechanics were unfamiliar to me.

'Once, though, my godson Nicholas, who was boarding at Stowe school, was staying with me for the weekend, and we realised he'd be late back if we went in the '26 Humber I was running then. So we went on the Vincent and got him back with five minutes to spare, and as we roared in to the school every window opened, and my godson's stock at the place instantly went rocketing up.

'After I had got into quite a serious wheel-wobble on the Vin, in 1990 I sold it at a Sotheby's auction for £7,500 – it was not concours, and the market had just peaked. I had retired by then, and I still hankered after a proper motorcycle. On Asian expeditions I had seen and heard Indian Bullets and thought, "that sounds fun", and I knew one or two had been ridden back overland to England.

'So at the NEC Show I sat on one, and it felt comfortable, and fitted me well. The 500s were just in, and the big single pot appealed – to be honest, I've never really cared for twins, I like to feel a thump between my legs. In many ways the Bullet was right for me, because I wanted a real motorcycle but I also wanted one whose history I knew. So I bought one new from a nice garage in Bristol, Hub Motorcycles. They fitted it with an Amal carburettor for me, and a pattern Gold Star silencer. I asked if this was legal, and they told me that they had a Traffic policeman among their customers, and when they'd asked him if the silencer was legal, because it did make a noise, he'd replied "Yes, lovely, isn't it?", and ridden off.

'I've only done about 1,500 miles on the Bullet. I've never had any trouble with it apart from a blown fuse, but I'm very aware of all those letters about them in *The Gun*, the RE Owners' Club magazine. The 500 does 70 easily, but one thing I have discovered is how inconsiderate modern car drivers are. At the beginning I kept to the left-hand side of the road like a bicycle – and was treated, and overtaken, like one. I try to keep to B and C roads now.

'Whatever happens, I shall always keep a motorcycle. I love having one in the stable, it talks to my Land Rover and my bicycle. And there are about ten days in the year when nothing else compares (except possibly a Type 33 Bugatti …). It's the sense of one-ness – you and the prime mover are as one. Maybe I'm rising 65, but I still like to have a really powerful motorcycle between my knees, to hear the rockers rocking, the tappets tapping, and the young girl on the pillion clinging on for dear life – there's nothing to beat it.'

Brando and *The Wild One*

This one was particularly dear to my heart, which is something that I hope still comes over as you read the piece. In fact it would not be putting it too strongly to say that, once, I was literally fixated on Marlon Brando. He gave me a voice, albeit a mumbling, third hand, elliptical, evasive one, during days as a teenager when shyness had combined with various shades of anger and unhappiness to leave me actually speechless a lot of the time.

So The Wild One *may have had plenty of flaws, but it did contain and distil images of an abiding power. And it still does. For, as if to prove the point, in response to my article there came a letter from one Erum Waheed, some 30 years younger than me but still smitten by Brando, 'the patron saint of "cool" British motorcycling'. Erum, a law student, went on to be our magazine's unofficial film critic. Here are some extracts from his first epistle:*

'In 1988, aged 18, with mild rebellion simmering and looking for a means of expression, I went to Madame Tussauds Waxworks of all places … I looked forward to the James Dean exhibit … he was all I knew of an angst-ridden icon whom I might relate to, to normalise (or glamorise?) my own angst … (Pop stars didn't really seem to count as they seemed so insincere.) But when we got to the Dean exhibit, I was disappointed … he looked like something I did not relate to, a Teen-Dream. Aaggh!

'Instead I noticed another exhibit. It was of a leather jacketed and peaked cap chubby dummy leaning against a pole. I'd heard of queers looking like this but somehow this image seemed different and distinct … the clothes,

expression and pose were the personification, articulation, if you like, of cool. The image seemed to be arrogant and exclusive but at the same time open to anyone who dared "join the club" of those who knew …

'I was surprised by the Triumph Thunderbird bike he rode, though. We used to live where they made them, until we moved to London in the mid-eighties – then, we had only known Triumph as "the motorcycle factory" or "the co-op" … I liked the look of the bike but at first I was uneasy about relating to a 1950s machine … Thankfully, the fifties style revival of the mid-eighties was in full swing … therefore a fifties style motorcycle was "in".

'No licence … but in the meantime, I acquired a cycle cap like Brando's and the obligatory leather jacket, but did not feel right wearing it without a 'cycle. After all, its beauty is in its functionality: not much point in wearing it for walking to the shops, I suppose! … I got my learner bike cheap enough, and after saving up, finally got my T'bird!!

'I later did a project which happily necessitated a study of the film … [in the last scene] giving his trophy away, Brando didn't say a word, not even a mumble … the enigmatic Kerouac-style hipster? Well, not entirely. I got the impression that his character, appropriately named John Straggler, was none too articulate … It was a good film, although you could see it had been compromised … I wonder where that original script by John Paxton is now …?

'As critic Rene Jordan said of Brando's performance, "His first impact is devastating … Every gesture is a signpost to a personal angst that cannot be verbalised. When it is, it becomes a mumble, as if the onrushing thoughts were smashing the structure of the sentences. The easy shrug, the tilted head, the roving eyes that can't look straight – all the elements are there …"

'No wonder,' Waheed concluded, 'generations are constantly hooked.' Couldn't have put it better, Erum.

If it's motorcycles at the movies, you can talk about *Easy Rider*, or even the great documentary *On Any Sunday*, or the pre-war comedy *No Limit*, but for many of us *the* bike flick is, was, and always will be *The Wild One*.

I first saw the film while I was a student at Oxford in 1963, although it was not to be unbanned in the UK for a few years after that. But cinema clubs could show movies without a certificate, so an approach to the University Film Society quickly got a result. Sitting on the hard benches in a tall Gothic lecture room of one of the Parks science buildings, I was carried back a further ten years (the movie was made in 1953), halfway across the world to the magical dusty backroads of California, to hear the heavy opening Social Realism music fade into a little melancholy jazz and listen to Marlon Brando's voice saying: 'It begins here for me, here on this road …'

The audience that night were mostly earnest film buffs in college scarves, including me – or did I wear the black Lewis Leathers Bronx jacket? – I

Wildest dreams – harsh reality.

think not, and the Norton Navigator was usually stashed somewhere unobtrusive until my third year, as the college required. Our sober gathering made quite a contrast to a 1954 audience of incipient Hell's Angels, a San Francisco bike gang called the Market Street Commandos, as related to Hunter S. Thompson in his seminal book on outlaw bikers: 'We went up to the Fox Theatre on Market Street. There were about fifty of us, with jugs of wine and our black leather jackets … We sat up in the balcony and smoked cigars and drank wine and cheered like bastards. We could all see ourselves right there on the screen. We were all Marlon Brando.'

Amen to that. I was already hooked on Brando as a role model. *On the Waterfront*, and especially the under-rated *Fugitive Kind*, had provided an awkward teenager with a way to talk and carry on. Stir in motorcycles …

you can believe that the following week Kings of Oxford were fitting cowhorn bars to the Navigator (shame about the two-tone rear panelling), and I was buying my first pair of 'Bans.

However … *The Wild One* may be the definitive biker movie, but it was very far from perfect, and one of the imperfections, though not one I was aware of as I sat mesmerised at the time, was embodied in that opening monologue. In a recent competent biography of Brando by Charles Higham, it was revealed that the star took on *The Wild One* because his hip liberal views had been drawn to an original screenplay which took a serious look at the rising violence in American society, stemming from pressures on young people that drove them to rebel, even to the point of endangering their own lives.

The truth about motorcycle hoodlums undoubtedly included that element, but was also a little deeper and darker. As Hunter S. Thompson observed, in the late 1940s 'there were thousands of [World War Two] veterans who flatly rejected the idea of going back to their pre-war pattern … It was a nervous, downhill feeling, a mean kind of angst that always comes out of wars … they wanted more action, and one way to look for it was on a big motorcycle.'

Soon enough came trouble, at Hollister in 1947 where a hill-climb turned into a town take-over and full-scale drunken brawl. As Thompson points out, despite the thousands of bikers involved, 29 cops had the thing under control by the following noon. But the incident sparked the nation's imagination, and formed the basis of *The Wild One*.

An outlaw rider's down-played account of Hollister illustrates some contradictions. 'We were just there to party,' he told Thompson. 'As for punching on citizens and stuff like that, we didn't do it. Sure we made lot of noise, and we chased some people who started throwing rocks at us. When the cops got panicky we put a couple of them in garbage cans and stacked their bikes on them, that's all.' The last sentence is surely a bit at odds with the 'boys just wanna have fun' image, and shows why West Coast bikers en masse would be more or less correctly perceived by straight America as more than a little bit out of control.

But despite Brando's serious intentions, Hollywood in the early fifties was a deeply compromised dream factory. It had already deballed the movie version of Brando's first great vehicle, Tennessee Williams' *Streetcar Named Desire*, by fudging Blanche Dubois' nymphomania and subsequent rape, and providing a happy ending. Now, just before shooting began on *The Wild One*, Jack Viszard of the Breen Office (Hollywood's self-appointed censors) refused approval of the script's first draft. Viszard was appalled by its sympathetic treatment of the motorcyclists, and said that if a gang like this invaded his own town 'he would shoot first and ask questions later'. He forced a new script on the project, which emasculated much of the film's message and mightily angered Brando, who had researched the part by hanging out with cycle gang members, and even arranged for some of them to be blended in to the cast. But he was trapped by contractual obligations into carrying on.

And it was Viszard who insisted that Brando narrate the 'on this road' introduction to the film, which was to emphasise that the town take-over in the movie was a one-off that could never happen again. But as Higham says, 'for Brando the whole point was that it could happen again; that it would happen again; that incidents like this would become typical as ordinary young men became increasingly crushed by society's pressures and deadened by the boredom of their lives.' The outlaw biker violence of the sixties, with gang rape (something *The Wild One* only hints at), castration, fatal shootings, and the public stabbing at Altamont, would seem to vindicate Brando's intuitions.

Since it was a case of no prologue, no movie, Brando worked out a way of expressing what he felt for the introduction. He delivered it in a semi-amateur Southern accent which doesn't appear anywhere else in the film. He also made faces throughout the recording in the studio. 'It was,' said the director Laslo Benedek, 'his own way of saying to the Breen Office "Screw you".'

But it wasn't enough to overcome Marlon's dissatisfaction with the finished, compromised picture. At the time he was so disappointed that he wanted to retire. He didn't, but after the Hollywood fudges of *Streetcar*, *Wild One*, and even, as he believed, *On the Waterfront* with its contrived upbeat ending – all examples in their way of 'society's pressures' – he was disillusioned with the movie industry, thereafter mostly regarding it as strictly a money-making exercise; and his genius has only been very sporadically evidenced ever since.

All this, fortunately or unfortunately, got by me at the time. I listened to the speech and watched the empty road, waiting for the growing rumble on the soundtrack and the moment when the bike pack would materialise from the distance and roar straight into the camera. I knew about this from a brilliant comic book version in *Mad* magazine, where, as in the movie, the gang fills the whole road, until an oncoming vehicle suddenly slices them clean down the middle, thus allowing the film's title to be modified to *The Wild One Half*.

Then it was time to feast the eyes on Brando moodily leading the pack, and on the bikes. At the time I thought Marlon's riding a bit tentative (angles of lean etc), but I wasn't allowing for the high-bar cruising style, and having subsequently been involved in mobile photo sessions, I now have some idea of the constraints he was under.

In fact Brando seems to have been a pretty sharp street rider, according to his mate Carlo Fiore. When they were together in New York in the early forties as the play *Streetcar* was opening on Broadway, Brando had bought himself a second-hand Indian vee-twin. While not an obviously nimble machine for the city, Fiore writes 'We tooled all around town on that bike, Marlon always in Levi's and ratty tennis shoes … He was an expert driver, and I realised it was really the most sensible means of transport for him. He slithered through the snail-paced, bumper-to-bumper New York traffic like quicksilver and got where he wanted to go in a hurry.'

According to Fiore bikers were rare in New York then, and taxi drivers began to warn one another about 'a crazy kid on a motorcycle who's looking to get himself killed.' He was stopped by the cops a couple of times speeding through Central Park, but he was already a cult hero from *Streetcar* and they were happy to chat and let him go.

His evident riding skills were perhaps in contrast to those of James Dean, the other tormented young teenage actor, who fixated on Brando's *Wild One* persona, bought a black jacket and a Triumph twin and slavishly imitated his hero, much to Marlon's irritation: 'he's more fucking me than I am myself,' the multi-facetted Brando grumbled to Fiore. The great director Elia Kazan was asked if he 'wanted to ride on the back of Dean's bike; I didn't enjoy the ride. He was showing off – a country boy not impressed by city traffic.'

Naturally, in *The Wild One* I liked Brando's 1950 Triumph 650 Thunderbird, lightly California customised with high bars, a big sprung saddle and pillion pad, and slanted Harley-style pannier frames for his leather saddle bags. According to Higham this was Marlon's own bike.

But it was a Harley that swerved stylishly and kicked gravel into the camera lens at the end of the opening sequence – I'd guess that was one of the real cycle gang members taken on as extras. Otherwise the motorcycle emphasis was mostly British, with three or four Triumphs, and AMC also represented, with an AJS single and a Matchless 500 twin in dirt bike trim, its big chromed 'M' badges on the tank screwed on upside down to make 'W's. This bike was said to be Lee Marvin's, though in fact it belonged to stunt rider Wally Allbright. In the movie Marvin, as the leader of the Beetles, a breakaway faction of Brando/Johnny's Black Rebel Motorcycle Club, chugs in on a Harley.

The Beetles, the name looking sideways at the burgeoning cult of the beatnik, and eventually inspiring a Liverpool pop group, are a curious mix. One of them conforms to the beats' wiggy-weird profile with a meerschaum pipe and a false beard, but a couple are genuinely mean, and it's their presence in town which tips the scale over into violence. The Beetles' bohemian diversity stands in contrast to the Black Rebel MC ('What are you rebelling against, Johnny?' 'Whattaya got?') who, conformist non-conformists, all wear the same black leather jackets. But a point in the original screenplay about the potential Fascist uniformity this symbolises is lost in the actual picture, mainly because Johnny's henchmen are played by little guys who appear to be refugees from a Danny Kaye movie, and feed him lines as sycophantically as Sgt Bilko's stooges.

By contrast, Marvin himself is quite palpably the real thing, an ex-Marine who flew open cockpit biplanes and rode his dirt bike for kicks. His character, Chino, deranged by booze from the word go, contemptuously spouts free-form dialogue at Brando ('Hiya sweetheart. Hey, what are you doing in this miserable gully?'), before hauling off with dangerous unpredictability and slugging him – or rather his double, as the fight sequences don't stand up to close scrutiny. With the studio insisting that the whole film be completed in an amazing 24 days, it's no wonder.

Brando's Johnny represents the outsider-as-victim version – 'My old man used to hit harder than that,' he grunts at the citizens beating him up, thus neatly dove-tailing Freud and the liberal it's-all-the-parents'-fault approach. But you can't imagine Marvin's Chino justifying his freewheeling, malicious life-style in this or any other way, or feeling the need to do so. He is that disturbing thing, a flat-out crazy. The real-life Hell's Angels picked up on this – Frank (not Westworth), the President of the San Francisco chapter in the late fifties and early sixties, bought Marvin/Chino's actual blue-and-yellow-striped sweatshirt off the studio, and wore it ragged when confronting Authority.

Then there's the love interest. The decent small town girl, the sheriff's daughter (played by sweet if a bit wet Mary Murphy), after some well crafted scenes illustrating the non-meeting of minds with Johnny-the-urban-hipster, is pursued at night, on foot, by the marauding bike-mounted horde (in a chase sequence so unlikely and extended that in the *Mad* magazine version, when they catch her, it's only to present her with a long-distance running trophy!). Rescued by Johnny, cruising off on the back of the Triumph with the moon filtering through the cottonwood trees, she melts, and is in a giving mood when they stop in the park.

But Johnny is first too rough, and then, oh God, maybe a bit ... intimidated? His hypermasculine hunkiness has already been established by a minor female biker girl called Britches who thrusts her spectacularly pointy brassiere at him and blubs about the good times they once had on the sleeping bag circuit. But I remember being rattled by the park scene's failure to uphold the machismo of butch bikers. The scene, while its abruptness constantly teetered on the edge of the ludicrous, did convey that leather and bikes might be a cover for some crippling insecurities and even impotencies in the gurl department – which was not what an inexperienced 19-year-old with a Bronx jacket wanted to consider *at all*. It's undeniable that Johnny demonstrates more concern when he sobs over his fallen Triumph than he ever does over the 'sad chick', though unfortunately this might just ring true with the majority of bikers ...

So in the end, is *The Wild One* just a tame artefact, a studio-licensed playing-at-rebels? Yes and no. Like all good art, some of the film's images subvert its overtly stated morality. What survives is some kind of allegory and coherent take on the West in the fifties – a town almost entirely made up of stout, materially-minded middle-aged male burghers, where the best (the sheriff) lack all conviction, and the worst (Marvin and co) are filled with a terrible intensity, from aimlessness and the incoherent energy of unfocussed anger.

The film's real strength, though, lies in the unforgettable moments created by Brando – the homework with real bikers paying off with utterly natural rhythmic dialogue, as when he explains the fatal accident with 'I did a big brodie, and I went out, and that's all.' Or when he enters the empty Bleeker's Cafe for the first time, his stolen trophy dangling head down by a thong from his wrist, walking slowly down the row of vacant swivel chairs at the counter, casually spinning them, the impatient and the dreamy in perfect balance.

The only possible response to materialist Amerika as represented by the town seemed to be embodied in Brando's enigmatic, magnetic sense of style, both his awesomely cool take-no-shit front, and the confusion and vulnerability he also managed to convey beneath it. Mere style may have

'Quarter-inch Whitworth ... Please, oh please ...'

been shown by now to be a partial and inadequate response to a complicated world, but it spoke to us at the time, and as Johnny might have said, 'What else have you got?'

And the ending, with Johnny redeeming himself by wordlessly returning the stolen statue to Mary Murphy with a dazzling half-smile, though Brando hated it as Hollywood phoney, does touch something in us that can still hope for redemption to come from women's kindness – as well as letting him roar off down the road on the T'bird to freedom … Now surely that's a window on the biker soul?

1959

Not much to add to this one, except a little context. Under the short-lived but excellent editorship of Claire Leavey, while Frank Westworth was away minding other titles, CBG *ran a few themed issues.*

One of them centred on the year 1959, which famously had been the one when sales of two-wheelers in this country had reached an all-time high. Happily I remembered it well, as it was also the year I passed my bike test (cars would have to wait another 12 years). Living today back where it all happened for me then, it sometimes seems like only yesterday …

Castro took over in Cuba, the space race got underway, and they opened the M1 – it all happened in 1959. But none of that counted for me against one red letter day – I passed my two-wheel driving test, first time.

Aged 16, bare-headed, wearing yellow leather gauntlets (a Christmas present) and a long grey mac, I was mounted on a Douglas Vespa 125 scooter – damaging admissions, or what? But I was still at boarding school, the only holiday work available was potato picking at £1 for an eight-hour day, and a scooter was all the aged p. would spring for. And in them days for us newly-minted Teenagers, it was like the old song says: 'Some like Cadillacs, and some like F'ods, And some like *anything* as long as it rolls.'

But it was also the way things were going then. The November 1958 Earls Court Show, where the models for '59 were unveiled, billed itself as 'The Show where the scooter and motorcycle finally met'. There had been no Show in '57, and the ones at Frankfurt and Milan that year had also been cancelled, so the innovations on view were quite striking.

The 'new superspeedsters' like the first T120 Bonneville, AMC's 650s, and BSA's A10 Super Rocket, were thought to be anticipating the upcoming motorways. The nation's very first section, the eight-mile Preston bypass in Lancashire, would be opened in December '58 by Prime Minister Harold Macmillan, Supermac himself, 'as a token of what is to follow ... the symbol of a new era of motor travel in Britain'. It featured the first special traffic signs with white letters on a blue background, 'designed to be visible to high speed drivers, with letters as much as a foot high'. Wow. A few weeks later the new bypass was to be closed by frost damage.

Supermac wasn't kidding, though. 1959 saw the Tory party reverse its long term policy of favouring rail transport over road-building. The closure of 230 railway stations was announced, and rail fares were to be raised by a cool 50 per cent. At the same time Government plans were unveiled for a road expansion scheme with an annual budget of £140 million, and of course in November came the opening of the London to Birmingham M1 motorway. We live with the results of that policy U-turn to this day.

At the Show, however, the targeted market was principally 'bread and butter buyers', ie commuters whom public transport was serving increasingly badly, plus more youngsters, and women. Continental scooters were already popular with all those categories. The famous peak British two-wheel sales figure for 1959, of 331,806 machines, concealed the fact that imported content was already high, and rising (54 per cent in 1957, 87 per cent by 1964). And of the 1957 sales total, while 75,000 had been motorcycles, 100,000 had been scooters, mostly imported. At least my Vespa had come in CKD form, and been assembled at the Douglas works in Bristol. On-the-road two-wheeler figures for 1960 were 950,000 motorcycles to 470,000 scooters.

But that didn't convey how universally popular the cheerful, stylish, non-threatening Italian scooters were, at all levels. My mother, knowing I was keen on two wheels, in an effort to head me off from motorbikes used to send me at school the monthly scooter column out of *She*, a mainstream women's magazine. I don't think you'll find an equivalent today.

So the British industry was finally, belatedly, stirring its stumps in that direction for '59. The scooter features of enclosure, weather protection, bright colours and light weight were all aimed for, with varying degrees of success, by British motorcycle manufacturers. The AJS/Matchless 'Lightweight' (sic) 250 went two-tone, as did the all-new Ariel Leader, which exemplified just about every one of those current trends. BSA came up with their light 250cc C15 and with the second 175 version of the Bantam, the D7 Super.

This 175 engine, as well as a pokier 250 twin motor, also went in the new BSA Sunbeam/Triumph Tigress scooters – Meriden's press folk were said to have scoured London looking for tigerskin tights for the models who publicised the Tigress at the Show! The production target on these scooters was 1,000 a week by '59, serious business, but teething problems plus a dry weight of 244lb versus around 180lb for my Vespa, meant that the BSA/Triumph effort never thrived. In truth the real scooter boom had peaked, and it was to be no go for the many, many new Villiers-engined

British scooters on offer, up to and including the Dunkley 'Do-it-all' Commercial Combination.

This did not stop some of the great motorcycle names charging down the enclosure road, now that Triumph's Edward Turner had started the ball rolling in 1957 with the bath-tub Twenty-One 350 twin. For 1959 Triumph came up with the 500 version in the 5TA, which spelt the end of the pre-unit Tiger 100, one of the great sportsters. On the Triumph stand with its 140 neon tubes and 19-year-old Mike Hailwood's Thruxton 500 Mile-winning T110, there was even a 3TA with a prototype Motoplas 'boot' which wrapped around the whole of its rear. They were crazy for this stuff.

Norton joined the queue at the trough with the unreliable panelled Jubilee 250 twin, and even Velocette covered their lower halves on the grotesque 'Sports' versions of their classic singles. Ambassador, Francis-Barnett, Panther, Sun, and Royal Enfield with its relatively stylish Airflow fairing, all covered up some of their motorcycles to greater or lesser degree.

A lot of these offerings look pretty silly now, and weren't that well-received by enthusiasts at the time. But they represented some sort of attempt to cash in on a brief but very real boom for motorcycling. As Supermac's 'You never had it so good' indicated, wages for male manual workers had risen during the decade, there was virtually full employment, and minimal inflation. And even more relevant for most motorcyclists was something the government did in the interests of winning the 1959 election, which in October the Tories would indeed do very comfortably for the third time running. After a long period of economic 'squeezes', in September 1958 the previous controls on Hire Purchase were removed. With rates dropped a point to 10 per cent and no more 24-month limit on repayments – and then purchase tax dropped from 30 to 25 per cent in mid-1959, so that bikes actually fell in price – sales went through the roof.

Even the weather conspired to help. From March to October 1959 the warm weather set British records for the century, and if August saw violent storms and floods in London, well, most people had bought their bolide by then. That 331,806 new bike sales figure was never equalled, before or since.

My main recollection of the weather involved the acquisition of the second-hand maroon Vespa, complete with windscreen, that summer. It set my mother back £25, I think. The nice man from Coronation Car Sales in Swindon arranged the insurance, and then came out with the scooter in a van. He took me up onto a steep ridge above our village with a longish straight at the top, and showed me the rudiments of the little 3-speed two-stroke's controls, with its twistgrip hand gearchange – a good idea, recently adopted by mountain bikes. He supervised my first few wobbling goes on it, and even showed me how to bump-start it. For training, that was it. Good thing there was only about a sixth of today's traffic around then.

Anyway, I continued to bumble up to that same ridge every day, to get in some quiet experimental riding. One afternoon in August I ventured down the long steep hill on the other side. Attempting a U-turn at the bottom, I stalled while still in gear. And couldn't get it into neutral to kick-start it again. So I pushed it up the hill a bit and tried bump-starting it. But whatever gear I was stuck in, the Vespa wasn't playing. Further and further up the long hill I pushed it. It was a very, very hot afternoon and I remember the wringing wetness and the burning face (embarrassment and chagrin as well as overheating) to this day. I was planning to get to the lane back to the village and freewheel downhill and home, but at the top I once more tried pulling in the clutch. The Vespa clicked easily into neutral, and started first prod.

Down the dead-end street of our little Berkshire village, sales of new motorcycles were not a feature, and in 1959 the mix of two-wheelers was probably relatively representative of the real-life country as a whole. There was a jolly farm labourer with a DR coat and a maroon beret who ran an agricultural A10 Golden Flash outfit – plunger? – can't remember. It took the hill up the village street with gusto. There was a no-good boyo called Robbo, the by-blow of a departing black US serviceman and a local girl, who came over from a neighbouring village on a filthy 350 Royal Enfield Bullet with oil baked and caked all over it and a fresh puddle underneath, every time he stopped to sneer at us and show off his cigarette smoking – a risky business that, given the Bullet's Kuwait-like fumes. But at least it wasn't panelled.

There was my friend whose British parents had sent him over from Argentina to go to Eton, billeting him with ancient, beady aunts. Going his own way, he acquired a well-used 350 Jampot Matchless single, but being both more thorough and a lot more skilled mechanically than I (you couldn't be worse), he seemed to spend more time rebuilding and decoking it than in the saddle. This would have pleased AJS/Matchless' ill-starred boss Donald Heather, who had famously declared on how that was what British motorcyclists liked to do on their weekends. But in this case it may have been just as well, since my friend was a highly skilled but pretty wild rider, as I would discover watching him on horseback in Argentina a few years later.

In fact it was rare that any of us, village lad or otherwise, had our two-wheelers going at the same time so that we could ride out in a group. The Vespa was pretty reliable, only stranding me once that I can recall, and capable of trips to Sussex and back, though the lights were the anaemic glow-worm variety. But there were a couple of Mist Green D1 Bantams in the area, with that impressive cockerel transfer on the cream-panelled tank, and something Villiers-engined – a 150 Fanny-B, I think.

Only once did we get it together for a burn-up – smoke-up? – with the other three strokers, along the base of the Downs on the old road to Swindon. I took my best village pal Anthony Austin on the Vespa's sprung-saddle pillion, and then experienced stark terror after he talked me into letting him drive. He passed the whole lot on the inside, snaking along the chalky white verge of the narrow road while the 125 screamed its guts out. But it was a great, memorable day, a real foretaste of what two wheels might have to offer.

In complete comfort.

We all had highly inflated dreams already, of course. I sent away for an enormous ex-RAF bone-dome shell which arrived complete with squadron crest. I also located a brand new tan leather US Eighth Air Force flying helmet, luxuriously lined in soft yellow suede. Worn together, the bone dome didn't wobble about too much, but I hate to think what sort of neck-cracking trouble I could have been in if I'd fallen off for real. Still, it helped you feel like a jet pilot – a 35mph jet pilot …

Our real heroes, though, were the paid-up rockers you found in Swindon. Brylcreemed coifs and sideburns, white silk scarves, ice blue jeans, winkle-pickers and, of course, black leather jackets – all way beyond the pale for even the most tolerant middle-class mums and dads. Though I think flick knives were still legal then, there weren't many other accessories available in 1959, so if you were magnetised by the sight of some swarthy cat with a big belt-buckle like a Triumph 'mouth-organ' tank badge, it was odds on that it was a real tank badge and he really owned a Triumph. Likewise the peaked caps some of the grease affected couldn't be bought, they had to be snatched from poor old bus-conductors and have the wire removed to get the proper floppy profile – sideways homage to the RAF again (or to the SS?).

Rockers generally were not to be trifled with. When three or four of them on big twins went by the family Morris Minor, you knew it. Almost more impressive were the spiralling trails of smoke laid down by the two-tone Leaders and, later, Arrows. But it may surprise younger readers to hear that there was no motorcycle/scooter antagonism at that stage – like I said, '*anything*, as long as it rolls'.

But Rockers did span a spectrum from exuberance to seriously bad news. A couple of years later I went to a rock and roll concert in Bristol. The front several rows were packed with Rockers and Teds, and unfortunately the support act, sandwiched between Johnny Kidd and the Pirates and The Killer himself, Jerry Lee Lewis, was – Heinz and the Tornadoes. Ex-Sputnik Heinz had daffodil yellow hair, and neither his falsetto voice nor the wavering notes of 'Telstar' impressed the grease one little bit. They pelted him off the stage with coke bottles, and only Jerry Lee's bravura wild man performance at the piano – he played with his heels, he hit it. with his forehead, he was crazier even than the craziest of the audience – pulled round the evening and turned it from ugliness to roaring exhilaration. Great balls of fire, all right.

Back in 1959 some of the other role models might sound a little unlikely today. It was not only the year of *Living Doll*, it also saw Cliff Richards' film debut in a home-grown juvenile delinquent flick called *Serious Charge*. He played the singing younger brother of the maximum JD, who, if memory serves, rode a Triumph. Indeed, it was Cliff who that year opened the rocker's Athenaeum, the 59 Club. Don't snigger, but he was a fair old rock and roller in them days – I still have the EP with his live version of *Move It* complete with delirious pubescent girls audibly screaming 'Gorgeous! Gorgeous!' from the front rows, which always used to crease us up at school.

It didn't make up for the loss of Buddy Holly, Richie Valens and the Big Bopper (who could forget his *Whole Lotta Woman*?) in February '59, but it was something to be going on with. Cliff's diminutive rival Adam Faith rode a Triumph round Soho for real, reportedly inspiring much concern among his friends, because he was so small and the bike seemed so big.

Adam too wore a single zip black leather jacket in a risible youth movie with a fair John Barry soundtrack, *Beat Girl*, which we all broke out of school to see. Scooter rider or no, the iconic significance of the black jacket grew and grew for me, and I gazed through the window of the shop in Swindon at the lancer-fronted Lewis Leathers Aviakit offerings, with the double row of zips supposedly so you could still do them up with an extra sweater underneath but actually, one suspected, an excuse for more metal to join the buckles, zipped pockets and push-studs in a symphony of lush black and silver. The cherry on the cake was these jackets' quilted scarlet linings. Had to have one, even at £9 18s 6d. By the following year I had done what was necessary, and as my poor old mother shuddered, came back from Swindon with the full-dress item.

Meanwhile, though I might be riding Italian wheels with a head-full of American dreams, Britain was still a speed king among nations. In 1959 Mike Hawthorn had been killed in a road accident on the Guildford bypass, but Stirling Moss won the Italian Grand Prix and Donald Campbell in Bluebird broke the world speed record on water. MV might be completely dominating the motorcycle world championships, but their winning rider was an Englishman, John Surtees. The first trials began for another revolutionary British invention, the Hovercraft, and a further necessity for the motorway age, sodium street lighting, was tested for the first time.

The British were still British, and the proposed route for the M1 was changed to save a forest. Then early in November the first 69-mile stretch of the London to Birmingham motorway opened. This was a new thing. On its first Sunday in action sightseers flocked to the area, picnicking along the approach roads. But within a week a fatal accident had claimed the lives of two British lorry drivers, and soon afterwards five Police Chiefs went public to say that in their view the new superhighway's design and operation were unsatisfactory. Just like the M25, eh? Same old same old.

It was not only the road's design, however, which was unready for the new decade. With no upper speed limit, the motorcycling press could speak airily of cruising at 90 on the motorways, on new tyres purportedly designed to permit this, though practical chaps like Ixion would query the absence of 'illuminated direction indicators' on British machines (we would, however, have to wait another *ten* years for them). But anyone who has tried sustained high motorway speeds on a British twin that doesn't have 'Vincent-HRD' on its tank, or 'Commando' on the side-panels, will know that it's really not on. British bikes had been designed with the existing, often twisting network of converted cart-tracks and Roman roads in mind. Versatility and good handling were the home-grown machines' forte, not high speed cruising. And from then on no-one at the top of British industry would have the foresight or the will to provide a really new generation of reliable big bikes.

And in August 1959 came the first pictures of the traditional British motorcycles' nemesis, the BMC Mini. 70mph (the saloon car's ton) and £500 were the vital statistics. Adventurously, my mother immediately bought one, and the change from the Morris Minor was very, very noticeable. The lively Mini meant that sidecar outfits and bubble cars were taken out at a stroke, even if an unofficial strike at Longbridge in September would halt Mini production and give another foretaste of the decade to come.

The other half of the pincer movement that was squeezing the industry came in some terms from the sinister charisma of the rockers themselves, allied with the motorcycle sales boom. In 1959, with 1.76 million two-wheelers on the road, motorcycle accidents rose 31 per cent on 1958, and a slew of scare stories on reckless coffee bar cowboys appeared across the full spectrum of the press. One ton-up anecdote which circulated locally will give you the flavour. There is a long stretch of road running downhill into Henley from the west, and three rockers were said to use this, late at night, for chicken runs. One would scream down the hill while his mates roared up it side by side, the three converging so that the solo rider had to rocket *between* the other two at a terminal velocity approaching 200mph. One night the downhill runner saw the headlights starting up the hill towards him, went for it, and only discovered far too late that it wasn't his mates, it was a car ...

Probably an urban myth, but one result of the scare-mongering and accidents would be the 1960 250cc learner limit. The '59 sales boom had already dramatically gone off the boil, and the new emphasis on small capacity machines provided a ready-made toe-hold for Japanese marques. 1959 had seen Honda's first, unobtrusive appearance at the TT, and the following year the Anglo-Japanese Trade agreement liberalised motorcycle imports – to the disgust of our Industry Association, who correctly perceived that there was unlikely to be much reciprocal liberalisation by the wily Orientals – and indeed in 1971, Japan would permit the import of just 266 British machines, while the Hondas flooded our streets.

So a good deal that was disagreeable had its roots in the seminal year of '59, but I'm afraid that I can only really see it as the start of something personally good. My village pal Anthony Austin became a Royal Navy frogman, and on his wages bought a succession of Triumph Bonnevilles which he rode to the max, until he caught himself one summer evening riding neck and neck with a mate, both doing over 90 down an impossibly narrow lane above Portsmouth. With marriage and fatherhood impending, then and there he gave up the game. That was Austin – he took it to the limit, and lived to tell the tale. Me, I blagged a Vespa GS for getting into college, and immediately rode it 6,000 miles to Greece and back, imprinting myself in the process with an indelible love of the long roads. And schizophrenic or not for a scooter rider, I wore the leather jacket. In my mind, I'm afraid I've been wearing it ever since. And it all began in 1959.

The Ace Cafe

From 1959 to 1999, the revival of the Ace Cafe neatly closes a 40-year loop. Once again there's not a lot to add to this piece, except that the Ace today continues from strength to strength, despite extensive damage caused to the place (and to moving spirit Mark Wilsmore's bike) by fierce floods in the spring of 1999.

The Ace has been further buttressed by the recent opening of Bill Crosby's London Motorcycle Museum nearby. Mark Wilsmore himself was a fascinating character to meet; as with most of our subjects, it was a real privilege.

There has probably been more hot air talked and written about rockers and ton-up boys than on any other scene in motorcycling. Both at the time and in retrospect, something which evolved quite naturally at grassroots, first had to contend with a barrage of paranoid projection which demonised the leather boys, and then with a lot of inflated myth-making that tried to turn them into some kind of rebel superheroes. Truth, as in war, was the first casualty.

So as I drove out early one summer Sunday morning to pick up Garry Stuart the photographer and visit the Ace Cafe, I tried to focus on a couple of basic truths. First, before 7am on that fine day, there were motorcyclists out, singly or in pairs, travelling at respectable speeds, their riders taking advantage of the early traffic-free roads. And you can bet that when they eventually took a break, if there was a roadside meeting place, be it lay-by or Little Chef, there would be a lot of pumped-up and enjoyable chat about bikes and biking. Second, as I approached through the woods to Garry's place, one tree by the roadside was bright with ribbons and fresh wreaths. Life on wheels is uncertain, like life itself only more so, especially if you take it to the limit; and that fact has a way of pulling things into sharp focus.

These are the elements in a continuous tradition.

The Ace Cafe, Take 1

In the late thirties, Britain acquired a new arterial road network. In 1938, the Ace Cafe was built north of Hanger Lane in West London, primarily to service transport using the A406 North Circular road. Being open 24 hours a day it soon attracted motorcyclists, though they would never be its exclusive clientele. The Ace, in fact, was part of a transport-orientated complex in the area, owned by one man and including a motor showroom and one of the earliest recorded car washes.

Badly bomb-damaged in the war during a raid on nearby railway yards, the Ace was rebuilt in 1949. Came the affluent fifties (relatively affluent – rationing in Britain only fully ceased in 1954), and this plus the wartime baby boom begat Teenagers, five million of them in the UK by the end of the decade. Motorcyclists had kept coming to the Ace – the Ariel Owners Club, for instance, was founded there in 1952 – but it was wage-earning working class teenagers, with access to British bikes now affordable via Hire Purchase, who really swelled their ranks as the fifties progressed. There was no financial slack though, so drinking and smoking were out if you were serious about speed.

Another feature of the era was rock and roll. This strand of the identity which teenagers were discovering for themselves, like a lot of it, was imported from the seriously affluent United States. The lack of recognition and the disapproval of the new music from grown-ups, as represented by Auntie BBC, meant that although you could buy records (my brother had a 78 of *Hound Dog* back in '56), pretty well the only ways to hear them first were either Radio Luxembourg, or listening to them on jukeboxes in coffee bars and cafes. The big Bel-Ami jukebox just inside the door to the right at the Ace (you can still see the bolt holes where it was fastened to the floor) became a crucial part of the scene; several Ace regulars started bands, or clubs, and big names either current or future often dropped by.

Hard riding was still the main event though, and the jukebox contributed to that, too, via record racing. In the length of a three minute single, bikes, usually after midnight, would blast out of the car park heading left and burn away northward. As described by Mike Clay in his book *Cafe Racers*, they would roar under the railway viaducts, shoot the Stonebridge Park lights if necessary, accelerate to a three-quarter mile 90mph right-hander, then take the climbing left-hander to the treacherous Iron Bridge, which had to be exited at 80. Then it was brake to 65 for a downhill left-hander, and finally a quarter mile right-hander to the Neasden roundabout, which was negotiated with everything scraping and sparking, before running the same route in reverse to rocket back before the record stopped.

It was do-able, but only just, and with total commitment. This, plus cafe-to-cafe racing, took its toll; Clay confirmed that in a single two-week period, seven riders lost their lives at the Iron Bridge alone. As the most prominent in a network of venues around the capital which included the Dugout at Golders Green, Johnson's on the A20 by Brands to the south-east, and the Busy Bee on the Watford bypass, the Ace began to draw Press attention, and official disapproval. If there was an upside to the street craziness, it was the way it honed the talents of riders like Triumph works star Ray Pickrell, Dresda man Dave Degens and JPN stalwart Dave 'Crasher' Croxford, all Ace regulars in their formative years, and the kind of riders capable of out-running the late night traffic police patrols which were imposed on the area as the wipe-out rate became impossible to ignore. Another result of the deaths and injuries was the 250cc learner limit of 1960.

The Ace's heyday was probably from the late fifties to around 1963, when the British motorcycling bubble had burst; though the hysterical publicity surrounding the place would peak in the next couple of years with the largely Press-created and inflamed Mods v Rockers rivalry. As I know from personal experience, before that there had been no discernible antagonism between scooter riders and bikers, and the fact that John Entwistle of The Who went to the Ace argues that the ideological divide largely sprang from the minds of hacks, though many of the lads would certainly run with it in '63 and '64.

Otherwise, how rough was the Ace, where the chairs as well as the tables were bolted to the floor? Like anywhere groups of young males gather, with a dusting of admiring females, there was horseplay and a bit of brawling, but what most remember was the buzz, the camaraderie and the plentiful laughs. If the Ace had a dark side, in those relatively innocent pre-drug, pre-lethal weapon days, it was more the wide/dodgy kind. It existed in the real West London world, where strangers were fair game and the big ones ate the little ones. It was probably not too advisable to visit the Ace on your own for the first time and leave your T110 unattended for too long.

Dodgy spares dealing landed at least one very prominent figure on the scene in the nick, though the police were unable to get him for bike bits but did so for cars'. My colleague Jim Reynolds, another West London boy on a motorcycle, stayed away from the Ace for those reasons. In '67 I attended a motorcycle maintenance evening class held in some bike sheds behind the late lamented British bike shop Hamrax, in Ladbroke Grove. The class was conducted by two regulars from the Ace, and what I mainly remember was their detailed instructions not on tappet adjustment, but on how to use false ID to con riding gear on the HP out of Lewis Leathers. A percentage of the Ace boys were undoubtedly likely lads.

After I got my first motorcycle, a 350 Norton twin, in 1962, a couple of times I turned off when riding from Oxford to my father's house in Twickenham, and cruised by the Ace. But I'm sorry to say that I never went in. Partly it was the above factors, and mostly just being a wannabe-rocker from the wrong background who knew nobody. The opportunities for making a prat of oneself seemed limitless. The lads did their own maintenance (and plenty of it), and sometimes construction as well, often to a high standard, as witness the best of the Tritons from that era; while I could only just about tighten a rear chain or change a cable.

But there was more, and here I'm probably going to make my own contribution to the bullshit and paranoia that has surrounded a simple transport cafe. It was also LMF – lack of moral fibre – which kept me away, because, ultimately, of the death thing. Black jackets with 'Coffin Cheaters' or 'The Overtaker Gets The Undertaker' on the back could be rightly understood even then as callow bravado, or the lads, like Dickens' Fat Boy, wanting to make your flesh creep (especially if you were their parents). In the absence of the replica Nazi regalia that came in later with the patch clubs, the metal skull-and-bones badge on the rockers' leather jacket was often a British

'Rider and machine ...

Army crest, that of the 17/21st Lancers, the 'Death or Glory' cavalry regiment (our family's view of this stirring motto had been somewhat adjusted before the war, when a young subaltern from the regiment had come to stay, and at bedtime plaintively requested a hot-water bottle).

But when it came to it, taking it to the fatal limit and not backing off was close to the real rocker heart. The closeness of death, that in the recent war had been so cursed and hated and feared as it destroyed families and blighted young lives, nevertheless proved to be a potent drug which some of a new generation in their turn needed to roll the dice with. After facing it, of course you never felt more alive.

When it came to it, I didn't want to die. Some of the time then I thought that I did, but when it got to it, I didn't; so I rode the Norton up to Aberdeen and down to Barcelona, but I stayed away from the Ace Cafe. As with most people, the place aroused powerful emotions. Its character then changed as the sixties rolled on and some of the leather boys transmuted into Easy Riders; drug dealing and its attendant nastiness was often attributed as a factor in the cafe's closure in 1969. Subsequently it became a tyre depot.

The Ace Cafe, Take 2

'No,' said Mark Wilsmore. 'There have been all sorts of versions of why the Ace closed, but in fact it was because the man who'd owned it and the other businesses since the thirties retired, aged 75. Though his son has told me that the old man was "stunned and shocked" at the speed it was converted to the tyre depot.'

… growing old gracefully together.'

If you've attended any major classic motorcycle gathering over the last few years, you'll probably have seen Mark Wilsmore, a self-effacing figure with lightly greased coif and wispy rockabilly sideburns, tirelessly handing out the Ace Cafe Reunion leaflets with their distinctive ace of clubs and black and white chequered logo. From the first Ace Reunion Day in 1994 on the 25th anniversary of the closure, when 12,000 bikes turned up, Mark has worked ceaselessly to get the cafe back in business.

The movement has been helped along by his September Rockers Reunion Runs to Brighton (25,000 attended last year), and since 1996 by a merchandise operation offering a small, thoughtfully selected range of rocker clothing (Lewis Leathers, Barbour etc), plus relevant props like white seaboot hose and Brylcreem, and Ace regalia. There's a website also – ace-cafe-london.com – plus a recently launched Ace Cafe Club. And 1998 saw the partial reopening of one section of the original building, on Sundays from 8am to 8pm. This followed the acquisition of the site and the building, and the granting of planning consent for a cafe/restaurant/memorial hall there.

The 1994 Reunion also coincided with the end of the old dual-carriageway as a primary thoroughfare, since a new, sunken underpass running parallel to it now carries the North Circular traffic. This leaves the old road running in front of the cafe site as a quiet spur off the main drag, no bad thing since it means that bikes, *en masse* or singly, don't have to ride straight out of the place into today's traffic hurly-burly.

We drove into the hallowed car park, which is big, built for lorries, at 8am, because that morning at 10 Mark Wilsmore was leading a run to North

Weald Sprint off the M11, but had agreed to meet us before that. Mark's own Triton, built for him by nearby West London British bike specialist Bill Crosby at Reg Allen, was parked out front beside a pukka Degens Dresda twin, but Wilsmore's commitment to the Ace means he hasn't ridden his Triton as much as he would have liked, and when we arrived he was just off fetching his everyday wheels, an eighties oil-in-frame TR65 Thunderbird 650 with a blue and white export tank. The Ace food stall, also chequered black and white, was open, so while we waited we drank tea and sampled one of Joe's excellent bacon-and-egg rolls.

The Ace itself is a long, low building. To the right, as you look at it, is a clock tower, over what used to be the entrance to the cafe section, where Len and Roy Mayes dished out the egg and chips and mugs of tea (with the sugar spoon chained to the counter). To the left had been a restaurant, which the lads were not allowed into and where even truckers had to be smartly dressed. Both these sections are still currently tyre depot, but later in the Ace's life an extension had been added to the left end of the building, at the same time as an upstairs section was built to provide accommodation for drivers.

So it was the extension which now housed the Ace's interim 'view-and-brew' Sunday sessions, with the walls decorated by posters, original photos and items like a tee shirt from the Ton-Up Motorcycle Club of Nashville, Tennessee (Mark: 'So, basically, we're not alone'). Mark's red-headed wife Linda sits at a table dispensing regalia and signing up Club members. Also on display are architects' plans, and a scale model of the building as it will be. The soundtrack is a rocking mix of oldies and people's own bands, like regular Stuart Osborne and the Guano Bats, though CDs have arrived of bands who play the right stuff from as far away as Finland and Japan. Truly they are not alone. Meanwhile upstairs performs the function of a clubroom.

'Everyone has a look up here,' said Mark as he took us up, 'but then they stay outside talking bikes unless the weather gets bad.' He led us into a spacious room, with the walls decorated by collages of blown-up period Press reports on milestones like the Mod/Rocker clashes, and dominated by a huge circular black and white clock at the far end, bearing the Ace logo. 'I was getting nagged all the time to put the clock back up on the tower over the entrance, and finally a group of local friends presented the place with this one.'

There were blow-ups on the wall of Press reports on Bill Haley's ground-breaking, riot-prone '57 UK tour. Were the Ace's music connections for real? 'Oh yes. Take Gene Vincent. [Vincent, Be-Bop-A-Lula man, was motorcycle through and through, having got not just his black leathers but his trademark left leg limp in a Stateside bike smash.] There was an early British band called the Houseshakers who used to come here – they went on to become Matchbox, who are still around. Graham Fenton was a Houseshaker, and when they were on the same bill as Vincent, all he wanted to do was come here. So Graham brought him.

'Otherwise the most famous of the groups who hung out here was Johnny Kidd and the Pirates. [Kidd, a local boy from Willesden, with hits like

Please Don't Touch and *Shakin' All Over*, forged what has been called "the only authentic rock act Britain produced prior to 1962", before dying in a car crash in 1966.] People still talk about his antics here, and the way he'd stuff all his money in the jukebox playing his own latest releases. I've also been told that the Beatles, before they were, got kicked out for playing the same Buddy Holly song on the box for half an hour. Screaming Lord Sutch and the Savages came here, and Robert Plant from Led Zeppelin.

'Also the generation that listened to rock and roll on the jukeboxes went on to open clubs. Big Roy from the Ace started the 2 I's in Soho [where Cliff Richard recruited Hank Marvin and Jet Harris for the Shadows], and late at night after they'd closed, he'd bring the crowd back here.' Seminal doesn't seem too strong a word for the Ace in terms of British rock.

So had Mark Wilsmore been there in the old days? 'No, I'm 41 – yesterday, actually. The Rockers are well into their 50s now [tell me about it], while the Ton-Up boys are 60-plus, reaching retirement – it's amazing.' A big bonus from the Ace Club newsletter has been its 'Backtrack' initiative, encouraging old regulars of the place to share their memories. In this way, plus tireless archive trawling, Mark has accumulated stories and photos which have never before come to light.

We looked at the faces from the fifties, achingly young and full of life. 'Look at him, so handsome,' Mark gestures at a Triumph-mounted Rocker, 'he still comes in, but he's an old man now.' Others have gone down, to the road or occasionally to drugs. But there are plenty of happier endings, couples married by the 59 Club's Father Bill and still together, or riders like Paul 'Heinrich von Tritonhausen' Evison, today an official in the Gold Wing Owners Club and still active in classic racing. But looking at the photos cannot leave you unmoved. How many roads must a man ride down?

Mark Wilsmore was born in Barnet, North London, and today lives in Hendon, 'though I spent a chunk of my youth in Bedfordshire. But I'd always had, since childhood, a lust – like, cor, look at that bike! My generation in the seventies were into 100mph L-plate 250s. I had many Yamahas which I crashed regularly, and the last RD250 stuffed me up a treat – or rather the car driver did … In fact there was a bit of a gap from age 20 to 22, as I spent two years in hospital because of that. Then the moment I passed my test, unlike all my friends it meant I could have a Brit – I got that Meriden Thunderbird in 1980. It was strange, because my own peer group just weren't into those bikes.

'Or the music. I loved Rockabilly – the punk thing passed me by completely. At first it was just records on the radio or the odd tour by "mature" icons, usually disappointing; but then I came back to London, working on building sites, and discovered I wasn't the only one. The Stray Cats from America in the early eighties lit up a lot of things. So with the bikes and the music, you'd be sharing the same enthusiasm, and then you started thinking "Why doesn't somebody …?" By the tail end of '93 I had a peer group into leather jackets etc, and the Ace was an icon. When I learned the date that the cafe had closed 25 years before, that felt like the key to doing something in 1994.' The result was the first wonderful Reunion.

But Wilsmore's previous career move had been a little surprising. 'I'd joined the Met as a mounted policeman. It was always horses. I'd wanted to be a jockey in Bedford, until I got too tall. Then I wanted to go into the Army, but my mother wouldn't allow it, because of people getting blown up in Ireland. So it was the police.' But not Traffic, on two wheels? 'No, the bike bit for me was always about leaning on the tank, even with wide bars …' As a mounted officer, did he ever have to supervise MAG rallies? 'No, I'd take the day off and be one of them.'

'I was mostly based in Hackney and Stoke Newington, but I'd be going out to Leyton and similar places three times a week for football matches. You wouldn't get back to your nick much before two or three in the morning, and that meant riding home through the streets out East late at night, with no lights, and no radio. You had to learn to use this,' he said, tapping his forehead.

So time-wise, how did he square the job with the massive work of reviving the Ace? 'To begin with, I was doing it after hours. But today, though I'm still technically in the police, a lot of get-offs, both from horses and bikes, mean that I now have osteo-arthritis. I've been discharged, but I have to wait for it to go through various departments. I've been in and out of hospital over the last couple of years for my knees and ankles; I also used to do weightlifting, yeah, pretty daft, which has taken its toll on the joints – I used to be 16 stone …' You look again at Mark and realise that he seems a slighter figure than he actually is, part of a self-effacing, almost hesitant quality, a lack of dogmatism which should definitely not be mistaken for lack of fire or of resolution.

But what of the poacher/gamekeeper paradox, a copper helping revive something that was quintessentially outlaw? 'Well, I think the Ace scene is now as British as the Yeomen of the Guard. Which is probably why it suits my personality – I mean, I eat this pasta stuff, but how do you fit it round your fork? In the seventies and eighties, if you expressed all that, you were considered a rightwing loony. Now it's almost righteous … which is a remarkable turnaround in such a short space of time.

'What I treasure here, and I think others do too, is that there's a known history to this place. When people come today, with all sorts of preconceptions, what seems to hit most of them when they come into the car park is the wonderful mix of machines – classics, musclebikes, Viragos, Harleys, Tritons, and all nattering happily together – it's bikes. Then when people come inside, that's when I want to transport them to the history of the building, by the gubbins around. What I'm trying to avoid is either a museum thing, or a retro thing. This is only a view, but my view, and after talking and writing to hundreds of others – the reason people bought a Triumph and came to the Ace is the same as the way today they'll buy the fastest bike they can afford, and then make it go faster. It's the same today as it's ever been. That's what's so marvellous about Hinckley Triumph coming up with the T595 … at long last.'

And the death thing, back in the ton-up days? 'I was pulling out the newspapers for '64 the other day. One of the broadsheets headlined with the Mod/Rocker Bank Holiday riots, but there was another piece, about the size of a Swan Vestas box. It was Saturday's paper, and so far that weekend, at least 30 people had been killed on the roads already. And it was reported as a minor detail. What seems to come through is that it was simple things, the worse roads, tyres, brakes, which were mainly to blame – and then you factor in being 18, with a powerful motorbike ...'

How many of the original rockers come by? 'It's hard to quantify. Every rider of that generation remembers the place, and it's a treasured memory, even if they only came once, or never even came at all. There were many groups of around half a dozen, hard-cores, at any different time. But *the* night was Thursday, when there was speedway at Wembley, and a lot of riders would go to the Ace, go on to the speedway, and then come back here and watch the excesses.'

And the dodginess? 'One guy still comes in on a Goldie he rode then. He had it nicked – there was a lot of that going on, no question – but he asked around, and then put the fear of God into some known faces, told them it was a different thing to having a bike off someone coming from outside. And he got it back again.' Aggro? 'The only violence I've been told about was a bit of a set-to one night, and a ketchup bottle cut someone's hand. There was a local regular, Tex Childs, a big chap, and he sorted it out, because the night manager had legged it. The next night Tex was offered the manager's job, and he took it. It was Tex that Father Bill Shergold wrote to, and that led to the 59 Club, which had previously been simply a youth club with Cliff Richard as its patron, becoming a bike club.'

And bang on cue, Tex Childs came through the door and hustled Mark out to get the run to North Weald underway. Mark winced quietly as he rose from the table, his joints suffering. Out in the sunny morning, with a police car in relaxed attendance, Tex marshalled the riders with a portable bullhorn – the Ace seemed well organised like that – and they were indeed all sorts, a Goldie blaring into life, streetfighters, cruisers, an ultra-elongated Sierra-powered trike whose technicalities interested the cops as they sipped their tea, and even a scooter, a heavyweight red Heinkel Tourist. After the run had followed Mark out as he swept away on the blue TR65, Tex recalled the ketchup bottle incident clearly.

'My mate Keith was joking with someone, using rough language, and this nasty little red-headed Scots bloke thought it was aimed at him, and went for him with the bottle. It was bad, he cut Keith's little finger tendon through at the wrist. We sat on the Scot hard.' At the time Tex, who still looks handy, was an ABA boxer. Today he's an honorary member of the 150-strong Triton Club of France, and of its Swiss equivalent, the Loud Mufflers.

Tex was one of a handful of wise and wily faces with long greased grey hair, sometimes in pony-tails, sitting dotted around the car park giving strangers the eye, as the sun shone benignly and a minibus-load of biker tourists from Squires cafe Oop North turned up and started taking photos.

Another arrival was a flame-hooded hot rod; in a recent development, the Ace has started opening on the first Wednesday of every month to host a custom car cruise, with a lot of bikes showing up too.

Mark Wilsmore has dealt endlessly with the Ace's owners and occupiers, with the Council, with the local Regeneration Board and with English Heritage (getting the building listed before the Golden Arches went up there). Then to qualify for funds for restoration, he had to come up with a Business Plan to show that the Ace's activities would be self sustaining – and Business Plans are difficult to do, and cost £20k to have done professionally.

Then it was back to the Council for the crucial Planning Consent, which required detailed drawings, traffic reports etc. Even now, with all those hurdles overcome, the way ahead is still not clear, with a lawsuit looming over the use of the name. Can't talk about that since it's upcoming, but what I can say is, the best of luck to Mark and his friends. Because all the effort has resulted in something which, for no clear reason, has great emotional power, and the emotions are no longer fear and loathing, but warmth and good memories. This is the Ace without tears, a place which, as Mark put it, reflects the roots, the roots of some things that a lot of us hold dear in a quiet sort of way. Listen, go there and see for yourself.

'Take a seat …'

CHAPTER THREE

My journeys II:
Sweden to Holland

This run, a mini-epic, took place in the summer of 1991, riding the same BSA A65 Star Twin I had taken on the Portugal trip described in Chapter 1. By this time, with its rebuilt front end and finally well-sorted front brake, DSU 792 was shaking down nicely. So the early hiccup described here came as, if not a complete surprise, at least a nasty shock, particularly since the alternator had been fitted by an expert. (You know the definition of an expert? An 'ex' is a has-been, and a spurt is a drip under pressure ...)

There wasn't room to go into much detail about the trip's destination, the BSA Owners Club International Rally, which that year was held in Holland. Rallies, which have been described as 'riding 500 miles to stand around in a field', are not to all tastes, but this was a good one. The campsite was very well-appointed, and if you were too drunk to remember what country you were in, there was even a windmill to remind you.

The Rally was excellently organised by the BSAOC of Holland, who had to cope with several emergencies, mostly precipitated by the heavy rain that fell on the opening Saturday when everyone else was arriving. Tireless and friendly, the Club gave each new arrival a hot drink and a goody package, with a programme, a plaque, and printed with the red Rally logo – a large towel. In view of the deluge, did this mean they had known something in advance?

Well over 300 BSAs attended, and activities included a trip to a beer factory (yes, the BSA Owners can organise a piss-up in a brewery), plus the ambitious 'Midnight Lucas Die-Hard Run', a 100-mile trip 'through a gorgeous, but pitch-black landscape'. During this, half the riders were taking an after-midnight break in a cafe, thinking the other half were lost, when the prodigals were led in by a friendly police car.

At the Saturday night hop, the Dutch proved themselves the most, ah, creative dancers. But the best sticker spotted was in Swedish, on the back of an M20 sidecar outfit. When asked what it meant, the pilot pointed to the two children in the chair, and translated: 'Sidecar drivers have done it already'.

I had come to the Rally without camping gear, as I had previously arranged with the organisers to hire a hut on site. But it was not available the night we arrived, so (now it can be told) I shared a tent with one of the Swedish girls. Blamelessly, as it happens, because I was very happy with my girlfriend then. But in view of the way she treated me later, I've often regretted that innocent Dutch night under canvas.

I'm just back from a North European run on the A65. We went up to Sweden, and then joined some Swedish lads and lasses to ride down to Nijmegen in Holland for a weekend at the 28th BSA International Rally. It was a trip marked by a string of lucky coincidences, and topped off with some firm new friendships.

The 1962 A65 Star Twin and I made our rendezvous at Harwich with my girlfriend and her young daughter in their metal box, and enjoyed a hassle-free 24 hour sail to Gothenburg aboard just about the most comfortable ferry I've ever been on. It was sunny in Sweden. Our two parties separated, aiming to meet up 200 miles away that evening at Vastervik, a little port on the east coast. Driving in southern Sweden proved to be a doddle – very low volumes of traffic and shame-makingly considerate road users, with well-cambered and gently curved roads, clearly signed. Other bikers always waved. The only difficult bit was the prevalence of automatic petrol machines, which needed clean bank notes and a degree in computer science to operate. I learned to look for stations with a conventional 'Kass' option.

Outside the town there were logging trucks, and triangular yellow 'beware of the moose' signs (though a Swedish friend later said that there in the south, deer are more of a hazard). There were white-trimmed farms and barns in the characteristic red 'Falu' paint, and the smell of wild flowers and the purple weeds by the roadside. There were lakes and lakes, and trees and trees and trees. After 70 miles I was just concluding it might be a teeny bit boring when the engine began to stutter, and I broke for a sandwich lunch.

After lunch things seemed fine, but when I switched on the lights (daytime compulsory, as they are in most of Europe now) the engine died. So I proceeded without lights (and in fact would only see one police car in several hundred Swedish miles – just as well, as no lights means a £60 fine). Things were all right at speed, but after 20 miles, slowing down for a village, the stuttering happened again. Another wait, a change of plugs, another ten miles, and the same thing again. I was getting the idea it was electrical, so changed the fuse and fiddled with the switch connections, but once again, ten miles later the engine was jerking and stuttering violently on the over-run, and I eased into a self-service Jet station on the outskirts of a little town, I didn't know where.

Somewhat desperately, because Swedish leaded petrol comes in two grades and I'd chosen the higher 98 octane kind, I was wondering if it was that which was proving indigestible to the engine. So I tried to top up with unleaded, hoping to redress the balance.

The cash-for-petrol machine, however, proved baffling. But before long a figure in overalls bicycled up out of nowhere and showed me what to do. This attendant stuck around while I tried to start the BSA again. But this time it wasn't going to start.

I was left 70 miles short of my destination contemplating a lifeless machine, with evening coming on, in the middle of a country where my only knowledge of the language came from Ingmar Bergman movies and the Swedish chef on the Muppets. Added to which, in my parsimonious way I had delayed the start of the RAC Eurocover, so that for less money it only covered the *last* ten days of the three week trip. Hmmm ...

The attendant, however, spoke some English, and once he'd roughly got

'We really need a bright spark ...'

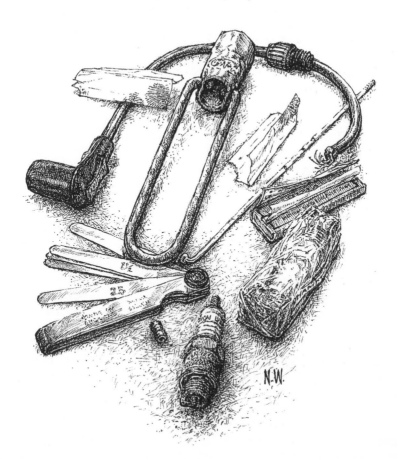

the picture, communicated it to the next guy in, a fair-haired chap on a green K100 BMW, a man with a moustache and a friendly if mildly perplexed expression. After that, things definitely began to look up, because amazingly, Inge Bergqvist turned out to be, just like me – a motorcycle journalist. The small town I'd conked out in happened to be the home of *Race*, Sweden's only *MCN*-type paper. Not only that, but Inge was slowly restoring a Norton P11A desert sled, and consequently knew that one of Sweden's few British bike specialists, Lugnets Motor, was located in the woods some 20 or 30 miles away. Since he didn't have their phone number and it was 4.30 on a Saturday afternoon, Inge reckoned he'd better go and look for them – he hadn't been there for five or six years – and arrange for the bike to be picked up. He whizzed off on the K, leaving me to contemplate this first example of Swedish hospitality to a complete stranger.

In just over an hour he was back, shortly followed by a van driven by a fierce-looking girl with dark hair and pointed teeth, who I knew from the Bergman movies should be called Gudrun. This was the daughter of Jonny Johansson of Lugnets. I felt a pang of uncertainty as we loaded the A65 and saw it driven off by strangers to the depths of the forest for the sinister-sounding hamlet of Grimstorp. But Inge gave up more of his time to buy me a coffee (damn fine coffee in Sweden), let me use the *Race* office phone to call ahead and reassure the car party, and finally got me onto a comfortable coach to Vastervik. If you have to break down, I consoled myself, this was the way to do it. Since I arrived only a couple of hours behind schedule, I got away without too much mockery from the female War Department about the reliability of old bikes.

Five days later I did the journey in reverse. I had the pleasure of meeting the staff at *Race*. Inge's parents were staying with him, and we pigged out on delicious pancakes his mother made, before driving to Lugnets Motor. Jonny Johansson's place was deep in the woods, down eight kilometres of smooth reddish dirt road. Jonny proved to be a friendly, shrewd, competent guy with a wry sense of humour. The A65's problem had been electrical. I should have paid more attention to an earlier whine from the primary chaincase which I had assumed was due to a chain in need of adjustment, because within the case the alternator rotor, three years after installation, had loosened off enough to have started brushing on the stator.

Jonny showed me the sorry stator, with a couple of its coils burnt out. He had substituted a good second-hand component, and secured the rotor with the correct washers. He'd also put my mind at rest by checking that it was not main bearing play which had caused the problem. When I asked if he thought his repair would get me the thousand or so miles to the Rally and home, he laughed and said it was a BSA, and he'd once seen a BSA's pistons liberate themselves forcibly enough to bend the frame downtubes! So who could say?

But he pointed out how well the new set-up was charging; and since I went on to ride the bike with the lights on for a 15-hour day, I have no complaints about Jonny's work. The £90 bill put a hole in my holiday budget, but since everything in Sweden is about twice the price in England, 90 quid for parts, labour, and a 50 mile van pickup didn't seem at all unreasonable.

After saying goodbye to Inge, on the ride back there was another happy coincidence. I passed an A65 and a Triumph T140 with Swedish plates stopped in a lay-by, and hung a U to check it out. The riders, both in the period leathers which Swedes seem to have access to, were identical twins (on twins). The Triumph, an immaculate '86 Devon-built 750, had gone onto one cylinder due to a duff coil. Happily I was able to provide a spare from my tank-bag, and, once the Triumph was running again, to ride off, childishly satisfied by the twins' 'who was that masked man?' reaction.

After a week's relaxation, it was time to head south alone again for the Rally. The Swedish language had remained a source of amusement – as we were giggling at the label of our first bottle of 'FAT' brand beer, the waitress had reassured us solemnly, 'Don't worry, it is pronounced "fart".' The Swedes themselves were always a pleasure to know, and I had arranged to meet a posse from the Swedish BSA club by Malmo at the port of Limhamn at 6am one morning, for the run to Holland.

The day before that there were some pre-flight nerves, but leaving Vastervik with a little fresh oil and some air in the tyres, the A65 was running reassuringly well. We put in a hundred miles of empty roads before lunchtime, and afterwards had some fun running with a couple on a ruby red Softail Harley with GB plates for 20 miles or so, before the long straights saw them pulling gradually away, giving me the benefit of that beautiful crackling exhaust note. The pace meant that I'd done the 240 miles to the port by 4.30, and I decided to catch the hourly ferry over to Denmark that afternoon, put in a few more miles, and wait for the Swedes next morning at the Danish ferry port for Germany instead, at a more civilised hour.

Now as I waited for the £10 Limhamn ferry, easing aching joints, the red Harley pulled in behind, and this was yet another happy coincidence, as Tony the pilot and his elfin Swedish wife Tina (who's saving for a Sportster of her own) turned out to live less than ten miles from where I did in Sussex. I also found out that my speedo was about ten miles slow – the 55 I thought I'd been doing to keep up with them turned out to have been closer to 65. Interesting.

They were heading on for a campsite they knew, so I followed the Harley off the ferry and through the traffic – a novelty after Sweden – round the south of Copenhagen, which with the Harley for company was fun and took my mind off a sore bum, and onto the motorway south. The A65, I noticed, got none of the usual interested glances while I was riding with Tony and Tina – well, what did I expect, running with a big red Harley packing a blonde on the back?

It was a beautiful evening, with the sun setting to our right as the fields around the road were harvested and the dusty smell of chaff carried onto the highway. We rode south at an indicated 60 (real 70?) and after about 50 miles this took its toll. I noticed with a shock that my headlamp had detached itself from its nacelle and was dangling by its wires down by the front mudguard. The second time this happened I fixed it on by winding silver duct tape all the way round – not concours, but the light was still working and the bike running remarkably well and strong. We got onto A-roads, clattered over some metal bridges and reached the site at Guldborg well before sunset. My ears were ringing, and the rubber bung giving access to the clutch cable had also detached itself (more duct tape). But I felt in good heart for the long run to Holland the following day, which would include 150 miles of German autobahn, a first for me.

Next morning I set off at 8.15 on the last 20 miles to the ferry at Rodbyhavn, figuring that if the Swedes had left Malmo at 6.00am I should pick them up at the port. After a few miles, however, the A65 spluttered and I went onto the reserve tap – riding with the Harley I'd neglected to fill up for 150 miles. I turned into the nearest small town, and, coincidence again, met the party of four Swedish BSAs, who were also looking for go-juice.

The club secretary who I'd spoken to on the phone briefly was 25-year-old Elizabeth Faijersson. She rode a red '69 A65 Firebird scrambler with high-level pipes. She was a Swedish blonde and all I can add is that though diminutive, she proved to be a skilled and tireless rider, and a very good companion, with an amazingly raucous laugh when provoked. The leader of the pack was Bo Andersson, a railwayman with slanted, slightly intimidating prize-fighter's eyes. I wondered whether his '53 B33 500 single, in a later swinging-arm frame, would match the 650 twins the rest of us were riding, but Bo proved to be the goer. We would each take turns at the front, but Bo would always wind up there again before too long, and the pace his 500 set proved just right for our mixed bunch. As to his forbidding looks, in fact it was Bo who was most careful if the Swedes were talking among themselves, always to translate the essence into English, which they all spoke excellently. All of them deliberately did this, another very welcome example of Swedish consideration.

Bo's tall and exuberant girlfriend Helen was riding a '63 A10 Rocket Gold Star, a genuine one – they'd traced the original owner who confirmed it had been the fastest bike in Malmo when new, though he had soon pranged it. It had been restored with a few non-original components, provoking some pundits at the Rally to dismiss it loudly as an RGS copy – wrong, chaps. It was in touring trim, the engine rebuilt with low compression Huntmaster pistons, though as the day wore on it was sometimes a bit of a handful for Helen to start.

Last there was Kjell, pronounced Shell, a benign gnome-like eccentric with a full beard and voluminous waxed moustaches (which proved to be excellent barometers for the weather, as one tip would droop when it was going to rain!) Partial to a glass of beer and a plug of snuff (not so eccentric, that – every Swedish supermarket checkout has snuff along with the fags), Shell was riding a very tidy 1951 A10 in silver and chrome. Since it was plunger-sprung with single-sided brakes, Shell was the natural tail-end Charlie, though from time to time he would roar up unexpectedly through the pack to the front, treating us to the Flash's gloriously rorty exhaust note.

Shell kept a note of the price of everything in a little book, and had declined to fill up when we did in Denmark, where the petrol was dearer than in Germany. His handbook told him the A10's four-gallon tank translated to 18.3 litres. In fact he scraped onto the ferry to Germany on the contents of his carburettor, and had a 300-yard push to the petrol station when we reached Puttgarden. After filling up, he tapped the pump gauge and observed 'The book is wrong'. The pump showed 18.4 litres.

I fretted a bit at first at the way time went by there on another stop, and had to remind myself that the Swedes had ridden 100 miles already. And in fact the only way to do the remaining 300-odd miles was steadily, in long stages with decent rests in between. I'm used to riding on my own, but this was one trip where the right company was a real advantage. Bo set off at a good 55–65mph clip across the flat lands of Schleswig-Holstein, and soon we were riding together on the dreaded autobahns, which often have no upper speed limit, so that Mercedes drivers can get their money's worth establishing a brutal pecking order.

The A-bahns proved to be surprisingly old-fashioned looking, like the early sections of the M1, and to begin with were two-lane only; I suppose this figures, since they were the first motorways in Europe. Our pace was quite OK for the slow and middle lanes, though when overtaking you definitely had to take a good deep look behind, as the natives could come steaming up out of nowhere. I held my breath once when Elizabeth moved out to overtake a camper and a speeding black Volkswagen pulled up literally inches from her tail-light, and stayed there. The other tasty local habit was cars bombing out from the side slip-roads and pushing onto the carriageway at full tilt, which split up our lot more than once. I was well pleased with the way the A65 accelerated, pulling round traffic strongly when needed. The two A65s were the only ones bothering with daytime lights, and for what it's worth, the others got away with it.

Mostly it was just a long tiring haul. I learned to know Shell's yellow backpack and Bo's red one, the silhouette of Helen's turned-down bars in the blurred mirror and the way Elizabeth smacked her hands on her thighs to restore circulation in her fingers; I was grateful for my Oxford foam-rubber grips when we compared hands after hours and the girls' were shaking helplessly from twin cylinder vibration. Occasionally a modern bike would stream by in the fast lane and provoke a brief fit of 'why are we *doing* this?'

We swung to the right around Lubeck and stopped for petrol and fluid replacement outside Hamburg. Rain threatened but then held off as we pressed on towards Bremen, aching badly, all of us stretching our legs out on the move to try and ease the pain. A service area beckoned after 40 miles but Bo tramped resolutely on in the muggy afternoon heat. Then around Bremen we met the tail end of the mother of traffic jams.

We were reduced to a walking pace with frequent halts, and the old bikes and particularly their clutches did not appreciate it one little bit – and the jam stretched away as far as the eye could see. So Bo took the correct decision and found a way to keep us moving. Not the foolish way, along the hard shoulder (and just as well, since a police car was there a minute later). But on the autobahn's 3rd lane the outside edge was defined by a white line, with another narrow strip of tarmac before the grass of the central reservation. We fell into single file and rode the laden bikes feet-up along that outside white line, giving some of the drivers stationary in the fast lane a bit of a shock as we roared past their open windows. When a car was too far over we snaked behind it, into the middle lane and then back through gaps onto the outside. It worked, and after nearly ten miles of concentrating hard, we were clear. Next morning we would all discover weeds from the central reservation jammed in our stands and left-hand silencers.

The next pit stop at around 4.30 outside Wildhausen was massively

Problem solving.

welcome, and we had a full and hilarious sit-down meal – not a bad idea if you're doing a long day, to double up lunch and supper. Setting off again at 6.00, at the next exit we left the motorway and blissfully regained long, straight, fairly empty A-roads. The two A65s settled in together behind Bo, and aches and pains were forgotten as we pushed on towards the border.

But after an hour Helen rode forward to tell us to slow down a bit, as Shell was having some gearbox problems. In Nordhorn, the last town in Germany, we had to stop. As evening fell we pulled into the train station's empty forecourt. Shell quickly had the useful inspection cover off the A10's gearbox, and came up with bad news. The clutch pushrod was half broken; and was going to let go very soon. He couldn't go on like that. We were so near and yet so far.

At this time, a sleazy-looking German dude in a little black leather cap and a Fiat open sports car had cruised by, turned round, passed again and then pulled in and parked. With a pencil moustache, zoot pants and a shirt buttoned to the neck, the skinny guy looked like a true Willie the Pimp, and the girls, who assumed he was after them, made rude remarks in Swedish about leather caps. Eventually he overcame our collective cold shoulder to say, extremely diffidently, that he owned a unit 650 Triumph, with a spare engine in bits, and although he was picking up his girlfriend for a sports car rally in Frankfurt and was pressed for time, if we thought he could help …?

Shell thought a Triumph's clutch pushrod would be different, but we urged him to give it a go. They roared off in the Fiat and returned 10 minutes later with the spare rod and some graphite grease. Willie got our collective heartfelt thanks as the generous agent for this last amazing piece of luck, and then he shot off and we set to work. The Triumph rod was a narrower diameter (which at least meant that it fitted) and an inch too long. But Worry-Wart Wilson was able to produce a hacksaw to remedy that, and Shell, fingers flying, chattered with satisfaction as we tilted the bike, the old rod slipped out, and in went the new one. It would work, at least until the Dutch autojumble at the Rally fixed him up with the real thing.

By 9.00 we were gassed up and off again. By now it was full dark, not my favourite time to ride old bikes. Alone, I would probably have settled for finding somewhere to stay and finishing the trip the next morning, but the Swedes were made of sterner stuff. They had clearly decided to do it in one go, and do it in one go they would. Even if Shell's lights were vestigial, and a duff dynamo meant that Helen didn't have any lights at all.

I brought up the rear, both to give some extra light to Shell and to make sure his repair stayed operational. Helen rode with Elizabeth's lights flanking her and Bo leading the way. We roared through the border post, which was completely unmanned. After some motorway, we rode steadily along beside a canal. The cold damp air from the water made me regret not having donned the overtrousers, and my creaking knees would remind me of this for days afterwards.

Slowly the miles, or rather kilometres, to Nijmegen ticked away. We went south over the new bridge at Arnhem, and by then I had had enough of

Shell's uneven pace and pulled past him to take up station behind Helen and give her some more light. Soon we crossed another bridge, and just before 11pm entered the brightly lit town of Nijmegen.

It would be nice to report that we rode straight to the campsite and a heroes' welcome, but it didn't work out that way. Bo led us confidently through the town and out the other side, but we were soon lost in the outskirts. We stopped briefly in a lay-by where fatigue made me very nearly ram the back of Helen's RGS. After a too brief look at the Club's map, which established that we needed to find the A271, we were off (and lost) again. Stopping to ask passers-by led to an elaborate wrong direction. Then Bo headed back to the middle of town. By now Helen, with the added strain of riding in the dark, had had enough, and at every traffic light would pull alongside Bo and let him have an awesome stream of berserker Swedish invective, at top volume. But Bo pushed on, out of town again. Cringing behind the combatants with Shell, by now I was ready for a hotel, a kip in the weeds (which another party of Swedes actually settled for), anything to get out of the saddle. But splitting the party seemed even worse, so we rode for miles and miles and miles, sense of direction completely gone, until suddenly we all saw the magic A271. Bo seemed to know which way to turn onto it, and then I spotted a beautiful BSA sign tacked to a lamp-post, and the side-road to the campsite.

It was just after midnight when we pulled up outside the big site's closed barrier. Being a Continental Friday night, though, things were still lively in the bar. The manager very decently found us a field with some other BSA early arrivals, mostly unit singles from Italy, and let us ride in slowly and finally switch off.

Helen stayed in a monster sulk till next morning, when Shell helped joke her out of it as he cooked us all porridge for breakfast, and before the heavens opened, we sat in the sun and laughed about the previous day's exploits, sharing a really good feeling.

Helen's right-hand exhaust was oil-splattered, Bo's loose primary chain sounded like a ball-bearing in a jam jar, and the night before my lights had reached the flare-and-fade stage, but nevertheless, after 19 hours on and off in the saddle for the Swedes, machines between 25 and 40 years old had completed a 400-mile day's run without major mishap. And at the end of that weekend I felt that I could fairly call these people my friends.

CHAPTER FOUR

Bikes at work

While most motorcycles now, classics included, are playthings for our leisure time rather than primary transport, there was a time not too long ago when a lot of people commuted on two wheels (though it seems that in the new millennium, rising costs and traffic congestion may be initiating a new cycle of such activity, with scooters firmly to the fore, as they were in the fifties).

Not only that, but two-wheelers were a part of the fabric of society, from the bright red BSA Bantams of the GPO delivering telegrams, to the constabulary's silent grey Velocette LE 'Noddy' bikes on patrol. I used a Bantam for courier work in London in the late seventies, and this chapter looks at other ways in which the bikes that are now classics have worked, and been worked on, for a living.

The first piece overlaps a little with Chapter 6, 'Made in England', as Harry Larner the wheelbuilder also worked at AJS/Matchless. However, not only is he a lovely old guy (in his 80s as I write this, and still building wheels), but the question with which the article concluded remains a valid one – ie once the old, craft-apprenticed, conscientious generation passes on, who will replace them?

One of the bonuses of the classic movement has been to create and sustain a healthy network of small enterprises, within which skills like wheelbuilding and trueing, hand-lining, electrical rewinding, and the hand-tuning of engines with wide individual variations, have all survived and in many cases are being handed on. Not to get too Luddite, but older machines are simple enough to mean that expensive equipment can be by-passed in favour of human skills – you don't need vacuum gauges to balance their carburettors, you can do it by ear and by eye. If you know how.

'Maybe this wasn't such a good idea ...'

Harry the Wheel

Harry's in the comfy chair in his Bexleyheath living room, wearing overalls and carpet slippers. The blue overalls are covered with tiny burn holes from the ash of his Hamlet cigars. Harry's grey hair is brushed in a shock, like Tintin, like an exclamation mark.

Around his feet lies the high watermark of a tide of motorbike wheels. The tide washes in at the front door, laps down the flat's hall and fills most of the living room. This is Harry 'the Wheel' Larner, but looking around the wheel-strewn room he knows that he's in for it shortly when his married daughter comes to visit.

The wheels come for repair from south-east London bike shops who know of Harry's reputation. Harry learned the trade while he was still at school from his father, George Larner, who had a motorcycle shop in Welling High Street. He's still using his father's tools today, and buys straight spokes and bends them himself, because of the variety of Japanese spoke patterns. Harry is 76 and was widowed two years ago, and he knows that he is probably taking on too much. A few years before, another wheel man locally had a heart attack while working, and Harry's wife told him then: 'You will not die like Fred Grout, with a bloomin' nipple key in your hand'. Harry hopes not.

Before the war he owned a 600cc Ariel Square Four, which he liked because you could work on it with the engine still in the frame. But it's neither the Ariel nor the wheelbuilding which makes Harry a figure of fascination for any enthusiast, on two counts. Firstly, he worked for 31 years in something we don't have today, a busy British motorcycle factory employing 1,500 people. And secondly, there's the way he went about his work. And still does.

Harry joined the AMC factory in Plumstead late in 1938. He was soon an approved inspector, and a charge hand. (In the hierarchy of traditional industry, foremen and charge hands were something like NCOs, standing between the officer class of management and the rude soldiery on the shop floor; charge hands wore a dust coat, while the actual foreman worked in a suit.) Harry's attitude had quickly told in his favour with a key figure at Plumstead, Bert Bassett, the works manager. Harry had gone in one morning with his own micrometer to do a job because the one he had been using in the factory was worn. Bert noticed, and even told him off mildly because his tool might get pinched! Pilfering was an occupational hazard both in and outside the factory, and together with wartime petrol rationing was the reason Harry gave up the Ariel and came to work on a pushbike – and even then had bits stolen off it.

On another occasion Harry noticed that three bearings for the 7R racer, the lightweight 250 and another model, all catalogued by AMC with different part numbers, were in fact the same component. 'Where did you take your course in Pelmanism?' asked Mr Morgan the works director. It was Harry's willingness to take pains that got him into inspection.

Varying with the seasonal flow of work, there were between 40 and 130 inspectors. In the war they worked both on the Matchless G3L WD singles, the Forces' favourite despatch bike, and the WD contract jobs for Ford, Rolls Royce, Colchester lathe and others; Harry's first job had been filing bodies for machine guns. Inspection consisted of putting thread gauges and fluid gauges on main working parts, like the fork tubes and sliders, to check for accuracy. Solex fluid gauges would be used for the main engine parts; they worked by the amount of escapement between gauge and object, on 15lb air pressure. The amount that escaped was measured on an extremely fine scale, with 10 thou showing up on it as over 1/10in, and 1 thou as about 2in. Hours were long – Harry would often have to begin at 7am, to have components inspected before the production line started at 8. But the result of a combination of good inspection equipment, good skills and pride in the work done, was the AJS and Matchless reputation for reliability and fine finish, which was confirmed by the factory service department.

Very little came back to service under warranty; almost nothing in terms of workmanship, although there were occasional flaws in the castings, which were always bought-in components as there was no forge at Plumstead. The expense of transporting unfinished castings for barrels, crankcases etc from Midlands firms like Bircal and Qualcast, or even local concerns like Stones of Charlton, was one more reason, like its inaccessibility and its four-storey structure, why Plumstead was not an ideal works. Harry remembered one crankcase half on a single which was returned for persistently weeping oil. It was porous, and the proper solution would have been to machine a new one to suit. But the foreman of service at that time was in a hurry, and simply took a hammer to the case in a crude attempt to seal it. When this was discovered, the foreman was fired.

One product they were particularly proud of was the AMC 500 and 600cc twins. Introduced for 1949, the 500 was precision assembled and finished to the AMC standard. In Harry's opinion the engine's unique middle main bearing was marvellous at stopping wear on the other two mains, though factory comparison tests did show that it actually slowed the engine slightly, so that it was marginally less free-revving than the BSA and Triumph opposition. However, at rebore time the centre web was found to have helped keep the pistons reasonably parallel in the bore, so that appreciably less cylinder wear took place than in their competitors' engines.

The call for more power towards the end of the fifties led the 500 and 600 twins to be opened up to 650, which proved a few millimetres too far for the Plumstead engines, in terms of both stress and vibration. Simultaneously the twins were being tuned to increase output, and Harry remembers the initial experimentation on camshafts that would give quicker opening times causing much concern, as cam followers used to literally burn up as bhp increased. For 1960 both the 500 and 650 cylinder heads were redesigned by Jack Williams, to good effect. Unfortunately with the resultant Gl2CSR 650, increased power led to a rash of crankshaft breakages. Any AMC buff will tell you that it was the introduction of nodular iron, the 'noddy' cranks, which cured this. Actually, they would be wrong. The crankshafts had always been of Meehanite nodular iron. The new specification was of SGI, spheroidal graphite iron, and there were even problems with the early versions of these. When they occurred, AMC turned to their contacts at Ford across the river in Dagenham, who had used SGI for the cranks of their ohv Anglia car engines. It turned out that with SGI a crank had to be ground in the direction of travel, for its microscopic particles had to 'lay' one way, like a cat's fur, or stress points and fracture ensued. After that, the breakages ceased.

One process for which Matchless had justly been famous was their paintwork, with three coats of enamel per item, applied by dipping or spray, and then each coat stoved on for an hour and a half in a large travelling oven. The process was carried out to Government rules and regulations, though today these seem environmentally a little suspect. It was true that there was an extracting exhaust funnelling fumes from the paint shop up onto the roof, which was also true of the ferrous dust from the polishing shop and the cyanide fumes from plating. Once on the roof, however, the whole noxious cocktail was simply discharged into the air to blow away over the surrounding town ... They weren't the only ones. Harry once paid a private visit to another part of the AMC empire, the James factory in Greet, Birmingham, which was situated in a green field. Except the field wasn't green at all – this was after Francis-Barnett had moved in with them and the James colour schemes had changed from all-red, and now Harry was astounded to see that thanks to a liberal discharge of paint fumes, the factory stood in a field of multi-coloured grass!

But the paint shop at Plumstead did do quality work, and for a long time without the need for an inspector, because the foreman, Charlie Day, was very enthusiastic and wouldn't tolerate rubbish. Only towards the end, when accountants and financial crises had finally reduced the three coats to two, was inspection necessary.

Which brings us back to the quality of Harry's own work. He sighs; he knows how what he's going to say will sound. But he has had no faith in any British government since the war, on two counts. British Standards were set up in the forties; yet recently he's bought a pair of garden shears with both a British Standard number and a Design Centre kitemark. One blade soon fell off; the holes for the rivet hadn't been countersunk. Harry did that job himself. Then he bought a small vice, also with a British Standard number. The jaws tightened at one end but not the other. He sent it back, but the replacement too was only just satisfactory because the jaws were so close and the winding mechanism so loose.

The other part of the problem is that native industrial enterprises like Plumstead may not have been perfect, but they did foster hard-learned skills now obviously lacking on the evidence of British products like the above. Now that they have been allowed to go to the wall, we have been delivered into the hands of foreigners. This is not an abstract chauvinist proposition. Harry reaches out at random and holds up an Italian wheel rim. He points out the egg-shaped hump where the steel has been less than precisely welded. The wheels usually go up to a point there, which is hard to get out, because squeezing it causes distortion elsewhere. Harry lays a micrometer across the rim at the point where the hump is. Then he does the same thing about nine inches further on. The steel rim there is several millimetres narrower, visibly so. In the past he has found variations of up to 3/16in. This is clearly less than ideal for creating a true-running wheel.

The demonstration left at least one rider convinced that he's going to have his BSA's old Dunlop rim re-chromed rather than settle for a foreign replacement. But it's also left a half thought, a worrying undertow. When men like Harry, meticulous craftsmen, are gone, who's going to take their place?

The AA man

I particularly enjoyed meeting Patrol Owen Edwards, as the AA call-box on his beat, just before Lamberhurst on the A21 London to Hastings road, used to be a landmark on the car journeys between family homes in London and Rye which were a regular feature of my childhood.

I have always been an RAC member myself, and the combination of old machinery and my lack of skill with the spanners has meant that over the years I have called on them for help more than once or twice, and often while fairly upset, after the dream of the open road had met the reality of mechanical malfunction. The patrolmen without exception were always friendly and unobtrusively considerate, and more than once made special efforts because they too had sympathy for British bikes. If they ended up having to ferry rider and bike back home, there were usually interesting or amusing road tales to hear from them on the way.

But in the nineties, the organisation changed its policy and despatched help for two-wheelers in distress from a network of motorcycle shops, which generally took a bit longer to respond. Apparently this was partly because the high cost of the bodywork on modern machines meant that specialist transport arrangements were advisable. But I missed the contact with those patrolmen, fundamentally kind men, and like Mr Edwards, the salt of the earth.

It was 31 May 1992, and Owen 'Knocker' Edwards hadn't been on an AA M21 sidecar outfit for nearly 30 years.

Owen, well into his 60s, was retiring that day after 39 years with the motoring organisation. His friends at the Basingstoke AA depot, where the outfit had been renovated, had organised a ride for him through Hastings and out to Battle. Because that had been part of Patrol Edwards' 'beat' with the sidecar for ten years in the 1950s.

'I felt at home on it right away,' said Owen. When he found the toolbox was empty, he asked 'What's the use of that?'; so the sergeant put some in. And as he proceeded along the front at Hastings, they found him a breakdown! The motorist in question turned out to be an old boy who had been an AA member for almost as long as Owen had been with the service, but who was still considerably surprised to see something like a time-traveller arriving, as the bright yellow side-valve BSA and sidecar chuffed to a halt, and the patrol in his smart brown uniform, shirt and tie, dismounted and got to work. And did he fix it? 'Oh yes,' said Owen matter-

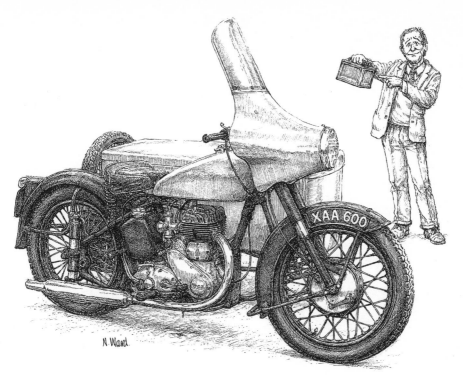

'Even now, they expect petrol – and a salute ...'

of-factly. 'It was an automatic choke that had been converted to manual, and the cable had slipped out.'

Owen continued on his last run at the 30mph which the AA had prescribed in the old days. But the other vehicles in attendance, including the BMW bikes they now use for work in built-up areas, had trouble keeping down to it. So Owen increased the pace to 45mph – 'but it's difficult saluting at that speed!' Owen spotted six old-style badges and saluted them all, but he didn't get a single acknowledgement.

As many readers probably know, the AA patrols' salute to badge-bearing vehicles used to be more than a formality. In the very early days of motoring, a 20mph speed limit and vindictive police speed traps meant that the first AA patrols, bicycle-mounted, would wave to their members to warn them of the traps ahead. After a 1909 court case ruled this to be illegal, they hit on the following drill: members were asked to stop and talk to a patrol who did not salute them – so he could tell them of any speed trap ahead.

It hadn't all been cheeking the rozzers, though. It was the AA who put up the first village name signs and signposts with distances (there's still a similar sign in our village, but the logo is the blue one, not the yellow one). In 1920 it was they who opened the first roadside filling stations – previously you had to buy your petrol in two-gallon cans. And in 1919 they commissioned the first motorcycle RSOs (Road Service Outfits). With tools in the sidecar, each patrolling 30 miles of road, they were miniature mobile repair shops, offering members roadside assistance.

Which is essentially where Owen 'Knocker' Edwards came in, on 9 March 1953. Why 'Knocker'? He claims he got the name so long ago that he can't remember, but perhaps there's a clue on presentation plaques he received 'From your many AA colleagues', for one features a large lump hammer and the motto 'If in doubt, give it a clout!' There are also cartoons depicting the time when Owen, attempting a tow, pulled the front bumper off a member's Reliant three-wheeler, and the frequent donations of coffee and cakes he received from old ladies along his beat. This popularity is entirely understandable. Owen is a Sussex man through and through, with a genial, Mr Punch-like face that would not have been out of place in one of Charles Dickens' coaching inns. Just the chap you would want to see if you were in a spot of bother on the roadside.

It was not like that, he says, back in 1953. 'I was a mad devil in them days,' and the devilry found its expression on bikes. After starting out on a hand-change 98cc Coventry Eagle with a wedge tank and pressed steel front forks, he graduated to a BSA B31, a big Norton single (which he didn't like or keep long), an Enfield 700 twin and a Sunbeam S8 and sidecar, his first outfit – 'I went through the majority of bikes, as kids did then'. But by 1953 he was running a quick Tiger 100; and indeed, after joining the motoring organisation he was ticked off severely for speeding on the Triumph after hours, and told he was 'a disgrace to the AA!'

The job meant stepping off a sports twin and onto a plodding 600 single and sidecar on which you were then forbidden to exceed 30mph, up and down (at which pace the side valve still only returned around 45 miles to the gallon). The slow speed was a problem at first, as it could send you to sleep – quite literally, for Owen, who nodded off on his first week and ended up in a hedge! 'It woke me up a bit,' he chuckles. 'I never had an accident after that.' If the AA outfits' stately pace caused a traffic jam, they were instructed to pull off and let the cars go by.

Standard riding gear was tailored to the pace. There were no helmets at that stage, just a peaked cap, with a white cover for the summer months. Likewise riding breeches and lace-up boots, with gaiters for the winter or socks in the summer. His early machine had no windscreen, and despite moistening the inside of his cap rim at the front to help stick it to his forehead, going down Park Street into Hastings the cap would sometimes fly off, and in his mirror would see some cars swerving to miss it, while others tried to crush it! But he loved the feel of the fresh air, and disliked the crash hats when they were introduced.

Owen's beat was a relatively busy one, because it included a section of the A21 London to Hastings road. But even in 1960 there was only a sixth of today's traffic, and there was a rustic flavour to the life. Since there was no radio link (suitable equipment had not yet been developed) Owen spent an hour each day at a standby point waiting for phone calls to say someone had broken down. Owen took over 'old Stanley's' AA box – and old Stanley's wildlife, which included a tame mouse, and birds which expected feeding and made the locals moan when they stole the seeds from vegetable patches!

He was expected to cover about a hundred miles a day to find members in trouble. With traffic sparse, the main volumes were on Bank Holidays, but even then top numbers might be just 2,000 vehicles a day. Owen knows this, because one of his duties was to count them! At least to count for ten minutes, and then phone in an average figure.

The rest of the time, people in the fields would wave, and some dogs bark, when they heard the chug of the M21 – Owen was known personally on his beat, treated as part of that one section of the road. He cared for it, reporting any surface damage to the Council so the 'lengthmen' responsible could see to it, and even keeping the road clean by picking up major debris. There was more time than today, to look around. Sometimes there would be only a couple of breakdowns to deal with in a week – now it can be ten in a day, or even in a morning.

Owen would 'put in' loose cattle and other stock that had got on the road; going down farm lanes was often easier on the bikes than on four wheels. He also attended accidents, including some nasty ones, but as he said, 'I used to be more happy doing the bandaging than writing them up,' for his education had been interrupted by the war.

The patrols' activities were supervised by inspectors, and in those days rules and regulations were quite strict. Like Thomas the Tank Engine and the Fat Controller, Owen would keep an ear open for Inspector Pick, who rode a Triumph – 'I used to hear that engine note a mile off.' He was once caught seeing to one of his own tyres and got a ticking off, as in the days when patrols worked directly from home, they were supposed to look after their own machines on their own time. Such maintenance included seeing to the primary chain oil, dismantling and cleaning the magneto's advance/retard mechanism, a tool check, and keeping the reverse thread on the front axle pin well greased every month, so that it didn't stick if you got a puncture.

The outfit had to be clean and your own appearance smart. In addition, though the early warning aspect had faded, every badge on a member's car had to be saluted, but you had to be especially watchful for the committee badges of the high-ups in the organisation itself, noting their direction of travel and the time, and reporting back on it to the inspector. This was a random check that you were out there as you should be.

Breakdowns were mainly cars, though Owen dealt with some buses too. He carried tools, petrol and water to deal with overheating and fuel problems, which predominated. But he never carried spares. 'You knew your garages on the beat, and got them there. You'd borrow a battery from them and take the money from the member, and give the garage a little drink if you got one yourself.'

However, a lot of people didn't have the money for spares, so Owen became good at improvising. One driver couldn't afford a new petrol pump, so to get him home Owen rigged up a gravity fed system by strapping a petrol can to his car roof. If a suspension spring had gone, he'd jack up the car and shove in a piece of wood, pre-sawed to length (or a brick, but they tended to disintegrate) between the chassis and the spring. He'd wire this around, and then tell the driver to take it easy going home – 'but they'd go off like the clappers anyway!' If a rotor arm went, he would rig up a construction using a medicine bottle cork, a drawing pin and a straight pin through the cork's side. Placed opposite the groove on the post, it would get you home.

The patrols' own machine, the BSA M21, Owen found very reliable, until the last years when there began to be a problem getting parts like rear chain sprockets. BSA ceased production of the 500cc M20 in 1956, and after that civilian M21s were available to special order only, as production was kept on solely for fleet users like the AA until the end came in 1963. The engines on the job bikes would do about 65,000 miles, then 'a new one would come in a crate and you had a day in to change them. There was a running-in period, but at our speed you didn't need it!'

The AA's bikes were purpose-built for their tough life. They used heavier

'Well, it's a long walk back to the house ...'

gauge spokes, special seats, tanks and rear mudguards, and forks off the A10 twins which were stronger than the standard M20/21 telescopic and would take an eight-inch front brake. They also continued to use the WD-type single spring clutch, as opposed to the standard fiddly six-spring item. They were quite comfortable machines, an important consideration.

Owen's complaints mostly centred on 'the wretched little gearchange spring', which broke frequently. Otherwise he had little trouble, though from 1961 the late bikes came not only with an alternator in addition to the dynamo to help power the radios then being fitted, but also with Motoplas plastic fairings and leg- and engine-shields. This plastic around the engine not only made the side-valve run even hotter, 'it used to channel water into the magneto like a funnel'. More improvisation was needed, cutting up old bicycle inner tubes and sliding them over the mag's cover for additional protection.

Owen had always been happy with the dynamo, possibly because in those days he started at eight o'clock in the morning, and 'as soon as it was night – home, James! We didn't ride after dark.' He was offered a late-type fibreglass-clad outfit for his parade, but turned it down in favour of an old one. And another ex-AA man writing in Australia detailed the drawbacks of the later machines – how the rain and snow whistled between the handlebar fairing and the legshields, how a 1961 engine assembled from spares had the carburettor flange on its barrel warped from new, plus both new brake drums oval, plus massive backlash in the mag gear train, and so on.

The radios signalled the end of this era, however. In 1963, as the man with the busiest roads, Owen was the first Sussex patrol to be put in a radio-equipped Mini van. The days of the beat, 'the old bike days, where you were on your tod,' were at an end – 'after that, you went where you were sent'.

'Then it was all go-go-go,' said Owen, who has paid a price for a busy life spent helping other people, today suffering from bronchitis 'from the years of fumes and that' – sadly ironic for a man who had 'loved riding bikes in the freedom of the air.' But he emphasises that though the organisation has changed as road conditions have, 'it's still a service, that's never altered. We've always been a team, right from then till now – modernised, but the old spirit's still there.'

The same spirit which was evident one night when Owen went to assist a car that had broken down with a pregnant, a very pregnant, passenger. As a condition of his employment, Owen had done a midwifery course with the St Johns Ambulance, so he asked her in proper direct Sussex fashion: 'Which is first – you or the car?' The lady managed a grin and told him: 'You're not touching me with them grubby hands!' So Owen fixed the car and got her safely to hospital. That's what I call a real knight of the road.

James Bond

Another facet of motorcycles at work has been their part in the Technicolor dreams which have fed this century's collective unconscious – the movies.

Prominent among the comic or thrilling roles that two-wheelers have played on screen has been their part in the films of that post-war icon, James Bond. 007's creator Ian Fleming had a wartime affair with a Triumph-mounted WRNS despatch rider who was killed in the Blitz; and he went on to write a well-researched Bond short story, 'From A View To A Kill', with both villains and the hero mounted on BSA WD M20s, though the plodding Army side-valve singles seemed thoroughly unlikely vehicles for high adventure.

On celluloid, though, the two-wheeled imagination could run riot. As well as Thunderball, *the movie under consideration here, Roger Moore's 007 was pursued on the piste by Yamaha XT500 singles with spiked tyres, and in the 1983 Sean Connery comeback* Never Say Never Again, *essentially a remake of* Thunderball, *a big nitrous-assisted Kawasaki featured spectacularly. The most recent bike chase came in 1998's* Tomorrow Never Dies, *with a BMW R1200C, the German twin's striking version of a cruiser, performing thrilling but unlikely-looking jumps between rooftops and through street-markets in Saigon. These fast-cut, well-made thrillers have you on the edge of your seat, but if you've ever paused to wonder how they get a bike to do those things, read on.*

Today, BSA's A65 Lightning may seem to qualify as Stodgius Maximus among British parallel twins, hardly rivalling Norton's Featherbed 650SS for class, or the T120 Bonneville for pzazz. But in its day the unit Beeza, Small Heath's flagship in the sixties, was quite sexy, and enjoyed media exposure to match. It was an A65 which Malcolm MacDowell, as English rebel youth personified, liberated from a dealer's showroom in the great anti-public school movie *If.*

It was an export Lightning Rocket which gonzo journalist Hunter S. Thompson rode, while running with the San Francisco Hell's Angels and writing his seminal book on the outlaws. And more recently Michael Elphick (or rather his stand-in) rode a White Lightning on the screens of our haunted fishbowls in the *Boon* series.

'Lightning Rocket' provides the cue for what was probably the A65's finest filmic hour, though. Preceded by the A10 Road Rocket and Super Rocket, and followed by the Rocket 3, BSA's associations with projectile weapons were perhaps too strong for movie-makers to ignore. At any rate, it was an A65 which the James Bond team selected for a bit of rocket-work in the 1965 film *Thunderball*.

The film, the first to put 007 in Cinemascope, was full of brill gadgets and special effects. Sean Connery was still playing Bond, and during the sequence in question the plot called for him to be stooging along in his own trick machine, the nail-and-oil throwing, machine-gun armed, passenger ejector-seated Aston Martin DB5. Then, sneaking up behind him, comes Count Lippe of SPECTRE, the maximum bad guys. But … Lippe has already alerted Bond to SPECTRE's current dastardly plot (nicking two A-bombs), and SPECTRE tolerates failure only slightly less happily than did the late female incumbent of No 10.

So when Count Lippe in his big Yankee Lincoln begins potting with a pistol at 007 in the Aston (not a brilliant career move anyway, given the DB5's firepower and armour-plating), he's in for a nasty surprise. Cos up from behind roars a gold-and-chrome BSA twin with four suspicious looking chrome tubes sprouting from its Avon fairing. And before you can say 'Tomorrow the World!', rockets streak from the bike and blow the loathsome Lippe and his gas-guzzler to a fiery grave by the roadside. Even Bond is too shaken, not to say stirred, to pursue the lethal biker, who soon finds a quiet spot by the riverside and dumps the offending bolide into the deep water. (No, no, in real life it wasn't the actual lovely Lightning they deep-sixed, just a mock-up made from an ancient A10.)

And then the black leather figure pulls off its helmet and holy moley, it's a girl! And one with long red-gold hair an', an' more curves than the old Nurburgring. Yep, it's SPECTRE's very own Fiona Vulpe, played by luscious Luciana Paluzzi, in a role which propelled the Italian starlet to prominence in Europe.

Apart from fulfilling a fantasy every biker must have indulged in once in a while (ie literally blowing the fat-assed tin box in front of you into the weeds), the story of this bike is an interesting example of the considerable pains involved in getting less than a minute's action onto celluloid. How do you set up a motorcycle to fire rockets? And how do you ensure the survival of the rider, let alone the guy who's driving the car which is blown up?

The top A65 for the UK that year was newly resplendent with twin carbs, and the Lightning name for this version echoed what was then the RAF's state-of-the-art fighter plane. The film bike was supplied by BSA, complete with contemporary 1965 plates bearing the number BOJ 443C – except that, as is customary with vehicles used prominently in a film, the number was apparently never actually registered. Fitted with a full Avon fairing in gold, to match the twin's finish of gold and chrome, including chromed mudguards and rear chainguard, the Lightning was an extremely handsome machine. That year's red-winged badges on the sidepanels had once been the tank badges for the pre-unit A10 Golden Flash, and this all-gold finish echoed that of the mighty Flash, surely Small Heath's finest.It's tempting to speculate that the solid A65 was selected, like a Hawker Hurricane, as a steadier gun-platform than the faster Spitfire-equivalent Triumph Bonnie.

But the truth is likely to have been more commercial. The BSA Group owned Triumph, and Group management was by then quite jealous of Meriden's charisma and sales success. Already Triumph's publicity department had been moved in with BSA at Small Heath, and big screen exposure for the Birmingham flagship was probably the order of the day. The rocket bike bore 'BSA' transfers on its fairing for those who were interested.

But the motorcycle selected had to have performance as well as looks, and John Stears, the movie's special effect supervisor, has confirmed that 'we shot that sequence for real. Real bike, real rockets and the car was doing something like 60, 70 miles an hour and the bike was doing about a hundred maybe – it had to be going that fast to get clear of the debris.'

First they needed a rider, and a suitable venue for the sequence. Initially BSA was to supply the Lightning jockey in the shape of Chris Vincent, one of their top road testers who was also a sidecar racing World Champion aboard A65-powered outfits. Publicity shots were taken with Vincent at Pinewood studios, but due to a combination of scheduling delays and Vincent's racing commitments, a stunt rider named (presumably by his agent) Johnny Walker ended up aboard the Lightning, suitably masked and helmeted to impersonate Fiona/Luciana.

In the same way, it had originally been intended to shoot the sequence on an unopened section of the M2, but delays due to bad weather meant that they ended up doing it at Silverstone. Despite valiant efforts to make the circuit look like a public highway, I do remember when I first watched the film noticing the sparse traffic, the road's odd colour and the ridged nature of its sections, and thinking 'Hmmm ...'

The next thing to sort out was the rocketry. The weapons selected were military Icarus-type projectiles, which had a range of half a mile as well as the benefit of being very economical, at $10 a pop to prepare! For conventional artillery use these rockets were ignited by electricity, and at first on the A65, spark plugs were tried. But for use on the bike John Stears in the end settled on dependable hand grenade-type percussion caps, operated in pairs by valve-lifter levers and Bowden cables mounted on each side of the Lightning's handlebars.

As mentioned, these were 'real rockets', and two carried a charge of black powder, while two were loaded with napalm! They detonated on impact with the target via either a rear-facing .38 pistol round or a 12 bore shotgun cartridge with the shot removed and black powder substituted. Though packing a real punch, the rockets could not be guaranteed to set off an explosion big and spectacular enough for the screen. So the boot of the car was filled with a hundredweight of rubber jelly, plus some five-gallon drums of petrol – which were then wrapped in cordite.

But ... someone had to be driving the car. This was the job for veteran stuntman Bob Simmons. With the above set-up the driving seat was clearly a bit of a hot-spot, so Simmons rigged a platform similar to a running board along the side of Lippe's car away from the cameras, from where he could control the wheel of the car out of sight, while a dummy 'Lippe' sat at the wheel of the Lincoln. Vital additional protection from the explosion was provided by a sheet of bullet-proof glass fitted between the dummy and the back of the car where the goodies were.

On the day of the shoot everything at Silverstone was ready, with director Terence Young and the crew set up for the mobile filming on the back of a (very) specially adapted vintage Rolls-Royce, with all but the driver's cab cut away and a wooden platform built around it and on the back, containing and protecting the cameras – a rig which presumably combined solidity, smoothness and a fair turn of speed. A fire crew and an ambulance were also on hand.

On the cry of 'ACTION!' Johnny Walker on the BSA swung up behind the Lincoln and fired the rockets. History doesn't relate what the recoil was like, but photos show the A65 well up at the front as the rockets fly, and later with scorch marks and minor dents on the fairing. This was indeed 'for real'. The rockets hit the car and on their impact Bob Simmons set off his own explosion, which demolished the back of the Lincoln as Walker on the A65 roared clear. It was a perfect first take.

But things are rarely that simple in the wonderful world of motion pictures. It had been a dull day, the rushes showed that the light had changed during the shot, and director Young decided he wanted to go for a second take. It took three days to rebuild the car and set up again. Once more Walker swooped in and let loose the rockets, perfectly, in a carbon copy of the first effort. Simmons again set off the explosives in the back of the boot.

But this time things went wrong, with thick black smoke and flame instantly billowing into the body of the car. The bullet-proof shield had failed.

With his clothing on fire, Simmons rolled clear of the car and into the verge, unseen by the crew who were intent on getting the explosion on film. The flaming Lincoln rolled to a halt with the dummy Lippe now burning fiercely. In the absence of the stuntman the horrified crew, including Terence Young, thought that the dummy was Simmons, somehow trapped in the car.

Desperate efforts were made to get into the blazing vehicle. Meanwhile Simmons, still unnoticed, collected himself and took in the situation. Quietly approaching the frantic director from behind, he enquired cheerfully: 'How was that Terence, all right?'

Young spun round, completely gob-smacked. 'You bastard!' he said with much emotion, 'You bastard, I thought you were dead!'

There was no third take. The Bond circus rolled on to the Bahamas, where in the plot, at the Jankanoo carnival Fiona Vulpe stopped a bullet intended for Bond. A shame, after she'd survived the rocketeering. When *Thunderball* was released and proved a big hit, John Stears received an Oscar for his work on the film's special effects.

Bond's Aston would fetch £100,000 when auctioned at Christie's, but the gold A65 lay neglected at the studios for years. It was eventually given to Pinewood's veteran PRO, Tommy Green. An ex-motorcyclist, Green spoke

'Keep trying – something should fit …'

of his grandson inheriting the bike, which by then almost certainly had been re-registered as GLA 427C. In fact after Green's death the A65 was sold on by his estate with only just over 1,000 miles on the clock, and passed through the hands of a couple of enthusiasts to the 'Cars of the Stars' motor museum at Keswick, Cumbria.

In conclusion, I'd like to send many thanks to Anthony Gould, Bond enthusiast extraordinaire, for his painstaking help in piecing this tale together. Meanwhile, if you see my thumbs twitching towards the air lever on my own A65 as the Volvo in front cuts in too close, you'll know what I'm thinking. 'Black powder or napalm, you Scandinavian scum …?'

Back from India

Another way that British bikes have been made to work for their living is as the chosen vehicles for long-distance travellers. The best-known example today is probably Ted Simon, whose ride round the world on a 1973 Triumph T100P Tiger 500 twin, as described in his best-selling book Jupiter's Travels, *captured the imagination of thousands.*

The existence in India of 'new' classics in the shape of the Madras-built Enfield singles, based on the sporting Royal Enfield Bullet built in Redditch from 1949 to 1962, should have been a spur for many riders to take the hard road from there back to the West. But as this story mentions, not a lot seem to have done so – successfully, at any rate.

With the Indian company under new ownership in the nineties, the Enfield's variable build quality is said to have improved recently, but a wait-and-see policy would probably be advisable. I once proposed to fellow columnist and ex-Royal Enfield Bullet rider Royce Creasey that we ride a brace of Indian Bullets out to India. His response was: 'Let's round up a mob of riders and ride them all back.' But as vehicles for adventure they do have some fundamental strengths, though the bottom line must be Giles Jackson's observation that for any long journey on them, 'one of you has to be a mechanic.'

A lot of English bikers must have looked at Enfield's imported-from-India 350 and 500 singles and thought, 'How about riding one of them back from there to here?' Yet when Giles Jackson and his friend Charles rode off the ferry at Dover last November and stopped at Customs to declare their Enfields, they were told that there was no need. They had to explain patiently that they were bringing the bikes onto English soil for the first time, and wanted to pay the duty and have that fact officially recognised, so that they could then get regular UK registration numbers for them. The Customs folk couldn't remember anyone having done that before. One Customs man, an ex-Panther rider, did finally recall them having enquired about the import drill before flying out to India. He told them 'I never thought you'd make it.'

The two friends had made it, though, and today Giles' red and chrome De Luxe model sits in the yard of the Gloucestershire farm where he lives, sharing the space with a banger racer called Penelope Pitstop, and Giles' big Guzzi. The Bullet carries 'AA-Upper India' badges, a Diva luggage rack with the rear end curving downward to protect the tail light, and at the front on each side fearsome OM triple crash bars like Neptune's trident which not only intimidated oncoming traffic but also served as a useful rack for carrying extra petrol or water. Otherwise there is little to show that this bike has recently put in around 6,000 very hard miles from a standing start.

The mileage has to be approximate because the speedo packed up at around 1,500 miles, one of many, many minor problems with the Bullets. 31-year-old Giles is an ex-Army officer from a cavalry regiment, though emphatically not like the cavalry officer in the infantry story who was 'so stupid that even his brother officers noticed.' A mixture of restless energy and patience, abruptly jokey as you could wish but also instantly serious about details which could be important, Giles might be summed up with the single word 'practical'. And his first rule for people contemplating a similar sortie is: 'one of you has to be a mechanic.'

Giles had been friends with Charles Booth-Clibborn since they were both 12 years old and starting at Stowe school. But they are in some terms an odd couple, since Charles works for an art-book publishing house, had only passed his motorcycle test a few months before they set out, and was not mechanical at all; in a naming-of-parts session towards the end of their trip, he still had trouble identifying the carburettor.

So all that side was down to Giles, but there's more to life, and long-distance travel, than bikes. Giles' second rule is: 'do your homework.' Thus before they set out, while he was gathering useful info on Bullets and kit, Charles in London took care of all the paperwork, insurance, ferries and visas. This was vital. 'Trying to get papers for Iran or Pakistan outside this country,' says Giles, 'is just not possible.' As it was, with one exception, everything went like clockwork. In addition, Charles' love of art was sometimes an asset; Giles might have found Iran 'pretty dire', but Charles' interest in the history and design of the mosques along their way added another dimension to the country.

The only negative reaction they encountered to their preliminary enquiries was from the UK importers of the bikes, who perhaps understandably not wishing to be by-passed by private enterprise, told them that what the two intended was illegal, and that they could end up in jail! Not true. Many good tips came from Giles' friends Franz and Peter, veterans of several trans-Africa trips by BMW.

On the advice of Hugo, another Bullet-traveller, they fitted filter elements in the fuel-lines, and a battery isolator to block the worst effects of the sometimes dodgy wiring looms. Spare piston rings, spokes, pushrods and several head gaskets (they were down to their last one by the end) all proved useful.

A spare rectifier was no help because, as Giles said, 'when I did need it, it had the wrong terminals.' He blames himself for not checking in India when he bought it. And then there were the 'Samrat' rockers, which on strong advice from Hugo the pair insisted on being fitted when they purchased the bikes new, keeping the original rockers as spares. Yet when they had their first free service, the Sikh who carried it out was aghast to discover the 'inferior pattern parts' in place! You can't win. In the event Giles couldn't be bothered to have them changed back, and the Samrats got them to England with no bother.

One final piece of lightweight kit was a credit card and a phone number. The latter was for Hitchcocks Motorcycles (01564 783192), who are as sound on Enfield spares as they are on Royal Enfields. From Iran onwards, one phone call would have had a vital part DHL'ed out in a matter of days. This back-up saved a lot of worry, as well as weight.

Weight was important, since as well as extra petrol and water on certain stretches, some camping stuff also had to be included. Unlike the BMW GS boys, who could ride a mile off-road into the countryside and laager up every night with no hassle, the Enfield duo mostly had to lodge in guest houses or customs posts, but sometimes there was no alternative to sleeping out. An 'Optimus' petrol-burning stove was a must for self-sufficient cooking. Franz had advised one without a pump, as sand gets in the mechanism. The makers say unleaded petrol only, but you can use leaded if you change the jet. A 'Starlight' tent by Jack Wolfskin, Thermarest inflatable mini-mats (oh yes), and integral-frame rucksacks which converted to suitcases to look reasonably smart for posher venues, were all worthwhile. (The friends had characteristically different approaches to dress code; Giles did the whole journey with just one spare pair of lightweight trousers, but Charles insisted on taking a Savile Row suit, and changing into it every night.)

Bike clothing taken from the UK consisted of only Belstaff waxed cotton suits (invaluable) plus light Rukka one-piece waterproofs, as well as open-face helmets with stick-on reflectors, not new but worn religiously however hot it got. One funky-looking way of combining light clothing with some protection when it got really warm consisted of skateboard knee and elbow protectors strapped on outside trousers and sweatshirts. Already familiar to Giles from Army days, the pads did save scraped flesh in the many tumbles taken.

Other luggage consisted of Frank Thomas FT Cargo panniers, to which Giles accorded the highest accolade – 'they were,' he declared, 'the absolute Dog's Knob.' With Velcro fastenings and integral fold-over plastic inners which completely excluded sand and dust, this was top quality soft luggage. The soft stuff was definitely favourite for its lightness, and because when a bike went down nothing broke; also it could be easily carried. The only negative point was security. But during their whole trip through the mainly Muslim lands, they never had anything taken. Incidentally, their Oxford Sentinel bike lock from England shattered when they forgot to undo it as they rode off for the first time, and only bent a couple of spokes as it did so. They had it welded up expertly by an old man on a Delhi street, who did his work on a length of railway line, with no eye-protection. They urged him to invest in goggles with the 60p he charged them, but he said he was going to buy food.

Luggage was held on by slim tie-down straps purchased from builders' merchants Travis Perkins and originally intended to secure ladders; they were bought long so they could be cut down to size. With bungees in Third World conditions your load bounces about and is soon dislodged. Bungee cargo nets, on the other hand, were fine, and very useful.

Army practice was applied again to maps. You cut off the bits you don't need, to save bulk; on the remainder you can put in your route etc, before sealing it with sticky-back clear plastic from Woolworths, which you can still write on the top of. That way maps don't disintegrate along the seams.

Maps were the first in an accumulating pile of bumf, the subject of Giles' third and final law: 'Keep every bit of paper, because you'll bloody need it!' – ie it might mean the difference between getting through a border or not. Franz also advised on a child's printing kit for, ah, improvising documents, but that's really only for Africa.

In reply to a query about weather conditions, they got a courteous letter from the Iranian embassy (headed 'In the Name of the Almighty'), no bad thing to be on their files, Giles felt. A more tangible benefit came from insurance. While it is almost impossible to insure vehicles when travelling east of the Bosphorus, personal health insurance is highly advisable, something emphasised by the story of an uninsured friend of Franz's who came off his bike in Africa and fractured his skull; not very nice anyway, and his parents then had to lay out £20k to have him flown back by air ambulance to the UK. The only people whom Charles could find to even quote on health insurance for this type of trip were Campbell Irvine, 48 Earls Court Road, London W8 6EJ; ring 020 7937 6981. But you do have to tell them you're travelling by motorcycle. This will add to your premium (£57 to the £161 per person Giles and Charles paid for their two months away), but otherwise they won't pay out.

Photocopies of passports and all visas in case of loss, and a record of their blood group, added to the paper trail. But on one final important document, they ran into trouble. A carnet de passage is required for any vehicle crossing frontiers outside Europe. Charles had set this up, and paid for it, in England, with the AA in Basingstoke – only to discover that the document could not be issued until they had the frame, engine and registration numbers of the vehicles. So they had to fly off to Delhi without this vital piece of paperwork, to buy the bikes.

They stayed with a business partner of Charles' father. As they set off for Madras Autos to buy the Bullets, their host loaned them his Hindi negotiator, a definite asset. 'He threw three fucks into the salesmen,' said Giles; money was slapped on the table, shoved away, notes removed from the pile, etc. Giles and Charles toured the shop-full of Bullets ('a fifties time-warp') for an hour or more as things got heated, though all parties negotiating clearly loved it, and in the end the travellers felt the benefit, paying just £850 for each bike! The last time I looked the retail price out there was around the £1,500 mark …

Paperwork set in again, since another important document was the bill of sale (mostly in squiggly Hindi), with both the price, and the machines' year of manufacture. The former was necessary at the far end to determine the UK import duty payable – they ended up shelling out some £220 each, 25 per cent of the price new, since the bikes, though very well used, were still technically only eight weeks old. Less scrupulous souls might have got the Indians to prepare an alternative bill showing a lower purchase price. The year of manufacture was needed for trouble-free registration of the machines in the UK, otherwise you would have to have an MOT, and would be assigned a Q-plate.

The pair could now fax the engine and frame numbers to the AA, who DHL'ed out their carnets. But – the Indian registration numbers had yet to be assigned, so they were still left with that bureaucratic nightmare, a blank on a form. Their host suggested taking the carnets to the Indian AA, but this led to three days of frustrating messing about, with men and machines ready to go, and the clock running in terms of visas etc. The Indian argument was that these were Indian bikes, so they wanted another £100 for an Indian carnet. Giles went up and down with the AA official, threatening to report him to Basingstoke and summoning up the ultimate insult – he called the man a Tricky Dicky. Giles prevailed in the end, but would strongly advise anyone else to get a registration number assigned in advance.

He would also advise taking more time than they did, putting in more miles in India, familiarising oneself and running in, and getting the three or four free warranty services due for a new bike. These can be arranged at any Enfield agent with no hassle about renewing defective components, and only the oil to be paid for. As it was, they headed north in a hurry, in one day doing the run to Shandigarh, a somewhat soulless modern city but heaven to the Indians. They arrived 'black and rather scared.'

The Bullets were 350s, for fuel economy, and in fact they saw no 500s in India. Though billed in Delhi as 'export' models, this did not mean they were off the separate export production line for machines aimed at Western markets. So they had the old-type front brakes ('pathetic'), and six-volt lighting ('a nightmare'). Worst of all, the six-volt system meant they couldn't fit an effective after-market horn, which are all 12 volt, to make their presence felt on the chaotic roads and counter 'the main threat' – nutters behind the wheels of some of the sub-continent's garishly decorated trucks and lorries, who thought it was hilarious to run anything smaller than themselves off the road.

In Shandigarh they had their first service at the excellent Mannohan Motors, probably also a good place to buy a machine. Charles' black and chrome bike was already burning a lot of oil, which they found was due to one of the rings having been fitted upside down. As the trip progressed, baffles came loose in one of the silencers, a pushrod broke, the head gaskets blew regularly, etc, etc. 'We broke down every day,' says Giles, 'but it was mostly small things.' All nuts shook loose regularly, but that was due to the rough roads and heavy loads. However, the build quality of the engine was not always encouraging. The pushrod's metal was unimpressive, and when the cylinder head had to come off, it revealed that the alloy hadn't flowed into the part of the head casting where the gas returned to the port, so that there was a large cavity. Finally, when one bike's charging system failed, the alternator soldering was found to be 'appalling'.

On the plus side, their puncture repair kits were never needed as neither bike suffered a single flat, and the hard Indian-made tyres, though largely an unknown quantity in the wet, showed no signs of wear. The chains and sprockets also stayed the course. The toolkit was good and very comprehensive, with only a few of those shaken-loose nuts it couldn't do up; a pushrod adjuster was included. The only extras necessary were a wire brush Giles purchased in Pakistan, sawed the handle off for lightness and used every day on the plugs, and a 'Bell' ring spanner for the head bolts 'which by God I needed!'

The engines performed happily on the nondescript oil ('You get what you can get') and on petrol usually dispensed from old jerrycans. They did about 300 miles to the tank-full, and one of the compensations of Iran was that there it cost only 60p to fill up both bikes. And the bottom line was that the Bullets did get them home.

Leaving Shandigarh and Amritsar behind, the two arrived at the Pakistan border, which took four hours to get through even with papers in order. It also provided an abrupt introduction to Muslimland, as a half litre of Scotch they were carrying was ceremoniously poured away. Videos, video cameras, cassettes and pictures of your girlfriend in a bikini can all give religious offence or arouse suspicion, and if you do take cameras, cassette players, etc, it's advisable to record their serial numbers.

Once in Pakistan, though the local mechanics were good, there was none of the specific Indian knowledge of Bullets, and no more free services. The country took about two weeks to traverse, rising early and riding every day; German BMW riders they met were amazed at their mileages, but it turned out the modern riders were spending much less time in the saddle than the ancient Brits, who in the two months' trip only had two days when they didn't ride.

Pakistan was the most lawless place they visited; most adult males carry arms, and the situation was particularly volatile due to the hotly fought elections then taking place. In fact the British Consul in Lahore advised the pair not to carry on east just then. Much of the place is still essentially tribal, so that you might have a visa, but around Quetta in particular, it might not be recognised by the local powers-that-be.

It was also demanding territory for the Enfields. In Lahore they had flipped a coin to decide whether to ride the valley road and then turn up to Quetta, or to take the mountain passes. The valley won, but then they took a wrong turning and ended up in the mountains anyway: fate. Climbing the rocky dirt tracks through the passes, on one occasion a bridge was down and they didn't notice until perilously late, so that Charles rode into the back of Giles' bike, not for the last time. Charles also fell off quite a lot, not surprisingly since most of his riding till then had been done on the streets of London. The fact that he stayed the course is pretty impressive.

This was nerve-racking stuff, with potential real penalties not only physically but also for trouble with the machines. In Lahore YMCA they had met a party of English riders on Kawasaki dirt bikes, stuck there for six weeks because a lorry had reversed over one of their irons and twisted the front forks badly, so they had to wait while the necessary parts were sent out from a breakers in Lincolnshire.

After Quetta came what is generally held to be the toughest section of the route East, the Baluchistan desert to the Iranian border. They had been told that the Bullets' rear cush hub rubbers might melt in the heat. Some Danes they met later, despite being on pukka moto-cross machines, were still planning to put their bikes on the train from Nok Kundi, the customs post just after the Iranian border, to Quetta, rather than face the desert.

Sure enough, as the Enfields hit the lonely desert road, first a sandstorm blew up ('the sand will have you off, but you're going slowly anyway,') and then one of the bikes broke down – no sparks. Acting on a tip they'd had from Mannohan Motors, Giles joined a couple of wires to isolate the kill-switch. It worked – 'otherwise we could have been there for days.'

Nearing Iran, fuel began to be scarce, though the pair in fact never had to resort to their emergency supplies of petrol or water. They had heard horror stories of Iran, so it was a major relief when the border crossing went easily; 'our big fear had been that we would be turned back, so once we were over we felt the cork was out of the bottle.' It was also a relief to find that the roads improved dramatically, doubling their width so that you didn't have to ride onto the verge to overtake. The only setback was that all the road signs were in Farseh script!

However, their visa gave them just seven days to do the 2,000-odd miles from the south-west to the far north-east of the country. The first night they camped alone in a medieval mud fort, and saw no tourists of any sort until reaching Esfahan, the only holiday place, where their smart hotel was still happy to have the Enfields wheeled into the lobby.

It was when they reached Maku, the border crossing to Turkey, that trouble struck. With the seven-day visas they had entered the country on Saturday morning, and reached the border on the evening of the following Saturday. To the Iranian guards those few hours over the limit were an insult, and things got nasty. Their passports were thrown out of the post, and the guards tried to order them back to Teheran, several hundred miles away. Giles had been in the Army 'and was used to being messed around' so he could be relatively patient, but the normally equable Charles was beginning to boil dangerously. They had to wait until one in the afternoon when a more senior man arrived. Going in to meet him was 'like the headmaster's study all over again.' The officer heard their story; then smiled gravely and told them that they had done wrong, but that he was going to let them through. 'At that point,' said Giles, 'I'd have drunk his bath-water.'

Once in Turkey, beyond the border on a lonely road beneath Mount Ararat, the west-bound travellers met a pair of their friends, BMW-mounted Anthony Wickham ('a bit of a turbo-head') and Simon James on a Suzuki, heading in the opposite direction. It was a Dr-Livingstone-I-presume situation, and only came about by good luck, as the next day Giles and Charles were peeling off from Erzerum for the south Turkish coast, and would have missed the eastbound party. They compared notes; Giles warned Anthony off the mountain road beyond Quetta, 'but they did it anyway, just to say they had!'

In the mountains heading for the Med, their only major mechanical mishap developed, with Charles' bike beginning to backfire badly under load uphill. At the next town, after playing with the ignition for a bit, Giles took the head off and discovered that the outer (stronger) valve spring had broken, and the bike had been keeping going on the inner one. They were carrying a spare spring, but lacked the means to compress it. No worries – a non-English-speaking Turkish mechanic went to the workshop next door to his and made them up a special tool which did the job. Giles still has it in his spares kit.

It was the end of October, and starting to get cold; and also Giles was 'getting jerked off with the bikes – my focus, my achievement if you like, was to get the bikes back.' After ten days or so the duo caught their ferry from Izmir up to Venice, where sure enough, after three days on the boat, as

'Phew – there's no such thing as free air ...'

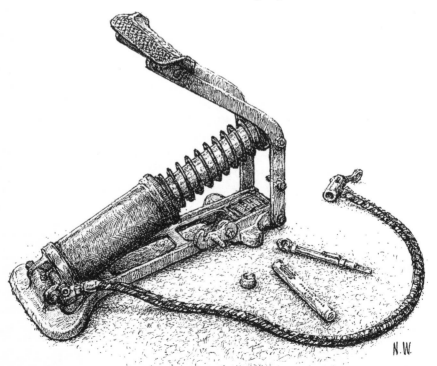

Charles' bike rode off it blew another head gasket. They parked in a lock-up garage by the port, and fixed it there. Giles' abiding cultural recollection of Venice was not the Canalettos or St Mark's Square, but the first sight for months of pretty girls.

They slogged north, and going through the Mont Blanc tunnel experienced culture shock of a different sort as for the first time they hit cold rain, and tugged on the Rukka suits. In Paris they stayed in an ex-brothel by the Arc de Triomphe, and in that bikers' town their Delhi plates drew a lot of attention. Finally, considerably knackered, they reached the last ferry, and the sight of the white cliffs was inevitably a very emotional moment; the two had known each other for so long, and gone through a great deal together to get the bikes back home.

Then, back in Blighty, with the Customs cleared and night coming on – the charging system on Charles' bike packed up. But the AA got them to 'friendly troglodytes in woolly hats' at Dover's Road Star Cycles, who fixed them up with a new, charged six-volt battery. Running on it for both spark and lights, they limped towards London, swapping batteries every half hour to keep them charged. As they reached town at 11 o'clock at night, with the lights dying and the unaccustomed fiercely fast traffic, Charles' clutch cable broke.

The last spare one was fitted in five minutes (by then they were well practised), and so with Indian plates and no insurance, they switched off their lights and rode the last two miles to the Kings Road unilluminated – 'and we didn't give a bugger!' They reached home by midnight. Not a bad show.

Police

There are bound to be mixed feelings for most riders about police motorcyclists. On the one hand they can be the men who deliver rude and expensive surprises when they stop you for speeding, bad driving, or a poorly prepared machine. On the other, they are riders like yourself, only highly trained and skilled and doing it for eight hours a day. Off-duty, most Traffic riders are realistic about real life on the roads, including some unfeasibly low speed limits, and emphasise the bond between all motorcyclists. They also tend to be enthusiastic about British bikes.

Triumph used to be the marque overwhelmingly preferred by the Forces, particularly the Met. I still remember one day in the early sixties when a gleaming Amaranth Red Speed Twin silently appeared at my elbow as I was riding my Norton past the Houses of Parliament. And the Traffic sergeant's withering look of contempt as he pointed out that my helmet strap was undone.

But the cops do have a lot to put up with. More recently I visited the Met Traffic Museum at Catford. A gruesome collection of post-accident photographs graphically demonstrated the results of some of the motorcycle-mounted public's recklessness and folly, which the boys in blue then have to clear up.

I was also told how the old, bulky Cossor R/T sets, mounted in place of the Triumph tank-top parcel grid, had presented a standing threat to the police riders' family jewels in the event of a front-end shunt. And how riding a Speed Twin, you never had to dubbin your boots, thanks to copious oil leaks, particularly from Triumph's unique 'tell-tale-tit' oil pressure indicator button. Then over the years there had been some deeply eccentric and impractical special equipment foisted on them, such as what they called 'the Fallen Madonna with the Blinking Boobs', a white PVC waistcoat worn by the Traffic man, with flashing blue lights mounted at around breast height – just the right place to blind the rider when they were switched on ...

Oh a policeman's lot was not always a happy one. But not boring, either.

I'd been thinking of investing in a new helmet. The old white Everoak (or E-R-AK, as the peeling stickers on the back put it) had been great. But the 'you're OK to race in it' sticker had expired before I even bought it, the cloth bit on the inside was coming out, and putting it on at that stage was guaranteed to turn clean hair to spaghetti-with-sump-oil-sauce in less than a minute.

But what to replace it with? There was one possibility, almost too radical to contemplate, which was to change to one of those newfangled full-face thingies. I had to admit that I'd never actually ridden in one, but increasingly desperate journalistic forays were now sometimes taking me out of the old bike ghetto and putting me aboard machines with, gulp, sustained ton-plus potential. At those speeds an open-face and a flip-up visor can sometimes feel a little, shall we say, prone to buffeting (I know, I know, get goggles).

Though I suspected I would stay with an open-face because that's what's comfortable for me in every way, there were other arguments for full-face lids. The best one I ever heard came from a motorcycle cop. He told me about the first week when the riders of his Traffic division had shifted from open-face (the same Everoak I sported) to full-face helmets.

Four of them, my friend included, were riding out in the city wearing their brand new brain-gloves. Round a right hand corner in front of them comes one of those double-decker car transporters. Narrow corner, transporter driver gets himself too far over to the right and suddenly the copper riding front and starboard has run out of options. Crashes into the front of the transporter, is catapulted up off his BMW and head first smack into one of the upright pillars holding up the second deck of cars …

Since it was head first, the full-face took the impact of the metal pillar, and amazingly the police rider got off without severe injury. Otherwise it would have been Goodbye Mr Chin, and probably Mr Mouth and Mr Nose too.

Policemen crashing may seem surprising, but according to my man, with only one exception everyone in his Traffic division at that time, despite being advanced level riders, had come off in their first three months on the job. And as the senior sergeant in a division with 18 City motorcyclists and 20 outside the urban area, he was the one who judged if a crash was blameworthy, and if it was, suspended the rider.

I'm lucky (or slow) enough never to have been seriously hassled on the road by the boys in blue, but my real reasoning in getting to know the sergeant was pragmatic. As a writer I'm completely promiscuous – I'll listen to *anyone* with a story to tell, and cops invariably do have fine tales and tell them in a memorable way.

To return to my friend the sergeant. Having started in 1967, he had ridden a fair number of British bikes, beginning on a '64 bathtub Triumph Speed Twin, and when I was last in touch was riding a Norton rotary Interpol 2 (which he liked very much but was realistic about). At one period in the

'… not completely oil-tight yet …'

N Ward

seventies he was changing round between Triumphs, Norton Commandos and the BMW R75/6s which the Division was phasing in. Not without the odd problem – at least one of the Boxer twins had to be fitted with stabiliser 'trainer' wheels until a rather short officer had got the hang of the Beemer's weight and bulk!

The sergeant rode 5TAs, T100s and Bonnevilles, as well as BSA Lightnings ('superb') and Rickman-framed Triumph 650s, with either Bonneville or the purpose-tuned single carb Saint motors in them. His Force also used 125 Zundapps and even BSA 250 C15s as divisional machines – ie Noddy bikes in the rural areas. But the sergeant's most memorable outing on a Ceefer was after he had gone on attachment to the Crime Squad, seconded particularly for undercover surveillance work.

Motorcycles were and are useful on tailing jobs, within certain limitations. Following a car is easier on a bike than on four wheels, but you do stand out more, though you can hide more easily behind other vehicles. For that reason there's usually only one motorcycle on the team in a follow (there are usually considerably more cars in a team than the two or even three you see in the movies).

The bike backs up the eyeball car, picking up visual contact with the suspect if that car loses it, and dropping back again when the car re-establishes contact. But bikes are not ideal in some circumstances – ie motorways, where, due to their conspicuity, ideally you need a fresh one at each exit; and even then, an experienced villain may throw things out by suddenly U-turning across a police crossing in the central barrier. The sergeant stressed that someone surveillance-conscious, maybe someone who's been busted that way already, should be expected to do anything at any time.

To maintain a bike and rider's anonymity, you change jackets and use helmets of different colours, and under them maybe a wig, or long hair sometimes up and sometimes down. You change number plates. A solo rider may acquire a passenger – in an anecdote so politically incorrect it was off the scale, the sergeant particularly recalled one WPC in this role, as the girl had the biggest nipples he had ever encountered, which poked into his back every time he braked!

Fairings were mostly out (too easy to identify) but panniers were in, as they concealed the necessary radio aerials, thin wires instead of the bungee wire type. Posing as a courier became a bit of a cliché and you couldn't get away with it any more. The bikes were wired in to the rest of the team and the rider could send/receive via a tit on the handlebars as on regular Traffic machines. This was fine until circumstances separated you from the bike ...

Most villains stick to their own ground, and once a suspect was 'housed', bikes were no use anymore. A static point overlooking the drum usually had to be a parked, apparently empty van, but this too presented problems. If you fit darkened see-through plastic panels to observe the house, at night any light used inside the vehicle will show through the panels. In the old days the sergeant rigged up a tank periscope which surfaced in a van's ventilator chimney.

Then again, people in the back of a van will make it rock on its springs when they move, giving the game away to a careful observer. So they used to weld nuts to the back axle, and once in position, screw down bolts to convert the suspension to rigid. The sergeant is a happily married man, but he did hear from single fellow officers that this system was also great if you and a female colleague wanted to get up close and personal, unobtrusively.

Once in a while, though, bikes came back into their own. One city centre watch culminated in a truck arriving outside the suspect house and beginning to unload hot merchandise. Close-up observation was necessary to make sure the team caught the bad guys with their hands full, and the sergeant showed me blurred photographs taken from the surveillance van of himself with long hair, wearing an old boiler suit and pobbling past the truck on a ratty old C15. Presumably the villains couldn't believe that the law would use anything that oily and noisy. A few minutes later, arrests were made. 'Good beans', as the sergeant put it.

Being a man who lives and breathes motorcycles, however, he soon returned to Traffic. Not content with riding eight-hour shifts as well as to and from home, the sergeant was part of one of the Police teams in the National Rally, contested the Circuit des Pyrenees on a Triumph-engined Sprite (which never actually finished), and did local and long-distance Trials, winning one of the major long-distance ones, twice. And there was also the Display team.

He and some other keen riders set this up in the early seventies, getting hold of half a dozen well-used Tiger 100 ex-patrol bikes with 60–80,000 miles up on them already. They then talked the city into converting them for trick riding, with some guys from a Royal Marine team coming up to help, bringing patterns for the metal stirrups which fitted over the footrests, for standing in. Otherwise they just stripped off fairings and panniers, shortened the rear mudguard and strengthened the front, and were ready to go.

They trained on a local airfield, and were soon asked to perform at the Royal Tournament, since at the time they were the only team featuring a double-act of motorbikes and police horses. The horses apparently loved it, staying docile amidst the noisy machines until the high point, the Crossover Ride, when they'd prick their ears, rear up on their hind legs and go for it! Sadly, eventual amalgamation with another Force brought an end to the team.

I always enjoyed my chats with the sergeant, though I was never quite sure if the Interpol parked outside my door when he came by for a coffee enhanced my street cred, or sent it through the floor. It never felt like consorting with the enemy to me, just with a particularly knowledgeable and experienced enthusiast.

Though one from another world. The sergeant once let drop that the day before he had been the second policeman on the scene when in heavy traffic they had arrested a guy who had gone ape with a shotgun in his home and

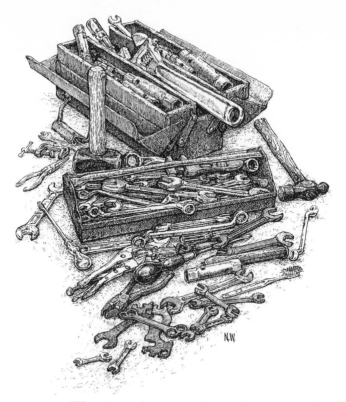

'There's one here somewhere ...'

then made it a double at his girlfriend's workplace. The man had surrendered quietly, even with relief, but it was then up to the sergeant to check the boot of the car. Not a problem, you might think, until he pointed out mildly that, given the guy's state of mind, it might have been wired for explosives. Not something one might care to confront at any moment of any working day.

It probably helped that he smoked a pipe, and was as laid back as you could wish, but also that he always spoke his mind. I might not have agreed with him about full-face helmets, but after that story about the car-transporter, I'll never forget his point of view!

T160 Saudi Service

More than most machinery, British motorcycles, built with often outdated machinery to idiosyncratic standards, required Tender Loving Care in the area of service to keep them going. British manufacturers and dealers expected most of this to be provided by the customer, and hadn't much time for those poor boobies who hoped they would be looked after. If you did find a conscientious, sympathetic mechanic, you were very lucky, then as now. By the seventies, with the benchmark of Japanese mechanical reliability and after-sales service established and the home manufacturers in steep decline, the over-stressed British designs in production at the time could not offer much hope of similar customer satisfaction.

One of the worst case scenarios it was possible to imagine got underway in 1975 when, in virtually its last gasp, the collapsing British industry exported several hundred of the final, temperamental three-cylinder Triumphs to the Middle East. Someone had to look after these machines. So, from scrambling in sleepy Hampshire to a job in the burning Arabian sands, shepherding some of the last 'real' British bikes ever made – Ron Moss was to have a strange and wonderful seventies. Almost as strange as the notion of using T160 Tridents as Saudi law enforcement camels …

Both Ron Moss and his twin brother Carl had grown up motorcycle mad, but with the manufacturing nexus firmly located in the Midlands, there was little bike-related work to be had in their area of Hampshire. So both completed apprenticeships in car mechanics, and then, as if by magic, in 1970 Norton-Villiers relocated their Commando assembly operation from Plumstead to Andover.

Both brothers secured jobs with what shortly became Norton Villiers Triumph (NVT). But all too soon, in April 1973, came the announcement from the group's chairman Dennis Poore that he was running down the Andover assembly plant and moving all Commando production to Wolverhampton. Despite a brief sit-in, from then on the Andover operation dwindled. It was sad, though neither brother had any illusions about Norton by then. 'On the Commando line,' said Carl, 'faulty bearings were fitted knowingly because the manager had to meet his production target. Every one would then have to be rectified under warranty.'

Meanwhile Ron Moss had gone to work at one of the surviving local arms of the company, Norton Villiers Europe at Walworth, east of Andover, in the service department. 'We had both been so pleased to be working in the motorcycle industry, and then doing competition at the weekends – it was brilliant,' said Ron, who had gone on from a Gold Star to a Victor scrambler, and then, naturally, to two-stroke AJS machines which were also developed at Thruxton. But like Carl, he watched as the Norton operation at Andover dwindled, and after a spell with NVT's service operation eventually left to work for Wooler Engineering for six months, converting Pacer cars to right-hand drive.

Then he heard a rumour about a job looking after NVT police bikes in Saudi Arabia. Ron applied, and despite no longer being a Norton Villiers employee, he got it. In 1975 the legendary police bike salesman Neale Shilton had negotiated a £1 million deal with the Saudi Defence Force to supply them with several hundred Interpol Commandos. But in the summer of that year NVT were forced into voluntary liquidation, and the only bikes they could supply to the Saudis were the final run of T160 Tridents, converted to Cardinal police spec. The first ones were actually sent out accompanied by a packet of Norton badges.

Ron's first trip to Saudi was a two-week stint in April 1976, to help assemble the initial hundred machines. Aged 23, 'and till recently catching a bus into Andover had been a big thing,' Ron went in at the deep end. Their jumbo jet flew into Beirut, where the airport was deserted and the city echoed with the sound of machine-gun fire. They landed at Jeddah in Saudi at night, yet walking off the plane was like walking into an oven. They only cleared customs after midnight, and the person supposed to be meeting them was not there. And Jeddah was 'a real dump'.

'People were sleeping in cardboard boxes. Every building was unfinished, because you only had to pay tax on a finished house. There were hundreds of cars just dumped at the roadside.' The Arabs just three years previously in 1973 had flexed their muscles for the first time, briefly interrupting oil supplies to the West. The result of taking a bigger slice of the profits from their own resources from then on had been an unbelievable explosion of wealth for the previously backward oil-producing kingdoms – and hence a casual attitude to consumer durables like cars and bikes. But at ground level things were rough. 'Car horns sounded all night. The weather was very, very muggy. In our hotel there were bare electric wires to the cooling fan, and the beds were all collapsed. It seemed like hell.'

One thing Ron did learn on that trip was all about triples. His companions were Les Williams, the legendary Trident engineer who campaigned Slippery Sam for several years and whose L.P. Williams shop remains one of the top triple outfits; and Jack Shemans, another three-cylinder Triumph guru who later worked with Norman Hyde. 'They were proper gents, and they really taught me the way around Tridents,' Ron confirmed.

His second trip, later on in 1976, was on a two-and-a-half year contract – serious stuff, because 'the Saudis took your passport, and you had to earn your exit visa every 12 months.' And Ron's motive? Making big money – they were paid monthly with a briefcase full of cash – so that he could pursue moto-cross seriously back home. The service contract on the

Cardinals was with the Dallah Company, who had a finger in many other activities in Saudi. Unfortunately this was not like working for the bigger companies, who had walled compounds with swimming pools and a comfortable lifestyle for their Western employees. Ron and the late Cyril Halliburn, an industry veteran known for his work developing the Gold Star, were put in a disused driving school on the edge of the desert outside Jeddah.

At first they were expected to sleep in a dormitory with the four mechanics, Egyptians and Pakistanis, who were assigned to the job; another aspect of the oil states' new wealth was the hiring of guest-workers from elsewhere in the Middle East to do the menial jobs, and since the mechanics were paid one-tenth of the Englishmen's wages, this would give rise to some friction. Halliburn had to fight to get them their own accommodation, and the problem there, as with much else, was that they had to rely on an interpreter for the negotiations.

Halliburn had retired, and like Ron was there for the money; he badly missed his wife and grandchildren. One of the old school, he persisted in addressing Ron by his surname. Things nearly got off to a disastrous start. Halliburn was proud of his physical strength, and for a demonstration, challenged Ron to try and twist his arm. Ron did it in an unexpected way, and trapped a nerve in Halliburn's neck running to his brain. The older man's eyes rolled back as he collapsed and fell, apparently dead. Visions of months in a Saudi jail flashed before Ron's eyes. Then after a minute Halliburn came to. He took that afternoon off.

Troubles with the Cardinals were not long in coming. The Saudi police riders were unused to the finer points of motorcycling, let alone to British bikes. They would habitually use the rear brake pedal as a footrest since it felt more comfortable, and the consequent drain via the brake-light would do for the battery in less than a hundred miles. The previous police machines had been Honda-4s, which had not needed choke or a pumped throttle to help them start on the button as the T160s did. And once their batteries flattened, the Cardinals would often simply be abandoned. On one machine the solder on the clutch cable went, and even this was enough to mean that it was chucked in a corner. None of the bikes that came back for service had more than 800 or 900 km on them.

Part of the trouble was that rather than Ron and the mechanics being able to make visits to the machines in service, it was ordered that the bikes had to be brought to them. 'Particularly from the holy cities of Medina and Mecca, where Westerners weren't allowed in; so the Cardinals were supposed to be brought out for repair, but a lot of them just weren't.' The exception was the month before the Hadj, the sacred pilgrimage, when the Mecca police sent them their bikes and the team worked hard to get them in gleaming, tip-top condition. But the machines then had to be sent back unaccompanied on a flat-bed truck, and they heard that at the other end, those in charge of unloading didn't know how to get them down off the wagon, so they simply pushed them off ...

Apart from such mistreatment, one problem arose from the quality of the gasoline available. Petrol in Saudi was incredibly cheap; at £1 for ten gallons it was cheaper than the (essential) bottled mineral water. But the best of it was two-star, and the quality went down from there. The result was bad pinking for the triples. Halliburn decided that the compression should be lowered from 9 to 8.25:1. To convince NVT of the problem, he gave Ron a week to thrash his personal test/demo bike, which was Ron's sole transport out there, until it would self-destruct. 'I was out there scrambling in the sand for a week, caning it every way I knew, but I couldn't blow it up! In the end Cyril told me to stop.'

On receiving Halliburn's memo, NVT agreed to the recommended change, but their solution was to cause another problem. 'The compression was lowered by skimming existing pistons, but turning the pistons down on a lathe often distorted their skirts. Where this happened, compression was going down past the pistons into the crankcases, and pressurising them. The chaincase was a sealed breathing system, back into the air filter. So compression was coming up there and lifting the throttle slides, even though the throttle stops had been taken off; this caused bad over-revving, and engines which wouldn't tick over. ' Cyril Halliburn worked out the cause of the problem, and another set of fresh pistons then had to be fitted to many of the bikes.

'We also did a mod on the alternators, to help cope with the abuse on the

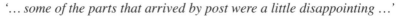

'... *some of the parts that arrived by post were a little disappointing ...*'

electrics, as well as the extra equipment – the Cardinals had two flashing red lights mounted on the crashbars, a siren, airhorns etc. They were heavy too, with the panniers, the base for the radio and so on. The windscreen made them tankslap between 60 and 70; if you were brave you could drive through it, but not many of the Saudis took it that fast. We tried to find out if the cause lay at the front or the rear; it was the front which wobbled, but probably the weight from the panniers etc at the back which caused it.

'The whole thing was frustrating; everyone was knocking the bike, but really no matter how good the bike was, it didn't stand a chance.' According to the late Neale Shilton, Cardinals were the last batch of Tridents produced in December 1975, and sent out in five shipments totalling 450 machines, with a further 130 stored in the Midlands and sold off in Britain during 1977.

If any of the above sounds like Arab-bashing, that was not how Ron felt about a culture which had produced chess, coffee, higher mathematics and the sublime architecture of the Alhambra. 'The Saudis were always friendly, though everything was *Inshallah bukra*, "tomorrow if God wills it", which is sort of like mañana but lacking the burning sense of urgency.' Ron did feel that the sudden explosion of wealth had catapulted people into the technological age with little preparation. 'They were coming straight from goat-herding, onto the highways.' A snapshot: one day Ron got a flat tyre, and as he reinflated it with a pump, a crowd gathered. 'They'd never seen a pump. All they knew about air was to go to the garage and push a button.'

Some of this was frightening. 'You'd see 12-year-olds going across red lights in a car with no doors. And if you as a Westerner got in an accident, it was automatically your fault; they knew this, and went for you! There were horrendous accidents; no one ever looked to see if anything was coming. Yet there was so much money. When we arrived there was a crude interchange we used to call the Donkey Roundabout in Jeddah; I went back there a year later, and they'd spent a billion pounds and put in a huge flyover there.' The wealth co-existed with old ways which were sometimes barbaric. 'You could go down to the souk and see people beheaded for murder, buried up to their neck and stoned for rape, or have a hand cut off for thieving. Gold bars were stacked openly on tables in the marketplace – no one was going to steal them.'

Ron's own lifestyle was scarcely luxurious. 'We used to bring in a lot of dehydrated food and cook it ourselves; we were there to make money, so we only went out for a decent meal once a week. You could eat well, with steaks from the US and so on. At one of the Chinese restaurants I used to clip their poodles and we'd get free meals.' Otherwise entertainment consisted of the occasional film show on the British Embassy roof, a once-weekly Arabic lesson from an Indian fellow-worker, and Halliburn, a British yo-yo champion, demonstrating his skills. Or riding out through the desert to Twenty-Nine Palms, by the sea, where you see camel trains away in the distance.

'I kick myself, now, that I didn't pick Cyril's brains more about Gold

Stars, or write down the stories he told – how BSA had given him five years to get a win at Daytona, and how he finally did it in the last year, 1954.' Before Halliburn left, he agreed that Ron could keep the demo Trident, and chucked it in with a consignment of unused Cardinals being brought back to the UK for resale. After that Ron was there on his own. With the bike service work running down, he began to work on another Dallah enterprise, doing the airport runway wiring. Labouring in 100-degree heat, he would watch longingly as the sole daily BA plane to Britain lifted off. 'Because you never saw grass out there, when you did come back you used to kiss the turf.' But things were improving. Twin brother Carl also came out to work, and Ron fell in with a crowd from an Isle of Wight Hovercraft company supplying the Saudi Coastguard, and moved into one of their bungalows. 'The Brits out there became better friends than your friends back home, because you relied on each other so much.' One of the Hovercraft guys would later be best man at Ron's wedding.

Dallah Avco also had a compound with swimming pools, tennis etc, but on Ron's final job for them it was back into tents, while he was working installing a ropeway up a steep mountain to take equipment for a weather radar installation to the top. When the ropeway was found to be insufficient, Ron flew with some of the material dangling under a Bell helicopter piloted by a barefoot American Vietnam vet, who skilfully turned the little chopper the opposite way to counteract the spinning load. Heavier material went up in a Kawasaki-built version of the Chinook helicopter, the vet hovering with the chopper's two rear wheels just resting on the mountainside and its body tilted for unloading; though once they did lose half a load of RSJs down the hill, when the cargo suddenly slipped.

In between these adventures, Ron on his travels had located some ex-police bikes for sale from a third party; for despite many being abandoned, it was sticky buying the machines while they still technically belonged to the police. Ron bought half a dozen Cardinals, as well as a load of Hondas which proved to be nothing but trouble; he dearly wished he had invested in some ex-police A65s instead. Then NVT's supersalesman Mike Jackson rang to tell Ron about a Finn named Terry Frederikson who had gone round various Arab police forces and tracked down hundreds of machines. Ron eventually had another five of the best, lowest-mileage Cardinals off him.

When it came time to leave Saudi, Ron did so in some style, driving home in a Straight 6 Chevy Camaro! He went from Saudi to Jordan and Syria, where he caught a ferry to Piraeus while his then girlfriend, now wife, Diane, flew out to join him. Together they spent six weeks going home, via the moto-cross Grands Prix in France and Italy. Once back in Hampshire Ron did return to competition himself, but also bought a house with his accumulated Saudi earnings. And with the van in which he transported his scrambler, he started moving furniture, the basis of the successful light haulage business he runs today.

Most of the re-imported Cardinals were sold by Ron to Croydon dealer Carl Rosner, but Ron kept his ex-demo bike for himself. Naturally it was in quite a state after the Saudi experience, but when Ron took the head off things were OK, so he had the frame stoved, and the engine then stayed under his bench for the next ten years. Once he finally got around to it, in a week he had the bike back together again.

After all the abuse it had taken in Saudi, ironically when he did then get it on the road in England it lasted less than two weeks before the plugs oiled up and the oil pressure light started flickering. Ron took the engine down again and discovered about an inch of play on two of the big ends, probably caused by the effects of condensation while the engine had been standing, eating away the bottom big end shells. By that time all the swarf from this had gone round the engine, so it meant a rebore and a crank regrind. He also had the head ported, fitted an L.P. Williams lightweight clutch plus electronic ignition, and double discs at the front – 'probably the most important item of all. Before that when I first went out on it, I came to a T-junction, hauled on the anchors and just kept going …'

With the tank resprayed in smart Cold White with gold-lined Sunflower Yellow flashes, the T160 is the nicest kind of reminder of Ron's desert days. After all, they did come through quite a lot together.

The Wall of Death

We round off the chapter with a tale of old motorbikes that work to entertain us. Nick Ward and I visited a steam fair in Nick's part of the world, and there we discovered a Wall of Death.

Somehow I had never been to one before. Once popular, there are now only two currently operating in the UK. The Wall and its front stage take eight hours to erect, while the show lasts just 15 minutes. But you definitely get your money's worth. Seeing and hearing the stripped, unsilenced bikes rocket up from the 45 degree starter slope onto the vertical sides where they race round at up to 55mph, horizontal to the ground and with a 25-foot drop if the bike should falter and centrifugal force fail them, is not something you forget in a hurry.

And all this on bright red Indian Scout vee-twins from the twenties! But apparently the US-built machines from Springfield, Massachusetts, are ideal. Their seat and tank are the same height, which makes them easy for the rider to move around on during the stunts; their footboards are easier to stand up on than balancing on a peg; and their leaf-spring front suspension provides somewhere to put your feet on when sitting across the bars. Also,

Indian tidied their handlebar layout by running all the control cables inside the bars, where the stunt rider's feet can't get snagged in them. The Scout's frames are massively strong, and their handling outstanding.

After the spectacle I should have interviewed these fearless showmen, but at my time of life it had been just too much excitement. I really needed a drink.

The steam rally was a big one, at Henham Hall, just over the border in Suffolk, which is a story in itself. This major estate and ancestral home of the Earls of Stradbroke apparently found itself without anyone to inherit it – until the legal eagles tracked down a distant relation Down Under, now known locally as 'the Aussie Earl'. A diamond in the rough, the present Earl has at least a dozen children (well, there's room for them), and still goes into his local with the cheerful Outback salutation of 'G'day, y'bastards!'

Entering Henham Park, Nick Ward and I seemed to drive for at least a couple of miles over dusty tracks before reaching the rally site of what must have been over 20 acres, and pitching into the very well attended 23rd Grand Henham Steam Rally. There was the sight and smell of smoke blowing from the mass of assembled devices – steam farm machinery and steam tractors, stationary engines, roundabouts and fairground organs, model steam boats and a miniature steam railway. If it steamed, it was there. Guest of honour was eccentric steeplejack Fred Dibnah with his own steamroller, but Nick and I had other fish to fry. We made for the motorcycle section.

Fearless tester Wilson takes the 'Wall-of-Death' machine for a spin ...

OH *NO!* THERE'S A ROUNDABOUT COMING UP...

N. Ward 97.

Despite our pal Slim Bartram saying that the following day, the Sunday, would have been a better one for bikes, that Saturday didn't seem bad to me, with everything from a Dunkley Whippet moped to a smart but well-used 1939 Brough Superior SS80 outfit, complete with Brough's petrol-bearing sidecar tubing. A fine marching jazz band was just leaving the main arena, so two glorious noises mingled as the motorcycles filed in there on parade. The sight of Slim's full-dress Ariel Leader, with his grand-daughter Tiffany grinning on the pillion, summed up what our kind of biking can be all about.

After that we headed for the Black Bull, a massive portable pub with wooden flooring, brought in on its own pantechnicon by Theakstons the brewers. But then our progress was fatally arrested by the sight of a BSA. A bright green and red rigid A7 500 twin to be precise, a pre-1950 long-stroke one with the Triumph-style screw-in rocker caps. It was standing on rollers next to a stripped yellow Indian vee-twin. Nick noted that both were shod with Avon SMs, 'so grip can't be the point!' Fired up on the rollers, the bikes' noise was used to pull in the crowds to the Motordrome Co Wall of Death. This we had to see.

We filed up a staircase, into the arena and onto the circular viewing platform, looking down on the plank-built cylinder of the Wall. This rose from a banked lower section; there was a yellow line halfway up the Wall, and its top three feet, just below the spectators, was painted white. In the centre of the pit there was a large tin box, white with a Red Cross and the words 'ACCIDENT FUND' painted on it.

When the first bike, one of a pair of Honda Benlys, fired up on open exhausts in the confined space, on the packed viewing platform the staccato roar got everyone's attention. After a couple of circuits on the banking, the bearded rider headed the Honda's maroon and cream tank unhesitatingly up onto the Wall. As the bike shot past below us, the planks we were standing over rattled violently underfoot, and you couldn't help remembering the excellent movie *Eat the Peach*, where a young Irishman achieves his impossible dream of building a Wall of Death out in the boondocks, only to have the bikes circulating finally shake it to bits!

It was thrilling again when just below us the pilot, grey-bearded like most of them, and with our downward angle of vision revealing pronounced bald spots – did this go with the territory? – took the bike right up into the white top section and then, the engine note changing, swooped down at full speed to the bottom. Each run lasted about a minute, and I noticed that the riders on the Wall never looked down. By way of a variation, they also ran a go-kart, meaning major plank-rattling as he too went up into the white danger zone.

But the star of the show was undoubtedly a red-painted Indian V-twin, which Nick identified by its quarter-elliptical springs at the front as a really early one. The engine note had serious BLAT as the red-jerseyed rider worked the left-side throttle, with its righteous din punctuated by unnerving backfires. He was smiling as his banking became even wilder, just before he took his hands off the bars. Soon, still at 90 degrees to the Wall, he was standing on the pegs with his hands clasped behind his back. Then he got a foot up on the ramp built out over the front wheel. Reader, hearts were in mouths. Then, in a crescendo of backfires, he went side-saddle – and again took his hands off the bars! I reckon you could have heard the applause in Norwich.

The finale was the two bikes chasing each other round the Wall together, provoking really serious plank-rattling and more gasps as one passed the other on the 'inside'. By the end of the spectacle we were all more than happy to toss coins for the 'accident fund' down into the wooden pit. Quite a way to earn a living, and just watching it drove us hurriedly to drink. The Black Bull put out an excellent pint of Old Peculier, and was big enough to comfortably accommodate the Dixieland marching band, Smokehouse Blue, as they came stomping in to entertain with some real Steam Music. One way and another the 23rd Henham Steam Rally had been a memorable affair.

'... the ignition was a little too far advanced.'

N Ward.

CHAPTER FIVE

My journeys III: To the Shetlands

Other than riding with the Swedes for a day as recounted in Chapter 3, the following trip was one of the few long ones I have ever undertaken with a companion. Motorcycling is an essentially solitary pursuit, so that's the way it suits most riders, me included.

But Sean Hawker had been indirectly responsible for my acquiring the BSA M21 side-valve 600 single on which I did this run, after I had tested his own bike for CBG. He had also meticulously rebuilt my M21. Ironically, therefore, on this one occasion when I was travelling with someone who could have fixed almost anything that went wrong – nothing did.

Sean's deep knowledge of the model had derived from using his one in 1990 to set out, with his similarly-mounted friend Martin Torpey, on a round-the-world trip. They had got into southern Russia, seen the earthquake damage in Azerbaijan, had a Russian factory stop work to enthusiastically turn up a new rear wheel spindle for Sean's bike (that spindle is still in place to this day), ridden into China and down to Nepal, and survived an incident in Malaya where, 60 miles north of Penang, Sean had flipped his bike and it had ended up in a river, upside down underwater.

They had called a halt, having worked for a while in Australia, after two years and 34,000 miles. 10,000 of them had been covered riding round Oz, where damage to Sean's magneto from the Malay immersion had finally led to his flywheel rivets loosening, which had meant a full engine rebuild.

So the travellers had come home to Bristol, but as voyagers from Ulysses onward have discovered, there were problems settling down – 'getting my head space together round here again', as Sean put it. He was still a fairly prickly and nervous individual when we took our trip north. I have been told that I'm not the easiest companion in the world either, and if you factor in a 25-year gap in our ages, you can imagine that as well as the good times, there were a few problems. The last night on the ferry, we had the makings of a serious falling-out when I was careless enough to try settling up for the work Sean had done on my bike with a cheque, after he had let me know several times that he preferred and needed cash.

But we patched it up and stayed friends, and Sean now runs his own business, CMES in Bristol, which capitalises on his skills, as it specialises in classic motorcycle electrics.

And the Shetlands? Magic. Read on.

It was off to the Shetland Islands with Sean Hawker on our M21s in May, for the 7th Shetlands Classic Motor Show. Why the Shetlands? Primarily because they were there, a good long ride within the UK with a clear destination; and also because the organiser had negotiated a really economical deal with P&O ferries. Even though in the weeks before we left, the little box to which the weathermen consign the islands seemed to be permanently obscured by stylised snowflakes.

And why the M21? Because that's what Sean Hawker rides, and I fancied some company on a trip for once, as well as a good outing to justify the

'Next time I'll set the tappets hot ...'

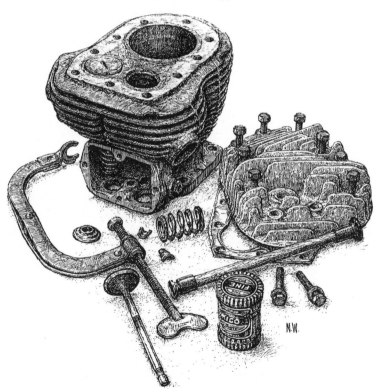

wedge I'd just spent with him on the old Beeza. And the 600 side-valve single's 'performance' meant that this trip would be done almost entirely on A and B roads, a fairly leisurely journey through Britain, an idea which definitely appealed.

My machine preparation consisted of cleaning the maroon monster, a first, and mostly a fool's errand which left tell-tale white splodges in semi-rusted and flaked corners. I never did get around to replacing the bike's ratty period plastic grips with cushioned rubber ones as Sean had recommended, but I did change the oil – we were both on straight 50, as Sean reckoned that would cope best with the side-valves' hot running over long days. And I was proudest of all of the 'covers' I cobbled together out of old inner tube and duct tape, wired over the top of the BSA's plunger rear units, to stop the bolts there rubbing through the back of my venerable Swagman panniers. Even if the result did add the final stamp of 'old nail' to this, ah, Show bike. Then I swung out of our drive onto the road, three hours behind schedule and with the mileage reading 56,172 – but the sun was shining. A good omen, and fine weather was to set the seal on our expedition.

The first leg was a familiar 80-something-mile run to Shropshire and Cleobury Mortimer, home of my *CBG* colleague Jim Reynolds. It was a happy ride, what with relief at finally getting underway and at the fact that the bike, loaded with panniers and a magnetic tank bag, handled and sounded all right, apart from a curious fluttering rattle when asked to press on past some dawdling drivers on the long Cotswold ridges above the Windrush valley. This was the first of a cacophony of weird sounds from the M21 which would provide much in-vehicle entertainment on the trip.

The last few miles from Worcester on were sheer delight, as cunning Uncle Jim has chosen to live in a place surrounded by a network of magnificent biking roads, a steep old town which is pretty without being prettified. Jim had purchased a bottle of what he called 'Margaret Thatcher' (Famous Grouse), and this combined with first-night-of-the-hols, plus the fine food and good ale at Jim's local, ensured that by the time Editor Westworth rolled in at the end of a 13-hour working day, his two columnists were perfectly, blissfully, *professionally* drunk, and capable of very little in the way of incisive, hard-hitting input, though I think we did manage some fairly inventive personal abuse …

Next morning Sean Hawker rolled in bang on time, if a little chilled, at 9.30am. His run up from Bristol had been 80-odd miles, so our mileages to the Shetlands would be the same. That day's destination was Carlisle, and we soon hit the fine winding roads from Jim's to Ludlow. These quickly let me get the measure of the Hawker riding style, which was to proceed briskly enough until the twisty bits, and then speed up.

This was his solution to the comparative monotony of M21-ing, as well as to having a competitor's reflexes (he does Trials and hill climbs) confined by economic circumstances to side-valve power. And the good bit is that you really can do it on a plunger BSA; they have, as one hackette put it, 'a wonderful cobby, sturdy, feel which made bends, while not exactly easy, a very satisfying experience.' Even with my unsecured, unevenly weighted saddlebags flapping about at the rear; Sean had proper pannier frames holding canvas bags. I could keep up with him fairly well, though a four-stone personal weight advantage and his non-stop flat-out approach did make him undisputed leader of the pack. However, for the first couple of days, since I had worked out the routes, Sean was happy to follow – a pleasant novelty, he said, for a guy who mostly travels alone, even if I did cruise at around 55, a bit slower than he favours.

After egg-and-bacon baps and tea at the Midway Truckstop at Prees, where the guv'nor had been well pleased with the recent spring *CBG* turn-out, we proceeded up the A49. The sun shone and rural England presented itself well, newly unfurled in green and yellow – daffodils, and hordes of roadside dandelions. Foolish young rabbits completed the picture by sprinting across the road. I also amused myself collecting place names. 'Highley' was a good one, especially when combined to make 'Highley unsuitable for HGVs'. Later high spots would be 'Conundrum' near the border (is it England or Scotland?), and 'Wideopen' on the way into wild and woolly Newcastle.

About 70 miles from the start, we could no longer avoid the M6, for negotiating the badlands between Liverpool and Manchester. The M21s proved well up to slow lane motorway travel, the trucks we shared it with being mostly patient and precise. We pulled in, a bit stiff and wind-battered, at Charnock services for an expensive but leisurely lunch, and a fuel-stop for me – Sean prudently held out for cheaper juice. My bike would return mpg between the high 40s and low 50s, the biggest determining factor seeming to be headwind; the whole journey north was done into a prevailing north-easter. Sean had replaced my M21's valve seats with ones which could safely be used with unleaded, and by the end of the trip I calculated that this meant I had saved about £15 on fuel. Useful.

After 40 miles we turned off the motorway and looped round onto the northbound A6. This was on advice from another colleague, Dave Minton, who regularly tests grown-up machines up there. I did wonder about the towns we'd have to negotiate, and we came straight off the motorway into the back of a traffic jam, which didn't seem auspicious. Sean had it sussed, though. 'School's turning out' – it's the same all over the known universe. After that we had little traffic trouble, road surfaces were great, and the major conurbation, Lancaster, seemed no bigger than a large town, with our route pretty well signed, and running beneath the imposing stones of a fine castle.

Beyond Kendal came the high-point road of the day, the magnificent stretch up and down over Shap Fell, a real biking highway. Then we slogged on the rest of the hundred-odd miles from the motorway to Carlisle. After a final roadside stop, I realised just how badly my lower back was aching when the M21 threw one of its periodic temporary 'won't start' tantrums. Luckily these didn't happen often, and seemed to be down to the need to tickle the carb after even a short stop, yet not enough to flood it. Meanwhile every kick sent painful jolts through a stiff, bruised lower backbone; the saddle's springs take minor bumps but they have to be attached to an iron frame, and this gives your spine a bashing on bad roads. Sean was suffering too. I was not sorry that Carlisle, which we reached at around what would have been rush-hour, proved to be in traffic terms 'like a Sunday', as Sean observed.

We then subsided into the excellent hospitality of Yvonne and Cyril Ayton, the editor of *Motor Cycle Sport*, enjoying a capacious hot tub, a couple of pints and a top class roast dinner. Sean and I were sharing a room, and I could no longer put off the revelation of a guilty secret – I was wearing a corset. Well actually a Held back-protector, made of flexible stretchy stuff, Velcro-fastened and with a semi-stiff armoured portion at the back. Bought for £25 with the plunger suspension in mind, it proved a real asset, so comfortable that you quickly forgot about it, and despite the Beeza's rudimentary springing I had no back troubles other than the bruising for the whole trip. It also kept my tummy warm. Sean's revelation

'… after the rebuild it fired first kick …'

N. Ward.

to match this, and amply confirmed by his girlfriend, was that he talked in his sleep. And how!

I was a little apprehensive about the next day's 240-mile haul up into the Highlands, as it was the make-or-break one, leaving just a hundred further miles to do to the ferry at Aberdeen the day after that. I still felt a bit groggy, and initially the day didn't help. We droned north on the A7, with the sky overcast and the north-east wind blowing hard against us. Crossing the border into Galloway it also began to spit with rain, and on the barren slope out of a new town we halted to haul on every available layer and then huddled in a bus shelter to snack on biscuits and apples. This was the bleakest moment, and chugging slowly uphill into the wind wasn't much better.

The antidote came in two parts. About 20 miles further on we stopped at the next town, desperate for a hot drink, and lurched into a pub. It was a plain enough place but well ordered, and made us welcome despite the deep-sea gear. Edinburgh was still 25 miles away and it was only midday, but we had hot coffee, then a wonderfully thick lentil, bacon and tomato soup served with warm rolls, and a steak pie with that crisp waxy crust you get north of the border. This really set us up; and then the sun came out. We stonked on until the Edinburgh ring road approached. I stopped for fuel at a Shell station but Sean, to his credit, wouldn't buy their petrol because of the company's recent behaviour in Nigeria and elsewhere, so declined to top up. Meanwhile a chaotic carload of crusties towing a decrepit caravan filled the forecourt with noise and cheerful obscenity.

It proved to be the last available stop before the ring road, and when I looked in my mirror after a while Sean had dropped way back; his fuel had got low enough so that a misfire had set in. We peeled off at the next exit, and just as well, because once we'd found a petrol station Sean noticed that the nut holding on the rear of his silencer had gone missing. Fishing out a Nyloc replacement was a lot easier than having to refit a hot exhaust system. We steamed on, and crossed the Forth road bridge (free for bikes) in good style and mild sunlight.

We pressed straight on up the M90, with the sight of snowy mountains ahead to lift our spirits. The motorway was a lot emptier and less fierce than its southern counterparts. We even overtook a few vehicles, including the crusties' caravan, whose back end we could now see was daubed with a rather direct message of just two words. We gave them a wave anyhow.

Sean had taken the lead, and he seemed to be able to wring that little bit extra from his bike, so I had to keep trying to keep up. This produced more frequent variations of the amazing repertoire of noises which my M21's engine produced, though these never affected its performance, just my nerves. The principal ones resembled: (a) a pair of ball bearings bouncing around in a steel sink; and (b) loose pieces of corrugated iron intermittently vibrating together in a stiff breeze. Then sometimes the ball bearings got into the corrugated iron. Later Sean suggested that the exhaust valve lifter might be loose, but at the time he just counselled, 'Don't let the engine labour. Rev it! They can't do more than about 5,000rpm anyway. And you needn't worry about wearing 'em out – M20s have been run as stationary engines for six months non-stop, and that was without the cooling airflow they get on a bike.'

The motorway ended at Perth, and from there the ride up the well-sorted A9 was grand. Outside Dunkeld we ran by the River Tay and, as the afternoon waned, watched fly-fishermen in high waders standing casting in the swirling brown waters. Soon I spotted my first Highland cattle, always a landmark moment on holidays in Scotland as a child. After a final fuel-stop in Pitlochry, where the bike managed to rip the buckle off the right leg of my overtrousers, we rode on through wilderness up Glen Garry, tired certainly but both having discovered that the pain in our lower backs had mercifully given way to numbness, and would never again be as bad it had been on that first evening. By six o'clock we were turning off the main A9 at Kingussie, and following the B road which parallels it through pine woods to our destination, the village of Kincraig.

Here Sean, no stranger to these parts, led us over a narrow wooden bridge and down a further couple of miles of wooded single-track roads, to a tall stone bridge over a plunging burn. There we finally stopped to enjoy the ringing silence and the last warm light, as the sun slanted down over the Cairngorm mountains to the east. The tallest of these is Braeriach; in fact it's the third highest peak in Great Britain, and our lodgings for the night were named after the mountain. Sean's friends Guy and Fee Johnson run the place, a comfortable guest house by the side of the Spey as it flows out of Loch Insh. Braeriach was being upgraded with fire doors when we arrived, and the joiner (who doubled up, as they do in those parts, as physics teacher at the local school), turned out to have once had a motorbike – an M20. We parked our gear and then tottered off for a couple of long ones at the Suiue Hotel, whose wonderfully lugubrious proprietor Farkie MacBane gave us dire predictions about the upcoming weather. Back at the guest house Fee Johnson cooked us a very welcome supper. Fee had come from Bristol, and confirmed my belief in it as a city of beautiful women.

I turned in early and enjoyed a really good sleep and a leisurely awakening in the big, warm well-appointed room. When I'd made myself a cup of tea, I drew the curtains to find, beyond the river, a view of the snow-covered peak of Braeriach crouched amid the mountains. Breakfast was three or four small, vividly coloured and full flavoured boiled eggs from Guy's chickens, but my eyes kept returning speculatively to a portion of polystyrene lagging round some exposed pipes. Guy obligingly dug out a length for me, and it proved just right for clipping over the M21 saddle's iron frame. It actually didn't make that much difference, but every little helps.

Though we had five hours to do the hundred miles east to Aberdeen, I was fretting to be off, and perhaps Sean's patience with my list-making, time-keeping approach was being rather tested, since his pride was his cool. It was a chilly morning as we set out, a red squirrel running in front of

Sean's bike on the road to Aviemore, where we turned off on the A95 to Grantown-on-Spey, and from there turned right, climbing a narrow road up to Tomintoul. From the start this route was one of the best of the whole trip, especially after Tomintoul, as the Lecht Road wound up over a high snow-streaked pass where skiing had only just stopped, then jinked down over the river Don at the Cock Bridge, and on through forest beside the water.

The twisting road was irresistible to Sean and it was fun trying to stay with him up and down the steep roads through the woods, watching out for the ridges of red dust that had blown onto the road while enjoying Sean's excellent lines and flat-out peel-offs, and as a point of honour trying to imitate him in not using the brakes through the bends. Under this treatment both bikes got hot and soon began to backfire on the over-run; by the time we reached the islands, the chrome on my silencer had been heat-treated to a yellow tinge like stainless, and the heat-resistant black paint on Sean's had begun to lift off. Eventually he pulled ahead and I let him, catching up gradually as we belted down hillsides that Sean said brought back the Himalayan foothills on his world trip. After a while we stopped in a little village at the post office, which advertised its own baking and sold coffee. Sitting outside eating pies in the sunlight was another nice moment.

After that, with 40 miles to go Sean really got the bit between his teeth, and I soon gave up trying to stay with him. I caught up when traffic thickened as we approached Aberdeen. The clutches on both bikes reacted predictably to town traffic, and it also seemed that the burghers of Aberdeen had not seen fit to dignify the Shetlands ferry with any signs to indicate its whereabouts. Eventually we stopped for directions, and then rode along the dockside until from the corner of my eye I spotted a cluster of interesting-looking vehicles behind a mesh fence, and turned left just in time for the ferry embarkation point. It was exactly 4pm, the check-in time. We'd made it.

Most of the waiting vehicles were headed for the Show, and they were a mixed bunch. Cars included the automotive equivalent of us, Terry Smith and his wife who had driven up all the way from Essex in a dinky grey 948cc Austin A35 made in 1955, like my M21. Eventually we rode aboard, and the P&O seamen on the car deck proved exceptionally friendly and careful of the bikes. The ship smelt reassuringly of fish, but was big and modern – 'romantic' said Sean of the lush dining room, where the excellent ticket deal meant that we took all our meals for free, and that's including £14 four-course dinners where you could help yourself to as much as you wanted. 'Those bikers canna half pack it away,' one steward was heard to mutter admiringly.

God is in the details – simple things like the tea, and the kippers, and particularly the porridge at breakfast, were all excellent. The cabins were comfortable too. A Force 4 blow was forecast, and later in the bar listening to some very fair MOR live music, Sean complained of the heat, left his drink and turned in early. My personal Ailment of the Day was a sore right hand and stiff sort-of tennis elbow from clenching the throttle wide open trying to keep up with Sean. For a couple of days it was bad enough to make lifting a cup painful. I really should have changed those hard handlebar grips.

In the night I woke briefly at three, and that far north the summer light outside was bright enough to read my watch by. Next morning, after a 14-hour crossing, we watched the low, treeless island grow larger through the portholes. We were midway between Scotland and Norway. We didn't have to worry about packing up, as the ticket deal on this 'mini-cruise' let us use the berthed ship as a floating hotel that night, and even provided good packed lunches as alternatives to coming back for the free lunches during the day. Not bad for around £125 per person all in.

On the quay at Lerwick in mild sunlight we were greeted by islanders from the show, and right away Sean scored! Pretty Marcia Irving needed a lift as her husband Les had made off with her 535 Virago, and she hopped onto the pillion pad of Hawker's M21. Then we rode and drove in convoy through the town to the show venue. The first of these biennial events may have taken place in a tent, but any doubts about the 7th Show being 'a haybarn display of rusty MGBs and a couple of old BSA Bantams' were rapidly displaced by the sight of the impressively large sports complex which housed it. Shetland seems to have spent the oil money held in trust for it in wise and dignified ways, resulting in exceptional social services and leisure facilities. Two vast gym halls were given over to cars and bikes respectively, and that still left an indoor bowls hall, a multi-million pound swimming pool (one of three on the islands), a comfortable cafe, and a bar and dance hall. And the Show itself was as good as any I've ever seen.

The bulk of the bikes on display were local. Shetlanders were 'the Chinamen of the North Sea', and work away on the boats meant that the islands' seamen could often afford a motorcycle when many could not. The bikes were arranged in a horseshoe leading from the earliest, a 1914 Douglas, to a 1995 Hinckley Thunderbird, with several interesting outfits occupying the middle ground.

Many of the bikes belonged to tireless salmon industry man Frank Johnson, whose machines ranged from that Douglas, to a '38 Inter Norton, to an interesting '76 Silk stroker, number six of just 138 Silks built. It showed signs of recent use, and even the Douglas had got a workout on this year's London to Brighton run.

'Many of the old bikes there don't run much, but I'd practised,' said Frank. 'When we reached Brighton and the traffic got bad, I made 1$\frac{1}{2}$ lanes by putting my elbows out! When I heard the tannoy announce that I was the furthest travelled entrant, I could have turned pirouettes in the saddle.' And his favourite bike? 'The Inter. She can stand for three months, and then just bark into life. I don't polish that one, just Waxoyl it.' For with the sea and salt breezes ever present, on the islands more than anywhere Rust Never Sleeps, and the fine finish on the bikes and cars at the show was the result of constant vigilance, and owners 'braving the rigours of their garages, as cold as only a Shetland garage can be', as the programme put it.

Frank was far from the only regular classic rider around. Big singles seemed to suit the islands. Terry Atkinson's everyday transport was a 1947 Norton Big 4 taken out to 630cc, which was occasionally prone to massive backfiring: 'we get worried that we might be responsible for simultaneous lambing all down our valley!' Maybe that's why he had recently acquired a new Enfield 500, on which he'd blown the piston while doing 90 the previous week. 'But it's still under warranty, and anyway, bits for them are so cheap – a new piston's only £35.'

Most of these riders had taken their Advanced tests, and we would see L-riders under instruction on the roads, as well as moto-crossers propped outside many houses beside the obligatory boat (a Shetlander has been described as 'a fisherman with a croft'). You may only be able to ride a maximum of 62 miles on any loop from Lerwick on the 'mainland' isle, but it's an all-day, 140-mile journey to the northernmost island, and the Classic Motorcycle Club is one of three in the Shetlands. This is riding country. The annual Simmer Dim rally in June, named after the light summer nights, would be a good time to check it out.

Emphatically not 'from outwith Shetland' was Joe Gray, the moving spirit behind the bike side of the Show. His family had been the motoring and motorcycling gurus of the islands since his grandfather at the turn of the century had opened the first garage, Grays Engineering; he had also written a book of island anecdotes with phonetic dialogue which is still read out with delight at local gatherings. Grays Engineering had serviced everything, cars, motorbikes, buses, and marine engines of all sizes.

Joe's bearded, aquiline face had the totally focussed yet calm look that seemed to be characteristic of the native islanders. I thought any tiredness around his eyes was simply due to the strain of getting the show together, but I was mistaken; in fact it had been just two days since he had been discharged from hospital after treatment for kidney problems, but he wasn't going to miss an event which he had been two years helping to set up, and he then worked harder than anyone, not just at the organising, but at making every visitor feel welcome. He certainly succeeded with Sean and I. That evening at the Foy (as they call a dance) for show exhibitors and organisers, it was Joe and his wife Hazel with whom we sat and chatted as a traditional squeezebox and fiddle band took the couples through wonderful dancing, culminating in a final 27-minute epic as the fiddler went ballistic. And they didn't even give us a hard time for not joining in!

The next day Joe took time out to show us the workshop which is built into the hillside beneath his neat house above Lerwick; the steepness of his drive means that all his rebuilds get an instant workout! Bikes that have had the treatment include his 1936 600cc Ariel Square Four; back in 1960 he'd bargained the purchase price down from £11 to £8, but had to pay an additional 16 shillings for bringing it down on the steamer from the north island. Via Grays Engineering he had a pretty good idea of the whereabouts of most two-wheelers on the islands; it was said that among those registered with the islands' previously unique PS-prefix numbers, Joe Gray knew them

'Welcome aboard ...'

all. And the islanders know him; interesting relics, old tool kits and bikes in pieces turn up unbidden on the Gray's doorstep.

Joe exemplifies the Shetlands tradition of self-reliance. Though he emphasised that most island enthusiasts have made good contacts on the mainland, he does his own electro-plating, painting etc, and also spokes his own wheels. Nothing unusual there, you might think, until he remarked mildly that 'we had some fun doing the 350 Rudge' (his 1932 Radial). I bet he did – the 350 Rudge was virtually unique in featuring off-set spoked hubs.

I soon sensed that the innovative Rudge marque held a special place in Joe's affections. Then Fraser Riach arrived for lunch on his 1939 Rudge 500 Special. Joe had first known Fraser when the latter visited Shetland in 1946 to teach local lads to swim (in the unimaginably cold sea). Fraser, clearly a hardy man still, 40 years on, had ridden the Rudge up from his Glasgow home. Later that night, as our homebound ship sailed past the remote fastness of Fair Isle, Fraser would tell me the true history and end of the Rudge which author George Orwell had used while living on the isle of Jura, writing *1984*.

Something else we already owed Joe was the way that he had encouraged us, the previous morning after we had arrived, to take advantage of the fine weather and take the M21s for a ride on the island. So, staying only to see the Show opened by *Top Gear*'s Steve Berry, we headed south, swapping bikes so that Sean could check out his handiwork on my machine. The road over the hillsides was long, almost empty and excellently surfaced, without even gravel on the remote tracks to spoil your line. This was later explained by the fact that Joe Gray's day job is to supervise their maintenance! The standard question for his men is: 'How would this be on a motorcycle?'

We saw vicious little Shetland ponies with supermodel manes, the corgis of the equine world, as they rushed down sloping fields or lashed and bit at each other in rough play. We turned off right to Bigton and followed narrow coastal roads by the sparkling grey sea in a loop round to the airport and out to the island's southernmost point, dodging sheep and coming to rest on the cliff top below the lighthouse at Sumburgh Head, one of the Coastal Weather Stations you hear each night on the radio. Sean said he'd like to visit them all.

The sun shone. I changed my spark plug, just to do it, really. We lolled on a stone wall, eating our packed lunches and watching the myriad seabirds wheeling below, gannets, guillemots and puffins. As a child the puffin was the one I always wanted from my grandparents' set of seabird place mats, because of its multi-hued beak; and only that weekend did I find out from an islander that the beak's colours are a mating display, not a permanent feature. Soon the birds were joined by several seals, their sleek heads lazily riding the surging swell. It was sunny, but the wind there never really sleeps, and we would both be chilled through by the time we'd ridden back that afternoon. In everything around, the sparse hills, the low-built houses, the spareness of the place, you sensed just off-stage the ever-present threat of long winter and hard weather. It made the fine day something to savour even more. That hour was the heart and centre of the journey.

It all went too quickly. Back at the Show on Sunday afternoon, with 38 stationary engines playing a silly symphony in the car park, there was just time for an hour with the automobiles, with plenty of exotica, but once again everything intelligently arranged to allow perspective on the evolution of the workaday likes of Austin and Morris. I fell for a '56 Vauxhall Wyvern, its cruisin' style based on the '49 Chevy and its 'wiper speed proportional to engine speed (in heavy rain, change down a gear)'! Boards full of archive photos of the island's buses over the decades, inching between snow walls or come to grief down cliffs, were particularly evocative. Outside, the Land Rover Club boys had some useful advice on the Series III soft-top which I'm eyeing up at home.

Then it was time to do a quick sound-bite for the local radio, and for the presentation from Steve Berry to Sean and I jointly of a handsome engraved silver plate as the furthest travelled motorcyclists (661 miles, to be precise). Now I knew how Frank Johnson had felt at Brighton. Steve told us we were really crazy; I told him that it takes one to know one. The Show deservedly broke records, up 500 on the previous event with a total of 3,124 visitors. Another memento for us were the Show mugs given to exhibitors, decorated by a map of the islands, with in one corner the UK reduced to fit in the same tiny box to which the mainland forecasters usually confine the Shetlands!

Then it was time to say our goodbyes, and ride back to the ferry for embarkation. As we waited in line poor Terry Smith jogged up perspiring. His A35 had chosen that moment on the quayside to dump all its oil via a loose pattern filter, and he couldn't find a replacement. I handed him my instant gasket and he tried that, but once on board, we heard the tannoy summon him ominously back to the car deck. But it was only to meet a man from the show – Terry had no idea how the guy had heard about his problem, but the islands are like that. The local, unbidden, took him back into town, located the correct filter and helped him fit it, all before the ship sailed. It exemplified the spirit of the place. The Shetlands have wildness, and wildlife, but the real jewels in their crown are the hospitable people who live there. They're well worth the trip.

Sean and I separated next morning at the dock gates in Aberdeen, he to return to Braeriach and then home via Birmingham, me for a leisurely trawl to explore the eastern side of the country. It had been good to have some company on the trek up, but I can't deny that the best riding for me came in the two sunny days which followed, as I rattled south at my own speed, a steady 55, with the wind now behind us all the way. On the long straights of the A1 south of Edinburgh I felt the flow of time, remembering an epic run in college days from Aberdeen down to Lincoln on my Norton Navigator. Then I stopped at a roadside stall called 'Elephant's Sufficiency' and fanged down a Venisonburger with redcurrant jelly. Quiet, well surfaced roads, and everything cheaper, that was the North; only days later when I got past Cambridge and was working my way back homewards through the traffic did I fully realise the contrast with what southern roads have become. But the North was also that night in Newcastle, gaping at the magnificent Tyne Bridge, eating in the Heartbreak Soup cafe and watching clutches of scantily clad, achingly young girls rush shrieking downhill to the quayside and the promise of £1-a-pint Student Night in the pubs there.

In the next morning's motorway rush-hour, or crossing the mile-and-a-half Humber Bridge, or on the empty sweep of a Lincolnshire plateau, I came to realise what was missing – any of the usual anxiety about a breakdown, as the M21's utter reliability brought peace of mind. A breather pipe came loose, and the clutch got a bit snatchy, but the engine never smoked, or faltered. Sean had done an excellent job. One lot of air in the tyres, two brake adjustments, and about a pint of not-really-necessary 10/50 oil, was the sum of the attention required until the moment when I swung back through my gateway again, the mileometer reading 57,662, just ten shy of 1,500 miles since the start. Good trip.

CHAPTER SIX

Made in England

The near-total demise of the traditional British motorcycle industry by 1975 is the factor which gives a clear shape, albeit a regrettable or even tragic one, to its story. Indeed m'learned friend Nick Ward thinks that it is this very cut-off point itself which makes classic enthusiasts so intensely interested in everything to do with their favourite machines, and the places which made them.

It is true that attempts to foster a similar cult of 'classic Japanese' motorcycles, following the reasoning that the generation now in their 40s would be interested in what they rode, or wanted to ride, when they were teenagers, have fallen pretty well flat. Nick thinks it is because Japanese bikes have progressed and improved in a straight line since the early seventies, so most people are interested in the latest and best rather than yesterday's heroes.

Interestingly, a friend who is the specialist in toys for the auction house Christies has told me that a similar phenomenon, obsessive interest in British toys and not much in imports, can be observed in that field, and for much the same reason: the great names like Britains and the Lines brothers' Triang ceased manufacturing in the UK at around the same time as the old motorcycle industry did, due to foreign competition, and that created finite ranges of well-made toys of which collections can be built up and gloated over.

Whatever the precise reason, the post-war boom, decline, and fall of the British motorcycle industry retains a possibly morbid fascination for many enthusiasts. While the broad outlines of the story are by now pretty well known, the real, inside story which resides in the details is still emerging via the usually oral testimony of engineers, executives, and voices from the shop floor. For instance, though it would be unkind to surviving relatives to go into details, I have been told that one particularly puzzling move by one of the major players can be explained by some very personal predilections on the part of that company's chairman!

The chapter begins with an extensive account of the AJS/Matchless factory at Plumstead, which in 1966 was the first of the major manufacturers to go down. I was there when they opened the exhibition about the works, and it was a memorable evening.

Made in Plumstead

Cross to the south of the Thames by the Blackwall Tunnel, turn left towards Woolwich and take the road that echoes the curves of the river it follows. Wind past the long grimy walls of the Royal Dockyard and soon you pass the Ferry, the Woolwich mosque, and the Plumstead bus garage. You're on one of the last squares on the eastern edge of the London A–Z.

Carry on down Plumstead High Street, through a couple of miles of post-industrial grimness, and you've passed the site of the offices and showroom on Plumstead road, and behind them the factory of 'Colliers', as they always called the old Associated Motor Cycles (AMC) works at Burrage Grove. This was home of Matchless, AJS and, latterly, Norton, until its closure back in 1969.

The factory was soon demolished. Today a technical college stands on the site, and there's not a single indication that since 1913 this had been the home of the firm with the longest unbroken production of motorcycles in the industry, and what was, even in the late fifties, the most modern plant in Europe producing motorcycles almost exclusively; a works employing over 1,500 local people, and in the peak year of 1955 producing 16,643 machines. From the reliable 350 G3L heavyweight plonking singles ('plonker' then meant something rather different than it does today) to Trials and scrambles winners and production road race machinery like the 7R and G50 OHC singles, plus works exotica like the AJS Porcupine and 7R3, up until the sixties all AMC machines were produced to a renowned high standard.

So it rankles with the men and women who worked there, many of whom were related to each other and who still live locally, that 'in its own country' the skills and industry of what was in today's jargon 'a centre of excellence' for motorcycle production have gone almost completely unacknowledged. In 1987 there was a move to name a new street near the site 'Matchless Drive', but the new home owners were of the upwardly mobile variety and rejected the idea. The road eventually selected for the title is some way from

'Colliers' – so-called because Matchless Motorcycles, which became Associated Motor Cycles in 1937 with the take-over of AJS, had been formed by local engineer and entrepreneur Henry Collier, and from then on his sons, Harry, Bert, and Charlie, were active motorcyclists and company directors. Many trace the decline of AMC from 'Mr Charlie's' death in 1954, and some even earlier, to the wartime crash that killed Bert Collier – as one man put it, after that 'Somehow the accountants took over more and more of the administrative work, until their departments were costing more than they could save.' A not unfamiliar story.

Things began to change on the recognition front in 1988 when the Mayor of Greenwich, John Austin-Walker, himself a one-time Francis-Barnett rider, came to the VMCC West Kent run. VMCC's Alex Brett and AJS/Matchless OC historian John Allen had been pressing the Borough for some time to commemorate AMC, and now the Mayor, who had been expecting scruffy motorcyclists, saw the smartness and dedication evident on the VMCC run. He commissioned a feasibility study, and the result was the opening on 19 February this year [1989] of an exhibition at the Greenwich Borough Library, 'Made in Plumstead', as part of an effort to celebrate AMC's achievements.

The exhibition was primarily the result of work by Fiona Davison, a tiny blonde 23-year-old who hailed from Middlesborough and had never been on a motorcycle in her life. But with questionnaires sent to a wide range of ex-AMC employees, followed up in some cases by interviews, Ms Davison assembled a really good range of unique testimony to the way things were at

'Commando at ease' (etching and aquatint).

the works. This was edited to become part of the exhibition, in the form of large wall panels with blown-up photographs and paragraphs of testimony sketching in themes like 'working conditions', 'fun and games', and 'what went wrong'. Fiona Davison did a fine thorough job, and served the locals well, letting their own voices tell the story before the tide of time swept it away forever.

Otherwise there were trophies, posters, tools, and three immaculate examples of the Matchless product – a 1938 vee-twin Model X, a 1959 G12 650, and, from Mark Stevens of Hy-Cam, the group dedicated to the Norton/Matchless hybrids of the sixties, a stunning red G85CS scrambler – though Mark said that it was a recent acquisition and that the silver Reynolds 531 lightweight frame needed attention.

On the night the exhibition opened, as many as possible of the ex-employees had been invited, and over a hundred of them converged. It was a genuinely warm and moving occasion, which Fiona Davison saw through a haze of fatigue as she had been up for 19 of the preceding 24 hours getting things organised. Meeting for the first time in sometimes 20 years, men and women stared at each other hesitantly or disbelievingly before recognition dawned, and soon people aged from 40 to 80 were talking with South-East London's own brand of humour about the old days. There was little sentimentality, and later when opinions were given it was usually almost diffidently; the more usual mode was jovial mockery of themselves and each other – 'don't believe a word,' and (in appeal, from one man scrutinising a photo of himself 20 years ago) 'Was I really that fat?'. The largely unspoken sub-text was true pride in what they had shared and helped to create. It was a privilege to be present.

Prominent in every way was the former works convenor, E. 'Tiger' Smith, a tall, imposing, upright figure with an air of command that absolutely belies his 78 years. Everyone joyfully recognised and remembered 'Tiger' – 'he was always a miserable sod,' one man laughed, but with affection and admiration. Hoarse-voiced, Dickensian, 'Tiger' had come to Matchless in 1925, and like Gerry Hartnell, a repair shop man who had joined the previous year, he could remember the power cut caused by the 1926 General Strike, and how a 980cc Model M3 vee-twin engine had been fitted up in the press shop, and all the shafts for the machinery had been run off it.

As well as his Union work, 'Tiger' Smith's job was trueing the wheels, and on a full day that meant 60 or 70 of them – at its post-war peak in the fifties, Plumstead was turning out 80 machines a day. He could also remember aspects of the not-so-good old days. 'The younger men here won't believe this – you used to have to clock on to go to the toilet. There was a one-armed chap sitting at a turnstile, like a station. He took your number and gave you a disc, and he had an old-fashioned alarm clock'. If you hadn't handed your disc back to clock out by the time it went off, a manager would let you know about it in no uncertain terms.

Time-keeping was always strict. 'A working day was 8 to 5.30, and you were allowed to clock in one minute after 8,' one man remembered. 'Two minutes after and you were late, and lost a quarter of an hour's pay. If that persisted they could say "We don't want a layabout," and out you went.' The point was well taken by some – at the opening, road-tester Alan Jones said that though he had lived 30 miles from Plumstead he was never once late, and his former superior Joe Allen had the records to confirm this.

Partly thanks to 'Tiger' in his Union capacity, and to works manager Bert Bassett, in contrast to some motorcycle factories, the post-war works enjoyed good labour relations, as all the interviews confirmed. In the fifties 'there were no strikes as such, just a couple of Union national one-day stoppages. There was the convenor and the works committee, so anything was thrashed out between them and management before it got to a stoppage'. There were hiccups, however – like one threatened stoppage over the absence of toilet paper.

Assembly line monotony lay beneath this: 'That was the reason for a lot of stoppages, it was boredom. If they could find something to stop the line and all sit there talking they'd do it'. The work was particularly relentless because, as one testimony makes clear, 'all the pay was based on bonus … they wouldn't stop [the line], they wouldn't lose their bonuses over you … The rate-fixer would come round and fix the rate for the job and the more work you done, the more money you earnt … It was up to you when the time-keeper came up. If you could string him along enough and convince him it was taking you that long, you could get more money on bonus. But they were very fly, the time-keepers, they got their stopwatch out and they watched everything. If you put a dull drill bit in, they would spot that in a flash, take it out and sharpen it. They wouldn't let you get away with tricks like that'.

The bonus system also affected attitudes to safety. 'They [the firm] were safety conscious, but we weren't. If you were on a bonus you couldn't put the guard on a machine because it slowed you down and you wouldn't make money. You put the guard on when the man was around and took the guard off when he went and got on with your work.' To the end, welfare at Plumstead was very limited. There was no sick pay whatever your length of service. There was a highly dangerous unguarded conveyor belt; sodium lamps, blacked-out windows left over from the war, and goods stacked at access points were all said to contribute to an air of suffocation within the works, and the services of 'Jean the First Aid Queen' from the nursing station, manned day and night, were sometimes necessary.

Some jobs were particularly 'gutty'. In the polishing room 'the front of their overalls was about three inches thick with grease, and if they came to visit me round the forge, it used to melt and drip off'. Polishing shop men suffered from two afflictions in particular; their noses 'would seize up, they used to go to hospital to have them cracked'. They also got piles, from the day-long straining. Conditions generally improved a little after the war, as labour became scarcer and had to be to some extent wooed by management, but they were never ideal.

'Tiger' Smith's Union chores meant that he had frequent dealings with the Colliers and with Donald Heather, the post-war managing director most associated with the company's decline. Like many of the men, 'Tiger' felt equivocal about Heather. The latter, like the Colliers, was at least a seasoned motorcyclist, and regularly rode the company's products. One man questioned recalled sometimes having to provide 'tea bikes' for the Colliers and Heather, ie machines built and tested that day, for the bosses to ride home and pass judgement on ('and woe betide the tester or quality control person if faults were found').

But Heather's commercial acumen was less impressive. 'He spent a lot of money for nothing,' said 'Tiger' Smith succinctly. 'I can't understand – and 80 per cent of the men here would probably disagree – the money that was spent on racing.' AMC took the decision to plough the bulk of their profits from war work – and profits on the WD G3 machines and on sub-contract work had risen from a mere £2,000 in one pre-war year to £80,000 for 1945 – into road racing, the development of the de-supercharged 'Porcupine' ohc twin and the 7R and G50 singles. To 'Tiger' this went against common sense. Norton, after all, had enjoyed their fabulous run of TT success – but in 1953 they still had to sell out to AMC. (As 'Tiger's words imply, however, road racing was popular at the factory, with an annual coach party leaving in the early hours of Thursday for the Senior TT – but back again in time for work on Saturday morning.)

One man at the exhibition opening who was involved in racing, but had a telling anecdote of his own concerning Donald Heather's lack of foresight, was Charlie Matthews. Charlie was an extremely well-respected engineer and mechanic, exemplifying the deep knowledge that continuity, working through with motorcycles, can bring. 'If you ever wanted to know anything,' said a former workmate, 'you went up to Charlie. He didn't have to look at drawings, he knew – he had dimensions, specifications, in his head.' Matthews ended up writing all the specifications for the Norton Commando, which few remember was designed and developed with a lot of Plumstead input.

Charlie had joined in 1928, and moved from repair to the race shop. As most men confirmed, there was little training as such except the on-the-job kind, by a senior hand to a keen youngster, with men starting wherever there was an opening, and the talented enthusiasts gravitating to the more interesting and better-paid jobs. Charlie was one such, asking questions and reading, and this paid off; he came to the race shop just after the take-over of AJS, and found the mechanics there in difficulty with the first cammy AJS that had come in for repair. They had it reassembled up to the timing stage; from his reading Charlie remembered a dodge which worked, and the foreman was highly impressed. Charlie became 'No 1 Houseboy' to George Rowley the AJS Trials ace, travelling all over Europe with him for ISDT events. He was also racing himself, with ex-TT winner Matt Wright as his sidekick, and the pair did quite well on R7s. Between times he worked with Wright on the AJS water-cooled V4 racer. After the war he was personal mechanic for racing star Les Graham, and the two grew very close. Charlie said that Graham, who was later tragically to lose his life on the MV-4, had one psychological fault in racing – no matter how he tried, his fastest lap was always his first one, even if only by a second or two.

'Don't look back …'

It was while travelling abroad with Graham and the Continental Circus shortly after the war that Charlie noticed the very large numbers of Europeans mounted on small capacity road machines. This seemed to Charlie to indicate a bottomless market for lightweights, and on returning to England he reported back to Donald Heather about it; but the latter just laughed off the information, calling Charlie 'a pessimist'. Remaining firmly committed to big bikes, Heather would dismiss scooters as 'a passing fad', until in the mid-fifties new sales of them had exceeded those of motorcycles. The AMC Group's response, a James scooter powered by their problematic own-brand two-stroke single engine, would prove too little and too late.

The company did invest in some up-to-date plant, however, much of it from Alfred Herbert, the Midlands machine tool giant. In the fifties Plumstead's heat treatment and inspection equipment, for instance, was among the most modern available in Europe. This was not so in every case, however – one man, Jack Hall, worked with the same linisher, a polishing machine with a sanding belt, from 1914 to 1969.

Another exception concerned welding. Frames were always of brazed-lug construction, and as J. Wren, a welder from 1957–69, pointed out, only old-fashioned oxyacetylene welding was used until the late sixties, when electric arc and Mig-welding came in via Reynolds, who built the Norton frames – and the old style was time-consuming. There was also no forge at the works, castings being bought in either from Midlands firms like Bircal or Qualcast, or more locally from Maybury's of Croydon or Stones of Charlton, who supplied the sliders for the Teledraulic front forks.

Another aspect of Plumstead that many employees felt could have been modernised to increase output was the layout of production. The factory consisted of three floors and a roof shop. The ground floor was the main production shop, warehouse, and dispatch. The first floor was where the bike frames were prepared for machining and plating, plus the painting, cadmium plating, and enamelling shops. The next one up consisted of the tool room, tool service department, and the cycle repair shop, and it was there that the testers brought the bikes back up in a large lift and carried out adjustments prior to despatch. Above that, on the roof, in one of two corrugated iron-roofed buildings in which workers boiled or froze, the frames were actually assembled and brazed together in the first place. So the progression was from the top to the first floor, from there to the bottom, back up to the second and then back again to the bottom, and it can be seen that this organically evolved layout was something less than ideal in terms of flow. (It was on the roof, also, that you could get a haircut from 'one Albert Beaumont Esq', just as the plating shop turned out chrome bicycle frames, tobacco tins, and even chrome plated electric irons, and the hardening shop produced wrought iron work and coal fire companion sets. Well, all [company] work makes Jack a dull boy.)

In general the technology which produced the famous AMC quality of finish seemed to have been a mixture of reasonably up-to-date machinery, and individual skills honed to perfection over the years. As one of those questioned remembered, this became particularly evident when the Plumstead works closed in October 1969 and Norton Villiers, which had been formed after the fall of AMC in 1966, moved production, now to be exclusively of Norton Commandos, to their new factory at Andover. 'They went down there and left the know-how behind. We had a bloke here who used to bend exhaust pipes on a machine. He had all these little bits of wood and stuff as he was bending them so they would come out perfect. And of course, when they got down there, they couldn't understand why the machine didn't bend the pipes right every time. It was the bloke's know-how; you can't buy this.'

Ironically the same thing had happened when the management had shut down Norton's Bracebridge Street home in Birmingham and in 1963 moved production to Plumstead, with just five of the Birmingham men moving down as well. There's a good story at the Exhibition from the one Norton owner already in the factory, who was assigned to assemble the first Norton twin, and, with the Press present to record The First Plumstead Norton, had got half-way through the task before he realised that the model he was working on was not a Dominator like his own, but a 350 Navigator, a completely different design.

Worse followed, when the multi-spindle drill that processed the Dominator crankcases played up, so that 300 sets of crankcases had to be scrapped because the drill for their central bosses would not run true. When the Birmingham operative who had handled the drill was contacted, he simply asked 'Didn't they take the plank with it?' The spindle's play had been taken up by holding a plank against it to stop it chattering ...

Beneath the Ealing comedy aspect, the growing Norton quotient at Plumstead, which inevitably increased in the Norton Villiers era and could always be justified as rationalisation and because by then Norton's name was better known, gave offence to the workforce. As Tony Denniss, who started as a draughtsman in 1956 and ended as chief designer on the P11 and Commando, said: 'Matchless had been a very well-built machine, so this Norton input was resented.' Harry Larner, an inspector, gave a concrete reason; he considered the amount of metal around the Norton twin's valve guides was insufficient, so that in production everything had to be absolutely precise for the valve guide to line up with the seat. He and others felt that the AMC twins were superior in that respect.

This resentment stood in contrast to the factory atmosphere, where all agreed that inter-departmental rivalry at shop-floor level was non-existent – or at least confined to the fiercely contested cricket series. As Mr Wren put it, 'each department tended to work in conjunction with other departments, as the majority of employees had pride in their product. The benefit of this co-operation was that every employee could see the end results of everyone's efforts and new models were often displayed in the factory canteen ... a deep sense of pride was felt ... co-operation often ironed out any problems in production'.

Those of the workers who rode motorcycles, and they were not in the majority, usually did so on AMC machines. While the G3 and G80 big singles were the backbone of the post-war range and cherished by many, there were also the twins, starting in 1949 with the very reliable and well-made 500cc Matchless G9/AJS Model 20 with their unique middle main bearing, spring-framed and with alloy heads from the start. Harry Larner detailed the care that went into the construction of what he considered to be one of the best designed twins on the road. The flywheels were balanced, and with them a pair of con rods were made and marked together, being weighed to within 10g of each other, and the same thing was done with a pair of pistons. All of this produced an exceptionally smooth-running 500, and later 600 twin, though much less so for the 650. Unfortunately the meticulous standards of preparation probably contributed to the fact that, according to publicity man Ray Kennard, 'the twins were said to have been produced at a loss since Day One.'

As mentioned, like all post-war Plumstead models these came in both AJS and Matchless forms, though differences after 1952, when the singles' magneto position was standardised, were almost entirely cosmetic. This badge engineering, as sales manager Jock West confirmed, with its separate sales reps, dealers, and publicity material, created a great deal of extra work. Publicity people eventually formulated the two marques' different images as 'AJS The Sporting Heritage' and 'Matchless – Incomparable Quality', but despite being near-identical in reality, there were still people who genuinely believed that one or the other marque went quicker. Tester Alan Jones thinks he may have an explanation. The bikes were built in batches by marque, and when whichever make it was came on assembly in the morning, the first batch would often have their timing set slightly out. By the end of the day, with the second make now being built, and the assemblers told by the testers of any problem, the timing would be spot on, and those machines would run better.

Not everyone rode; parking outside the works was not very secure, and thieving could extend to components as well as whole machines. More than one tester left his bike for a few minutes on a slight incline and returned to fire it up, push off the centre stand and accelerate away in the approved manner, only to finding himself rolling gently backwards because someone had made away with his rear chain!

Riding AMC was not just brand loyalty, as there were discounts available to employees on machines and also spares, as well as being able to get service jobs done on the spot. There were evidently also other fringe benefits. While some felt that 'there were little fiddles, but they were very hot on the door', another judged 'the pilfering was terrific. Chaps in the spares department were sending parcels of spares to agents and they were sending out parcels to their own address', and another stated that 'I've known people walk out with a complete engine and got Ted the doorman to hold the door for them!'

There were more legitimate compensations for the hard graft at Burrage

Grove, from a good meal in the canteen for 9d, through the 'Wills of the Week' competition to the children's Christmas party and the Band Concerts on the stage in the canteen (in the sixties there was a rock group called the Ajays), and not forgetting the Chrysanthemum Society, the darts, and the cricket – 'cricket was the great thing down there'.

This family feeling in the works made the end all the harder to take. There was wide perception of the usual reasons, from the detailed – 'what did bash our works was when the motorcycle insurance got put up' – to the generally accepted, the passing of the Collier family, followed by mismanagement and specifically complacency, 'our machines not keeping up with the changing times' or with the Japanese. Robert Hutchings knew things were going badly 'the day they dismantled a new Honda in the racing department, and the mechanic came into the engine shop and said 'Pack your tools, Bob, this thing is built like a watch.' But nothing prepared the workforce in 1969 for the actuality of closure. 'I've not often seen grown men, of 50 and 60, actually break down and weep. But when they heard the news, there were lots of tears that day.' And on the evening of closure there was not so much a leaving party as a 'drunken orgy, but I think that was the only way those men could have left.'

'Engine oil, gearbox oil, fork oil – but I can't remember which is which ...'

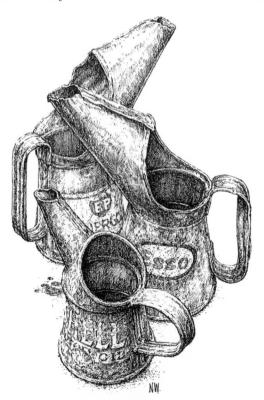

It's hard not to feel sadness at the waste, having seen the enthusiasm even now spring into life in the faces of men often in their 70s but with highly specific knowledge, skills, and judgement still fully intact. The only consolation is that the exhibition, plus a rally round the old factory testers' route later in the year, gave some belated acknowledgement of how important the area once was to the motorcycle industry. 'And,' as Fiona Davison's commentary concludes, 'of course, there will always be the motorcycles themselves to stand as testimony to the skills of the Plumstead workforce.'

Norman Peach

Vincent twins stand in the pantheon of British transport in a position roughly equivalent to Rolls-Royce motor cars and the Supermarine Spitfire. Their charm included something the English have always valued: effortless superiority. They could outperform every other production roadster of their day without, metaphorically, breaking a sweat. The fact that their vee-twin engine configuration with its slightly uneven galloping beat was at the time (but not today) unfashionable to the point of apparent obsolescence, gave their achievements even more of a mystic, atavistic tinge.

So it was a tonic to talk to the quietly realistic Norman Peach, who worked for the Stevenage company as a road-tester during the golden period of Series B, C, and D manufacture, and to hear him declare that 'So many people today think that Vincents were made to jewellery spec. But this wasn't true – they were financially constrained production things.'

Read on, for an insider's story.

Norman Peach had what many enthusiasts might regard as the best job in the world – road-testing brand new Vincents in the fifties.

Today [1999] Norman is 74 years young, and the contents of his garage say a lot about the man. There are a couple of Oriental step-throughs for use locally ('shopping trolleys'). There's a BMW K75 for the convenience ('it's like a car – just use it'). And, naturally, there's a Vincent. Not a twin, but a 1950 Comet single, rebuilt by Norman's good friend and fellow road-tester at the Stevenage works, Allen Rennie. The 500 was put together with practicality in mind, with a full Avon fairing, a later Series D lifting handle for the centre stand, coil ignition via alternator and distributor, winkers, mirrors, and a luggage rack with top box.

'The extra weight doesn't help the handling,' said Norman, who was well aware of the Comet's already rather stolid nature. But he did appreciate the practicalities. 'I and Ted Davis [the former chief development engineer at Stevenage and a bit of a Vincent guru] have road-tested Club people's bikes and made out authentic replicas of the original road test certificates for them. The sticklers for originality have no mirrors or indicators, and on today's roads you feel very vulnerable.'

There's a tinge of sadness to Norman's possession of the Comet, as Allen Rennie passed away from a heart attack in August 1998. Rennie had already had a bypass over ten years previously, but a month after the operation had joined Norman on a bike trip to a Continental rally. 'Allen was well known to the Dutch and Germans. There were 70 people at his funeral, and 12 of them came on Vincents – that would have pleased him.'

We sat in Norman's front room in Stevenage Old Town, where he lives alone, as sadly his wife too had passed on a few years ago. Though a little breathless, Norman's dark hair, shining eyes and relaxed alertness all belied his age, though he recognises that 'the Club has got much older. There's really only Ted and me left from the old days. If people don't talk to us – where are they going to get it?' Norman proved unsentimental about the 'snarling beasts', though clearly holding them in deep, proud regard. So as winter darkness gathered outside, we sat and talked about Norman Peach's life at Vincent.

Norman grew up in Buckden, a village north of Stevenage, and as a lad before the war had worked as a grocer's assistant. Already keen on motorcycles, he joined the wartime RAF as an airframe fitter, determined to get engineering training. Returning from a three-and-a-half year stint in what was then Rhodesia, he spent his demob money in May 1946 on one of the first 350 Triumph 3T twins from the local motorcycle mecca, Bryants of Biggleswade. With his parents' encouragement, he spent that summer taking the long leave he was due, and riding the Triumph.

His parents had also sent Norman *The Blue 'Un* and *The Green 'Un* while he was serving overseas, and he had seen Vincent's notice announcing the need for skilled men when production of the Series B twins got underway. So in October he contacted them and had an interview with works manager Jack Williams (later an influential designer at AMC, and father of Norton racer Peter Williams). 'Jack was also ex-RAF, and happy to take on qualified RAF folk. He was one of the nicest chaps at Vincent, a man you could talk to.'

The winter of 1946/7 was a bitter one, and soon Norman's ride to work involved a 30-mile run each way up the A1 on snow-packed roads, but the Triumph coped well and gave no trouble. He started on cycle assembly under foreman Ted Hampshire, at the Fisher's Green works, which had been put up by the Ministry of Supply to make wooden wings for aircraft, and then leased by Vincent in 1945. Vincent's own war-work had taken place at the original works off Stevenage High Street, which they retained. Norman saw the first four Series B production twins on the floor, before they were road-tested by Jim Sugg, a pre-war TT rider and Vincent's chief tester.

Under test, Sugg found the twins' wheel-trueing was suspect, leading to some unhappy handling. 'The wheels were being built by a batch of women who had been doing bomb fuses during the war. Ted Hampshire asked me if I'd had any experience with wheels, and when I said I'd done bicycle wheels and so on, he got me to fetch all the wheels out of stores, replace the punctured ones – the majority, because they'd been putting them on with tyre levers – true them up and make them fit. This was during the worst of the winter, a period when we had no electricity. A lot of people had been sent home, but I did this work during the blackout period, as well as helping shift motorcycle assembly to the High Street, with other stuff going to Fisher's Green.

'By March 1947 I was asked to establish a wheel-building department, and I soon had four men working under me when production got going. But I told Ted Hampshire I didn't want to spend the rest of my life wheel-trueing. I was often given a twin to take home at the weekend. [It must have been an eye-opener. One of Norman's colleagues, Alan Sargent, later a senior engineer at BSA and then Norton, told me how, on his first runs on a Vincent twin up the Great North Road, 'suddenly there were bends where before on other machines the road had been straight.'] And if they were getting behind with road-test, I would assist till they had caught up.'

A good life, but for the company there were set-backs. Early in 1947, the firm's founder and presiding genius, Philip Vincent, suffered a bad accident when the gearbox seized on a Rapide he was testing. 'After the accident, PCV was like a little boy; his voice had gone funny, and he had a nervous tic, shrugging his shoulders all the time.'

Unfortunately this was soon followed by one of the company's several financial crises, so that production was slowed. Then in 1949–50 there was a slow-up of the export of twins for the police in Argentina, where PCV's family had made their fortune. 'There was at least one batch of twins, already road-tested, which were then stored in a barn until things picked up.' (Wish they were still there …) Another inhibiting factor was the machinery. 'Most equipment post-war was rather worn out. It wasn't until the early fifties, when production increased, that they got some more up-to-date stuff. Till then, it did hold things up.

'So many people today think Vincents were made to jewellery spec. But this wasn't true – they were financially constrained production things.' It is well known now that there were considerable variations between the performance of individual machines, with some of the 45bhp Rapides faster than some Black Shadows, which theoretically put out ten more horses. Norman laughed. 'We used to say at the works, if you built one and blueprinted it, and then put one together out of junk bits – you'd probably find the junk one was faster!'

1949 was a good year for Norman on a personal level, as he married his wife Joyce. She was a Stevenage girl whom he had met at the Six Hills motorcycle club, 90 per cent of whose members were Vincent employees.

'Joyce was secretary to the buyer – a right swine. Philip Vincent did tend on his own to be a pretty easily led character. After the departure of Phil Irving and Frank Walker [the MD put in early on by PCV's father] he tended to surround himself with toadies. This buyer was a drinking, cadging sort of character who did very little work; he was always down at the Cromwell with the clique who carried Vincent along with them. So his second-in-command did most of the work, with the buyer himself really only being in the office much at Christmas time, to make sure he got the gifts from sales people ...'

And PCV himself? 'Even though I was in charge of wheel-building, Vincent would only talk to Ted Hampshire. I probably only talked to him three or four times in the 12 years I was there. He seemed to have no idea of the normal working chap. He'd had a sheltered upbringing, first in Argentina and then at Harrow and Cambridge, so he had never come in touch with ordinary men. He always seemed very diffident, too shy to stop and chat in the works, almost afraid in fact, so he would only work through subordinates; the only people he would get involved with were his managers.'

Phil Irving was the opposite. The down-to-earth Australian, a chief engineer whose input into the design of Vincents equalled PCV's own, had returned to Stevenage from Velocette in 1943 and would stay until the Series C was finalised late in 1949. 'When they were developing the first Lightning racer, Irving was involved. There was a panic on to build 21-inch front and 20-inch rear wheels for it. We'd got them laced in the afternoon, but when they were ready for trueing it was knocking-off time. I stayed on to do the job, and Irving stood by the other side of the bench, talking and handing me cigarettes until it was done – that was the sort of bloke he was.

'There was a foreman named Bill Brown, a little man of about five foot two who was in the Salvation Army. He'd had no engineering experience, but after a while he went to Letchworth, did a training course as a manager and was re-employed by Vincent. Cliff Brown, no relation to Bill, had been the engine assembly foreman, but then he transferred to the test house to work with his brother George, the famous sprinter and racer. Dennis Minnett, a pre-war Brooklands Gold Star winner, took over from Cliff until he was put in charge of the Lightning assembly gang, so Bill Brown took over as engine assembly foreman.

'One day Irving came storming in, picked up Bill Brown and pinned him physically to the wall. "Mr Brown," he said, "if somebody writes in to tell me there's something like a dog's cock in his timing cover, what exactly am I supposed to say to him?" What had happened was that there was a jet and a holder which screwed down into the top of the timing case, restricting the flow of lubricating oil to the camshafts etc. The holder was shouldered, but Bill Brown had decided that this was causing problems, and he'd had it linished, so that not only did it indeed resemble a dog's cock, but instead of restricting oil, it was letting oil through. And many Vincent owners were mechanically capable enough to strip down their engines and realise this. To my mind, even today, if you own a Vincent, you've got to have a reasonable amount of mechanical expertise.'

Early in 1950, with Series C production getting into its stride, the company decided to move engine and cycle assembly, which included Norman's wheel bay, back to Fisher's Green. 'I'd always worked in the High Street, so after the move, in April 1950, I told Jack Williams that the wheel section was running itself now, and I'd like to go on to road-test. It was to be a permanent transfer.'

This coincided with another important step for Norman – getting his own first Vincent. 'I talked to Jack Surtees [father of John, and himself a big London dealer], who used to come up often collecting machines from Stevenage, about changing my 3T for a Sunbeam S8. "You don't want one of those," he said, "they're no quicker than your Triumph. Why not have a Vincent?" So I talked it over with Joyce, and we went down to Surtees' shop in West London. I had a pre-war 350 New Imperial racer which I'd picked up for £20 and that interested Jack, so he agreed to take it, and the Triumph, in part exchange; but I would have to pay full price for the Vincent twin – which was £325.

'Back at work on Monday, Ted Hampshire, who was now on the sales side, said to me "Why don't you buy one through the works? You'd get a useful discount, and all you'd have to do is sign a paper to say you won't sell the bike within a year." Joyce agreed, so we went back to London, to Conways, another big Vincent dealer where again we knew someone, and sold the 3T for £110.' Not bad, considering the Triumph had served Norman well, covering over 20,000 miles in four years. 'Power on the 3T was a bit limited with a pillion passenger, but on one trip to Scarborough with Joyce, all the way from Stevenage we were only passed by two other vehicles: a Vincent twin, and a Jaguar.' Norman's subsequent experience was less happy with parallel twins, such as a Constellation he owned in 1961 ('a sod to start'), and an A10 he rebuilt. Norman found that they both simply vibrated too much at the 70-plus speeds to which Vincent twins had accustomed him.

Back at Stevenage in 1950, working by now on testing, he and a colleague went through the current batch of production bikes and chose one with the best features, such as heads cast by John Gale, which had quietening sections between the fins. Then Norman road-tested it himself, so that no-one else had ever ridden it – not many other owners could say that!

This first of Norman's Vins was a Series C, but that was not his absolute ideal – and, with his access to road-test bikes of all the post-war series, he was in a better position than most to assess the matter. 'I have always maintained that the best-handling Vincent was the Series B Rapide, with a 3.00x20-inch front tyre. The B's Brampton fork was lighter than the Girdraulic.' The latter had been PCV's own design, and was the distinguishing mark of the C Series, though initially a few C's were built with Bramptons. 'The Brampton people had been told that production of the different-forked versions would carry on in parallel,' said Norman, 'but that was only to get them to keep making the things until Girdraulic production was ready to take over. The Series C with Girdraulics was taller at the front, which to my mind made handling less positive. Another result of that was that the C's dual side/centre stands had to be lengthened, since with the old stands, once you had parked, the damper unit in the Girdraulics gradually extended itself at rest, and the bikes sometimes toppled over …

'The Series B's fork and wheel gave hairline steering – but that was presupposing good roads. Later, in 1959, I bought a Brampton-fork Series B, modified it with a Series D rear frame, and with Joyce plus luggage, went on one of Ken Craven's tours of Spain. But a 300-mile day's ride on the Spanish roads of that time left me with very sore wrists, from the Brampton girders. At least the rear end was fully damped. I used solo springs in the Armstrong unit which the D fitted, but also with a length cut off the smaller bore Series D front fork spring and fitted inside the rear unit's standard spring. Also, as well as the D's standard single rear unit, I fitted another Armstrong unit outboard of it, because Vincent's proprietary units on their own did tend to shed oil on Continental tours – it had happened to me on my first time out, on a Comet. On the B, I played around with that layout, and it did improve things quite a lot.

'The Series D rear set-up was definitely better than the B and C's, a bit lighter and with more travel – but the trouble was the D's bloody awful seat. It had been made straight, to reduce height a little, since the new springing had raised seat height and some shorter riders could find it a bit of a struggle. So the D's seat was fairly shallow, without the B and C's shaping. And what we found on unenclosed D's was that, wearing a newish waxed cotton suit, under acceleration you slid sharply backwards along the seat – you had to brake, or the bike got a lot further away from you than you wanted!'

Though Norman may have preferred the B's Bramptons, there was no question about the Girdraulic's strength. 'In 1949 one of our testers, Henry Pinnington, an ex-racer, was killed testing a Series C. He'd been doing 90 (there was no upper speed limited on unrestricted roads in those days), when a Devon saloon car pulled out of a side turning and drove straight across the road in front of him; the bike ended up inside the car. The driver was a local councillor though, so they blamed the mad motorcyclist. When the C was brought back to the works, although the front wheel had been flattened against the engine, and the steering stem had burst through the steering head, the blades of the Girdraulic fork were still virtually straight.

'That incident made the insurers insist that Vincent testers all wore crash helmets, though I'm not sure what good they would have done at those

'Just look at my nails …'

speeds. In fact there were surprisingly few incidents. George Brown did have a crash once, going to Hitchin; the police collected his bike and said he'd been doing 120, but that was because the speedo needle had gone round and jammed against the stop – even George would have been pushed to top the ton on a Comet!'

From then on, Norman worked at road-test. 'Each man had his own battery, exhaust pipes, speedo, and, usually, his own seat, so that those production parts didn't get any wear or mileage. We would collect a bike; they came to test with just assembly oil in them, so we would fill the oil tank, squirt oil into the filter chamber, and usually remove one rocker cap and squirt a quarter of a pint down the pushrod tube into the timing case. We also always had to slacken off the banjo at the bottom of the crankcase for the main feed to the oil pump, to make sure that oil was getting through. That was because, once, the cut-off on the main oil-feed from the oil tank, which blanked off the tank if the pipes were to be removed, had been re-inserted the wrong way round …

'Initially we'd check the tappets so they were approximately right, ie so you could spin the pushrod when the valve was closed. Once I called at Bryants of Biggleswade on a test bike to pick up something, and Jack there said that the bike approaching had sounded like an old Rudge, you could hear the clatter a mile off – that was probably on initial test.

'We'd fit the battery and exhaust, check the brakes were roughly OK, start up and set the carburettor approximately. Incidentally, starting was never a problem – there's a technique, of course, and it's surprising how many don't have it! Too many people stop three-quarters of the way down their kick – you have to give it a little flick at the end, to get the flywheels going – I could often do it for customers' bikes when they couldn't, and the bigger the chap, often the more difficulty they seemed to have. Brute force was not advisable, as Vincent kickstart splines were the same size as on the previous separate Burman gearboxes, and not truly adequate unless the kickstart was really tightened down.

'We would fill up at our own petrol pump at the works, and start. On the initial run I would do ten miles, through the lanes, so that I used the gearbox quite a lot to free it up, and could check the clutch action. On return I would probably collect another bike and do its oils etc, until the first one was cool enough to reset the tappets, before taking it out for another 40 miles. Personally I used to go somewhere quiet, like Knebworth, and readjust the carbs out there, since if several of you were doing it in test, it was awfully difficult to hear what yours was doing.

'We would return, do any necessary adjustments to the brakes etc and check things over for tightness, then have a cup of tea before doing another 40 or 50 miles more to complete a test of approximately 100 miles. There was never any fiddling to do less than that [which was not unknown at other factories], though the other way about, some testers were rumoured to go off to Wales on test bikes at weekends! No, it may sound prissy, but owning a twin myself and realising what they cost, with most people using their wartime gratuities to get one, I used to try and test them as I hoped someone would have if it had been me that was going to buy it. And today with the Club, of course, I've now met several owners whose bikes I did test when they were new.'

Hazards of the trade? 'Vincents were so much faster than anything else, but people still wanted to take you on – and when you're road-testing a new bike, you didn't feel inclined to prove to a flat-out Speed Twin that you were still in second.' And the police? 'I was done twice: 39.1mph in a 30 limit once; and then after a dash back to the works, I'd done 60 through a village – 60 doesn't seem much when you've been doing 90, does it? – and realised there was a car following me. Well, people would tuck in behind you sometimes, so I didn't twig for a bit, and then just as I was shutting off, he gonged me. I had no mirrors – in those days you used to think you were young enough to turn your head around! I was fined £3 – things were more reasonable then.'

By 1954 there were occasions in the company's uneven fortunes when production ceased temporarily, and Norman went back to wheel-building; and then to preparation for PCV's last throw, the radical all-enclosed Series D. 'I always felt that the faired Ds would be vulnerable to cross-winds. Then in June, in TT week, Jim Sugg came to me in a panic and asked me to go to

Ipswich and pick up a batch of Oilite bushes. I took a faired D, and was then delayed there as the depot had closed for lunch. I was very keen to get home and hear the TT on the radio so I came back like the clappers, cruising at 90 over that open eastern country, with its high winds. But the D was very, very steady even at those speeds.'

Another D-related incident saw Norman sent on one to the film set of George Orwell's *1984*, to evaluate the bike's suitability in the story as a mount for the Thought Police. 'I was on a Black Prince, in a black Belstaff suit with a black helmet. They offered me a job, but I told them I preferred road-testing.' In the end the VOC rather than Stevenage would provide the ten Ds which, with their bodywork modified and the soundtrack doctored to remove their healthy engine-note, provided memorably menacing mounts.

The D, of course, was Vincent's swan-song, and production ceased late in 1955. 'At the time we all felt that there would be no future for Vincents after five years, the period you were legally obliged to provide spares for a defunct model.' After working as head of service reception and technical information until 1958, Norman's career moved elsewhere, but the Vincent beat went on. He's appeared with Ted Davis riding Vincents on *Top Gear* ('and both our bikes were Brampton-forked!').

And he will continue to correct errors about Vincents, or they'll be perpetuated. For instance? 'One of my first jobs arose from the fact that they had found that when they put the drive chains on early Series Bs, because of a dimensional drawing error, the only way to get the chain on tight enough was to have it at full stretch from the start, with all the adjustment used up. So Ted Hampshire and I decided to take a bastard file to the rear fork and cut a quarter-inch slot so that the spindle could go forward enough to connect the chain up with two links removed (PCV wouldn't hear of using a half link). So some early ones had two links less. To justify this, it was announced that it had been done to allow for tyre growth at high speed, and also for a larger tyre to be fitted. That was the excuse, but those were the facts.'

I hope Norman will be around to tell the truth about the legend that is Vincent for a good while longer. Because no-one is better qualified. Norman Peach knows Vincents inside out, and he loves them, warts and all.

Tony Denniss

I mentioned in the introduction that during the eighties I ran a Norton Commando, which was perhaps the most satisfying machine I ever owned.

So it was particularly fascinating to be able to talk to Tony Denniss, who had been intimately involved in both the genesis and development of this 'stopgap' model which had ended up in production for nine years, and had seen the traditional British industry out. Tony would go on to work on the rotary-engined Nortons, but that was very much another story.

Some moments in this job leave one feeling very privileged indeed. One such came recently. A few miles from the MIRA testing track, in a Midlands garden bright with autumn sunlight, there stood an absolutely original Mk I Fastback Norton Commando. And next to it stood its keeper from new, Tony Denniss. Who also happened to have been a prominent member of the development team responsible for the Commando, which to my mind is the ultimate British roadster twin. Who better to talk me through design features of the 750 Norton, many of which he himself had implemented? Privileged, or what?

Tony Denniss today is a gentle, soft-voiced, rangey individual, with something of the look of John Surtees, but taller. A chartered engineer approaching retirement age, he shows no signs of slackening pace. Though described by an ex-colleague as 'a bit of a boffin,' then as now he was also an active rider. The Commando shared lawn space not only with two hyperactive Yorkies and a brace of caged finches emitting curious calls, but with a sparkling maroon '53 pre-unit Triumph twin. Curiously, for a long-term AMC and Norton employee, Tony was always a Triumph enthusiast, running a T110 and T100C at the start of his career, down at the old Matchless works in Plumstead. There were no comebacks, Tony smiled, 'and I could always borrow a Matchless or Norton from work.'

Tony's life with the motorcycle industry began when he was in his mid-20s, in August 1956. Already a draughtsman and mad about bikes, he literally knocked on the door of the Plumstead works, was interviewed by head draughtsman Horace Watson, and went to work two weeks later – possibly because, when he'd been told by Watson that the job would not earn him much money, Tony had said that if they'd take him on, he would pay them!

After gaining experience on assembly drawing, he worked with the 15-strong drawing office team on the first G2 'Lightweight' 250s, and AMC's new range of Piatti-designed two-strokes, their unsuccessful attempt to bypass Villiers. One thing of which he became very conscious was that styling was all done in-house.

'The draughtsmen's pride was that if given a brief, they could style it themselves. The results, as on the G2, looked neat, but not striking. I thought that with a professional stylist, the bikes could have been more successful.' This would be one of several areas where the Commando would break new ground. Meanwhile, the company was becoming strapped for cash, and even detachable chromed panels on petrol tanks were replaced with cheaper large 'knee-knocker' badges to copy Triumph's 'mouth-organ' ones. 'After that AJS and Matchless were very largely styled by Lucas,' laughs Tony, since the electrical giant also made the plastic tank badges for them and the rest of the industry.

Tony stayed in the drawing office till 1960, when it became obvious to him that he needed further formal training. So he then did 18 months of graduate training in the factory, progressing through the different departments – tool-room, grinding shop, heat treatment, laboratory – and making useful contacts with personnel who, since he was in his late 20s, gave him a bit more respect than they did to the young apprentices.

After that he took over the running of the drawing office, still under Watson until the arrival from Velocette, as design department chief, of Charles Udall, who supervised work on the Atlas 750, as well as on his own design for an 800cc dohc twin engine in a modified Featherbed frame, codenamed the P10. Horace Watson worked as a draughtsman on that one, so Tony became official drawing office manager.

This was the period of the Norton/Matchless hybrid models, and not a happy time. 'I could see the company was on a hiding to nothing,' Tony recalls. Norton, another part of the AMC group, had moved down from their traditional Bracebridge Street home in Birmingham to Plumstead, late in 1962. After AMC's own 750 twin engine had proved to have too little meat for effective oil-tightness, the Norton Atlas engine took over in a range of models mostly aimed at the American street scrambler and desert racing market, like the N15CS and the P11 desert sled. 'The things were tall, they vibrated and leaked oil,' says Tony, 'but the Matchless dealers in the US had to be given something, and AMC had no money to do anything really new. Those bikes at least sounded nice ...'

The P11, which involved shoe-horning a modified Atlas engine into the ultra-light G85CS single's chassis, occupied Tony's design talents for a while. 'To ride those P11s you had to be really brave, and about six foot three,' he says. The first ones used to split their alloy oil tanks, which continued on as part of the alloy rear mudguard, so that when they fractured oil went straight over the rear tyre. The four mounting bolts, each at an odd angle, strained the tank to begin with. Failure rates had the Berliner brothers, AMC's American importers, up in arms.

Tony was at home, sitting in the smallest room pondering the problem, when his eye fell on the toilet-roll holder. It came to him that since they could not correct the angles of the tank's mountings, the problem might still be solved if they fitted it on two bars, each wrapped in rubber, which could articulate, the top one to be located under the seat.

Testers under development shop veteran Wally Wyatt had been breaking the old mounts within about 300 miles. Tony instituted a test sequence with his new design which involved riders in relays going up and down the local dual carriageway to Plumstead, with three hours each at the maximum vibration period, around 70mph in third. Setting up HQ in an AMC truck parked in a service station, Tony stood on a footbridge looking down on the test bikes. The new mountings never broke. They produced kits to retro-fit to existing machines, and that sorted that.

AMC finally went under in August 1966, and Dennis Poore's Manganeze Bronze Holdings company took over a few weeks later. Poore himself was a remote figure at this period, in contrast to his later fortnightly visits to the Norton works at the old Villiers factory in Wolverhampton. The changeover at Plumstead was managed by Manganeze Bronze's vice chairman John Neville, with assistance from Bill Colquhoun and accountant John Moore. Neville was a tall man with a strong personality, a decorated war hero who impressed everyone.

The decision to drop the old Matchless name and organisation may have been taken by Poore, but it was Neville who implemented it, with some style. A mass meeting was called in the big canteen at Plumstead and everybody, from sweepers to directors, was ordered to attend. The directors had put tables up on the stage at one end of the canteen, with a seat there for Neville, as hundreds of workers milled around the canteen floor.

'But John Neville arrived in a big car with a flag on the front, and came in from the back,' Tony remembers. 'Being well over six foot tall, he marched through the workforce, climbed up on a canteen table and did a "gather round, chaps," just like Monty, leaving the directors up on the podium. He told everyone straight that the old company was bust and that the directors were to blame, and said that they had to be out of the building by five o'clock that evening! And they were gone, except for Charles Udall.'

Meanwhile the elements which would result in the Commando were beginning to assemble. Manganeze Bronze had taken over Villiers the previous year, and hired back one of their previous talents, Bernard Hooper, as chief designer. Poore had also employed ex-Atomic Energy and Rolls Royce man Dr Stefan Bauer, who had been his tutor at Cambridge, as head of the team to come up with an urgently needed new motorcycle to revive the fortunes of the Norton name. Tony Denniss went up to Wolverhampton to meet them, and got on well with both. The late Dr Bauer, whom some found autocratic, he considered 'a wonderful man and a real gent'; and one of the wonders of the Commando story was the way that Midlanders like Hooper and his assistant, ex-BSA man Bob Trigg, pulled together as required with the Plumstead people, at a time when Londoners and Brummies did not get along too famously.

Self-effacingly, Tony says that Hooper was 'very diplomatic with me, so we got on well,' but a lot of it appears to have been down to Tony himself, whose diplomacy was also being exercised within Plumstead. With the scaling-down of the factory underway, his brief was free-ranging, and Udall had put him in the development shop with Wally Wyatt. 'I played it very softly with Wally,' Tony explains. 'He was a highly experienced hands-on chap, and if you handled him carefully, he continued to produce and share good ideas.' Wyatt had already been responsible, chiefly by means of work on the cylinder head, for upping the power output on some works 750 Atlas engines from 50 to 58.5bhp, and beyond.

This suddenly became highly relevant. Dr Bauer had already sketched out his notions for a new frame, which featured a massive 2.25-inch spine tube and relatively lightly stressed twin downtubes; the Villiers drawing office had drawn it out; and frame wizard Ken Sprayson at Reynolds Tubes would build the prototypes. The engine intended for this was Udall's dohc P10, and work on it was accelerated. But Hooper found that it was heavy, vibrated, and that its very long cam-chain (90 links, about 3ft, as long as a drive chain) provided problems. Also, after some prototypes had been run, the cammy engine proved to produce no more power than an Atlas, and certainly not the Wyatt-developed Atlas. But this is the reason a Commando frame is so high, and its engine fits in so easily – it had been designed to take the taller P10, on which work continued.

At the same time Bauer, who was not a motorcyclist, had been for a ride on the pillion of a Norton twin, and had returned shocked by the vibration which Tony and most regular riders took for granted. Bauer's reaction was timely, though, as both the high compression parallel twins of the sixties, and the presence of Japanese middleweights for comparison, meant that the 'V word' had begun to be mentioned critically about British bikes, in the Press and among enthusiasts. At the next of the meetings for the project team at Plumstead, which were held every three or four weeks, Bauer asked: 'Have you tried rubber-mounting the engine?' In fact Wyatt and Tony had already done so, but had got nowhere trying to control the tugging of the primary chain.

Bernard Hooper also attended these meetings, and phoned up after one to say that on the train back to Birmingham he had thought about bolting the engine and gearbox together and rubber-mounting them as a unit. Tony said he couldn't see it, citing his previous problems with chain-lines and tugging, at which point Hooper mentioned that his idea would be to attach the swinging arm as well to the engine plates at the rear of the engine/gearbox package, and rubber-mount the lot. Tony therefore sent him up several old Norton engines and gearboxes to play with.

Some months later, Hooper rang to say that he had a system operational. Tony rode up to Wolverhampton on a P10 prototype for comparison, and jumped straight onto Bernard's prototype bike, an Atlas with its frame converted with the rubber mountings. He returned from his ride completely convinced. Hooper was by then being assisted by Bob Trigg, who was 'young, good-looking and an ex-Ariel apprentice. Bernard Hooper could ride but he was essentially a boffin, while Bob Trigg put in the practical touches. It worked quite well.'

Then in another break with accepted practice, Wolf Ohlins, an advertising agency previously uninvolved with motorcycles, were brought in to help with the styling. As mentioned, Tony had long perceived the absence of specialist styling skills in the industry as a lack, and certainly for this ground-breaking, breakaway project, looks which emphasised its novelty without straying too far from tradition would be a real plus point. Bernard Hooper has said 'Some of [Wolf Ohlins'] suggestions made us laugh, but others were good.'

The initial Fastback-style bike was all silver, with an orange seat featuring distinctive wraparound 'ears' to marry it visually to the tank, and 'green balls on everything', which puzzled people until they realised that this was the new Norton-Villiers corporate logo. The machine was suitably striking, yet with lines that were fundamentally right, and once modified a little for practicality (ie production frames and most cylinder barrels were black not silver), there were few penalties deriving from the stylists' input. Tony says that one was a slightly restricted steering lock/turning circle compared with the Triumph T120 Bonneville, which it was his aim for the Commando to equal or surpass wherever possible. Few would deny that the Commando is a handsome motorcycle.

By now it was June 1967, and the team were under further pressure, as chairman Dennis Poore was emphatic that a new model must be ready for display at that year's Earls Court Show, which was in September – just 11 weeks away. It was also said that Poore had taken a ride on a P10 prototype, and returned convinced that the engine in its existing form was not viable. So the decision was taken to go with the Wyatt-developed Atlas, modified, rubber-mounted, and tilted forward in the Bauer frame.

However, an essential point about the Commando was that in the eyes of its creators, it was still a stopgap model. And this would soon be used by some within the company to justify the failure to implement solutions which

Good vibrations.

N Ward.

already existed for some of its problems, on the grounds of cost. An example of this was a simpler Vernier system for adjusting the Isolastic rubber mountings; the Vernier system had been designed from the start, but would not be introduced until 1975. But a stopgap was how everyone on the team saw the machine at that time. For example, Dr Bauer for simplicity wanted American (Unified) Threads standardised throughout the Commando, but Tony Denniss drew the line at converting the engine in this way, he said, arguing successfully that the Atlas-engined Commando was only there for a couple of years, till something else came good.

The Villiers works at Wolverhampton, accustomed to making motorcycle engines but not whole motorcycles, and still busy with the industrial engine side, were by now struggling in their attempts to get the project into production. 'The Commando design was largely done at Villiers by Bernard Hooper,' Tony states clearly, 'but they got so far and it got too much for Villiers, they couldn't do it.' His boss John Neville told Poore that 'Denniss at Plumstead can do it, I have every confidence in him.' Neville then phoned Tony to say that 'everything to do with Norton is being shipped down to Plumstead from Wolverhampton, and I've told the Board that you can do it – you are going to be able to?' There could be only one answer, but Tony then 'rushed to Wally and said, we're in it now, we haven't even finalised the design on the thing yet. It seemed like three lorry-loads of stuff which came, as well as two Villiers draughtsmen, because we got not only the Commando project but all the other bikes as well.'

It was panic time, but the work went well. One additional problem was naming the new machine. Dennis Poore held a competition for all group employees, with cash prizes, for naming the bike, plus a powerful version of its engine, and also the new rubber-mounting system. There was fierce rivalry on this within the Norton-Villiers group. 'Villiers and AMC didn't get on very well,' says Tony with masterly understatement. 'It went back to the days of the trouble over the two-strokes' (the unsuccessful Piatti motors which had been intended to undercut Villiers, but ended up, in a humiliating climb-down for AMC, having to be assembled by Villiers due to lack of two-stroke expertise at Plumstead).

'When Wolverhampton later took over the Commando, some of their people, particularly production people, wanted to get their own back.' This would blight the model's progress. 'Both sides were proud of their production methods. When we wanted more power with the Combat engine, I knew from work with Wally at Plumstead that this would require the RHP barrel-roller main bearings, to cope with flexing cranks. But Villiers were very much mass-production oriented, and said that the bearings were unnecessary – they could always blame Bernard Hooper when things went wrong' (as they did, spectacularly, with the Combat engine in 1972).

But back in '67 it was AMC people who came up with two of the three names, 'which really upset Villiers – they were given a third prize, for political reasons.' Plumstead draughtsman Terry Weatherfield had an Austin 1100 with Hydrolastic suspension, which gave him the idea for the Isolastic name, and Combat was also a Plumstead suggestion. The main name, though, came from a Villiers director out in Australia. Tony was up at Wolverhampton when the man, who was also visiting, remarked, 'I think, Commando.' Tony reminded him of a previous James two-stroke scrambler which had borne that name, 'but that didn't mean much to the guy, and he prevailed with Poore.'

The new bike somehow got to the Show on time, and it was a sensation. As journalist David Dixon wrote at the time, 'no new model introduced in the last decade has made such a big impact as the Norton Commando.' It would win a Castrol design award of £1,000 for the Isolastic system, and be voted *MCN* Machine of the Year for the next five years. However, the twin would not reach actual production until April 1968, and meanwhile there was much work to be done. 'We took three prototypes round MIRA with some good Plumstead test riders, experienced Trials and motocross men,' though not the previous AMC ace Bob Manns, who was currently working at BSA/Triumph on what was soon to be the Commando's main British rival, the Rocket 3/Trident.

'The price of the Commando was determined by Bill Colquhoun,' says Tony, 'and fortunately the triple was to be even more expensive' (£466 v £614 in 1969, and the differential would remain throughout most of their production lives – one reason why I was never tempted by a triple). The industry was a small world, and around this time the two groups arranged a highly unofficial meeting, with some BSA/Triumph men, including Bob Manns, bringing triples, and the Plumstead crew coming on the Nortons. 'And each rode the others' bikes. I knew Bob Manns from his AMC days under Hugh Viney, and though he was a very quiet man, I could tell he liked the Norton, and I was pleased. I rode a triple, and I thought it wasn't as smooth as a Commando, and heavy too.' The highly experienced Manns soon joined Norton-Villiers, where Dennis Poore would refer to him as 'my chief test pilot'.

They were not out of the woods yet, though. The first version of Dr Bauer's frame began to fracture in quite a big way. As mentioned, the chassis' lightness at just 24lb had been partly achieved by using light downtubes, which with the massive spine taking the major stresses, were intended mostly to support the engine and cope with lateral flexing. But frames began to break, first at the top of the downtubes and then at the front of the tank tube, particularly at a welded U-shaped gusset just behind the steering neck. At first, with the aid of a graph showing the incidence of cracks, Tony tried making the tubes thicker, though by careful increments, as he hated weight. For testing they used the Fighting Vehicles Research Establishment at Chobham, which had both a concrete block 'suspension' course, and Belgian pave.

Their test lap included 400 metres of each, and within three laps the first Commandos had completely lost the damping in their front forks, with oil pouring out; after another three the frames would begin to break. Tony had a system involving a petrol tank with the front cut off so that they could see all around the head lug, since they soon knew roughly where fractures were going to occur. He would ring Ken Sprayson with his increased thickness requirements, and would have the beefed-up frames within two days. The Nortons began to manage more test laps, but some frames still broke, and it was now well into 1968, so some of them belonged to customers in America. The real solution came with Sprayson's suggestion to triangulate the bottom of the steering head with a small horizontal bracing tube to a point further back on the frame spine. 'I was unhappy because of the weight,' says Tony, 'but I tried it to appease Ken. And from then on, we couldn't break the frame.'

At this point in our chat it seemed appropriate to go out into the garden, where Tony had wheeled out the Fastback model he had got new on 22 January 1969, and subsequently ridden for just 8,625 miles. It was an export model – most early Commandos went for export – and what was subsequently known as a Mk I, the models made until March 1969. This meant that the famously over-engineered footrest hangers were painted black, as was the rear brake pedal (and on home models, the fork shrouds); and that neither the rocker box covers nor the fork legs were polished. Another visual clue to its Mk I-ness was the points/distributor housing, located behind the cylinders in the old magneto mounting position. 'There are two needle roller bearings in there,' says Tony, 'but they wore, and the bearing centres were so close together – it wasn't a wonderful idea.' Wally Wyatt supervised the introduction of points mounted in the timing chest, initially for the March 1969 'S' models.

The fibreglass $3^1/_4$-gallon tank, being for export, carried a 'Norton' transfer rather than the early home model Fastback's circular badge. The tank was also finished in amazingly garish (but then fashionable) metalflake Burgundy red with panels in 'quicksilver' metallic, which you could hardly believe was factory original if you didn't know that it was definitely so. A real period finish.

Starting at the front, Tony pointed out the chromed ring surrounding the headlamp shell. 'Fastbacks initially didn't sell well in the USA. We thought they should have a sports touch, so we added the ring, to take a stoneguard grid over the headlamp.'

The front brake was the twin leading-shoe drum effort, not replaced by a disc until the '72 Combat-engined Roadsters and Interstates. 'Wally Wyatt had originally done this brake for the P10,' said Tony. 'But since I was a Triumph enthusiast, I said it had to have an air scoop, like the Meriden twin leader – even though it then had to be blanked off on the home models, to keep out the rain! Yes, I liked Triumphs,' he added, 'but I was determined to bring out a better bike than the Bonneville, and I think we did.'

The alloy primary chaincase was interesting for a number of reasons. The old Norton twin's pressed steel cases had been replaced by alloy cases on the Atlas engines used in the AMC hybrids, but those versions had been secured by numerous screws around their periphery. However, as well as his Triumphs, Tony had owned a Royal Enfield Constellation, and freely admitted that this had been the inspiration for the single central-bolt fixing found on all Commandos until the final 850 Mk III.

This chaincase was simply sealed around its edge with a sealing band, and inevitably was found to bow if its central fixing bolt was over-tightened, and then to leak oil. 'So,' said Tony, 'we arranged that the back end of the chaincase was cast at the foundry so that it tapered out and was shallower at each end. This was carried out by Lavenders, who had done a lot of casting for AMC, and it worked until production was transferred to Wolverhampton, who didn't bother with this; so the case leaked.' It's one example of why many rate the few thousand early Commandos made at Plumstead, before production ceased in July 1969 prior to the move to Andover, as the cream of the crop. Some of these Plumstead Commandos can be distinguished by a P-suffix to the engine number.

Still on the chaincase, the Atlas engine had always had its primary chain inspection plug at the bottom of the cover, but Tony moved this to an easier-to-check position at the top. Wally Wyatt came up with the idea for another small screwed plug on the case's alternator bulge, giving provision for strobing, in conjunction with timing marks inside. And also inside the case, Tony made sure that, unlike AMC alternator machines, the stator was put on the back half of the chaincase, so that you could check clearance with the rotor – which, as he pointed out, was the way Triumph had been doing it since 1955.

The twin carbs had a balance pipe, an idea going back to Norton in their Bracebridge Street days, but up till the Commando the pipe had sat at the bottom of the carbs, where sediment could accumulate. So Tony moved it to the top. He was also responsible for the stylish finning on the carbs' curved alloy downdraught intakes.

The plastic catches on the toolboxes of these early models were one of many details in which they differed from the later '71 and '73 750s which I owned – and they looked more reliable than the Dzuz-style fasteners found on those. The big, period, circular Zener diode located behind the box was another authentic detail.

Tony had a hand in the choice of the Commando's large paper air filters. The prototypes had suffered loss of power as soon as filters had been fitted. Tony remembered that one of the former AMC draughtsmen was then a rep for Crosland Filters, and immediately asked him over. The man said that in his experience, the bigger the filter they used, the better; so Tony tried the biggest that would fit, and it worked without loss of power.

Returning to that flamboyant fuel tank, Tony said that its fibreglass construction became illegal after 1974, and though the law prohibiting all but steel tanks was recently repealed, hand laid-up fibreglass types such as this would still be illegal – unless, as here, they had been fitted as original equipment. Tony also pointed out how these early Monza-type fuel caps hinged at the front. This was convenient for the rider when filling up or checking the fuel level, but in the event of a crash the petrol could fly out over the rider. The caps were later changed to a rear-hinging type, partly as a result of product liability suits after accidents.

On the handlebars, the green button was a Wipac headlamp flasher, an idea of Tony's which was a unique feature on a motorcycle at the time. They had tried to tell him that it would be illegal, but he thought it was a nice touch.

The rear footrests came off a James, with the rubber mounting for them off a Mini. Beneath them are old-style conventional Norton silencers, something Tony would alter shortly afterwards. 'There were no real noise regulations then, and without the Norton baffles Wally Wyatt found the bikes went much better. So I worked out, partly by taking temperatures in the pipes front and rear, that if you reversed the baffles, it went really well, and you still had some proof of restriction if a policeman stuck his truncheon up the pipes!' This was to be the basis for the internals of the 'S' type and Roadster's reverse-cone 'peashooter' silencers.

'At least some of the oil should stay in …'

Beneath all, there was the centre stand, an interesting over-centre design with, on its left side, instead of a solid extension, a long, rigid *spring* sticking out. This is strong enough to use to lower the stand far enough so that you can get at the solid peg on the stand behind it; but being a spring it can't dig into the tarmac when you're heeled over for hard cornering. Clever stuff, but 'eventually we had to make the stand itself wider, because of the less than even surfaces found in foreign markets.'

The year 1969 was a high point for the Commando, which was popular, powerful, and, unlike later, thanks to Tony featured a decent kerbside fighting weight of just 420lb. The 750 Norton was selling well, and its prospects were apparently bright. In fact the model's future, and that of Norton itself, would be a chequered one, and the next 18 years of Tony Denniss' involvement with Norton were not to be all smiles. But happily this likeable, mild, but extremely clear-headed man survived 30 years in the motorcycle industry, and in good order.

Wilf Harrison

Having started out riding Nortons, somehow I became at first involved and then obsessed with BSAs, and by extension with the BSA Group's home, the 28-acre site at Small Heath, Birmingham. Ironically, the one time I ever visited the place was in 1969, before I had become interested in Birmingham Small Arms and their two-wheelers; I was there on firearms-related business.

I found that Birmingham itself was another country, somewhere you could get a shave at a barbers as a matter of course (I had come up at very short notice), where smog lingered and they still sold chestnuts from braziers in the city centre; it reminded me of the London I had grown up in over 20 years before. I was just back from America, and the place seemed incredibly antiquated. As with the city, perhaps, so with the company.

At Armoury Road works itself the next morning, I do remember the sight and the staccato sound of a pair of unit big single scramblers on test round the perimeter track, and the way smoke from the cold engines' exhausts and the sharp smell of burnt oil hung in the mist that foggy morning. Ten years later, by the time I did get hooked on the place, it had been pulled down, a possibility that would have been as unimaginable to me that morning as it would have to the 5,000 people who worked there. One of them was Wilf Harrison.

As my studies of the British industry deepened, it became clear that despite Norton's racing pedigree and Triumph's charisma, for good or ill the heart of the matter had resided with 'the Giant of Small Heath'. The subject is a complex one, but Wilf Harrison was one who saw, closer up than most, the shift from solid service and reliable products to misguided management and final disaster.

Wilf Harrison was BSA through and through. From a job as correspondence clerk in the service department, he rose to be service manager at Small Heath. And then, in a sideways move in the sixties, he became export sales manager, a vital part of the marketing thrust that saw their motorcycles sales soar overseas before the Group was mismanaged into extinction.

Not many men combined the technical expertise necessary for effective service, with the very different skills needed to sell; yet in the view of one industry insider, Wilf as a salesman was 'always better than his opposite number at Triumph'. He liked the product; he owned and rode BSAs himself, and road-raced them for a while. In fact it was Harrison who, famously, was told by BSA's autocratic and insensitive final MD, Lionel Jofeh, 'I would rather you didn't come to the senior management dining room in motorcycle attire'! Some boss of a major motorcycle manufacturers ...

And finally, after founding, with his former colleague Peter Glover, the successful import/distribution company Harglo, he has remained friends with the people to whom he used to sell BSAs, as well as with fellow veterans from the company. With his canny, even wily features, Wilf is still clearly not a person you'd want to try to put one over on, but at the end of a long career, a rollercoaster ride of commercial disasters and successes, the overwhelming impression is of a contented man.

In 1949, after National Service in the Army and a dispiriting year clerking with Birmingham's Department of Education, Wilf's wife-to-be, the shrewd and spirited Dorothy, pointed out an advert from BSA in the local paper which read: 'Versatile young man required, interested in motorcycles'. Soon Wilf found himself one of 25 correspondence clerks at £5 a week in the company's service department, which was then located at the old Lanchester car works in Montgomery Road, a quarter of a mile from the main Armoury Road works at Small Heath.

The service department was a major enterprise in itself, at that time employing over 320 personnel including mechanics, storemen, and illustrators, and despatching over 50,000 items world-wide each day. To start with, much of the correspondence concerned pre-war bikes and BSA cars. Customers could bring their machines directly to the department, and the staff often had to show people how to start big singles (so it's not just us modern softies!).

After six weeks the department's manager, John Balder, demanded to know why Wilf didn't have a pile of letters outstanding in front of him, like everybody else. Finding that it was because young Harrison knew something about bikes and could write letters, Balder offered him the job of section leader at £7.50 – 'the biggest percentage wage increase I ever had,' laughed Wilf. After that he was moved on to control of the commercial office, which included the illustrators, and this represented his first technical involvement.

Not everyone was as dedicated as Wilf. One clerk opened a Post Office account for himself in the name of 'B. Small', easy to adapt from the 'BSA' on the torrent of postal orders which were often used to pay for spares from the department. The guy was eventually rumbled and went to jail, but you can't keep a good man down; on his release he bought an old car, and sold eggs from it outside the service department. John Balder's advice to Wilf as a manager was 'don't put temptation in people's way', and he never forgot it.

Given the shortage of everything in those days of post-war austerity, Wilf had to wait a year before there was even talk about a motorcycle for him. One of the first was a C11, a workaday 250 single. One day Wilf went with his then fiancée Dorothy to her aunt's farm, where a pig had just been slaughtered. Returning that evening with Dorothy on the pillion clutching a large parcel of fresh pork, taking a steep hill at 50mph the big end seized solid; Wilf was catapulted over the handlebars and Dorothy was also spat off. 'Are you all right?' called an anxious Wilf when the dust settled. 'Yeah,' came the reply, 'but where's me pork?' First things first … It was not to be the last prang which marriage to Wilf would involve for the lady he calls 'Dolly'. The most recent came a year ago when he was landing his Rotax 503-powered microlight aircraft, and shaved off the undercarriage. In the ringing silence which follows these events, Dolly looked at him and said simply, 'Don't do that again.'

The C11 gave way to a B33 and then a ZB32 Gold Star ('one of the cheap ones'), both of which Wilf used to race at a couple of meetings a year. Next he got a 1951 A7 Star Twin roadster; but then Dorothy's brother was killed on a bike, so for her parents' peace of mind Wilf agreed to put a sidecar on it. 'It was a No 22 BSA chassis, and we sat Dolly in it on a sheet of brown paper, drew round her, and told her that was how much room she'd have. David Tye [one of Small Heath's ace competition riders] had Harold Tozer's ISDT sidecar outfit, and we modelled it on that. I built the body, screwing and glueing the wooden frame and putting the aluminium panelling on. Dolly was a wonderful passenger, leaping about –' 'I'd been trained,' said Dorothy, 'by Peter Glover [already a friend and colleague of Wilf's in the service department] and he'd been a racing passenger.' Eventually a 650 engine would be substituted for the 500. The chair proved strong. Once when touring in the West Country, an Austin A40 braked abruptly in front of them and they rear-ended it. The car's steel bumper was dented, but the sidecar was undamaged.

'When we eventually sold that outfit,' Wilf smiled, 'it had to go to someone whose wife was no taller than Dolly. We got a car, but that was a disaster. So then we got a 650 swinging-arm A10. We were told we couldn't

N. Ward.

'… getting a good spark …'

put a sidecar on a swinging-arm machine. But I'd been in one driven by Len Crisp of the development department, who was very quick. So I put on a Watsonian with a sprung wheel; it was good, though not as much fun as the early outfit.'

'You and Pete were a lethal combination on that one,' Dorothy chided gently. Wilf grinned. 'It used to roll the tyre off on left-handers, so you could hear the rim hitting the road before the rubber rolled back on as you straightened up.' In 1955 the couple took the outfit on a tour of the Continent, flying with the bike to Le Touquet on a Bristol Freighter aircraft. Through Belgium, Germany, Austria, and over the Brenner pass to Italy they went. By Lake Como they stopped outside a posh hotel, totally covered in road dust and feeling badly in need of a bath. 'We weren't sure, but then the flunky came down the steps, took our old army pannier bags and led us in; he never batted an eyelid.' Due to spirited charioteering, in Geneva after little more than a thousand miles the bike's rear tyre was already scrubbed bare and they had to buy a new one. Later when the competitive David Tye was told this, he turned up at service on his own outfit and showed them the brand new rear tyre on it. The following Monday when he returned from a 600-mile weekend trip round Wales, 'there was nothing on it – scrubbed bare,' laughed Wilf.

Back in service, general manager John Balder decided that the department had got too unwieldy, and created the post of service manager for Wilf, with the redoubtable Al Cave as spares manager. 'Al has been my personal friend ever since he came to service from the bicycle side in 1956. Typically, the first time we met was when he helped us out after our car had broken down. When he was works manager at Small Heath, and even after the company folded, he really looked after people, things like going round to cut the grass for a widow if someone had died.' In 1958 service moved into the Waverley works which had previously housed BSA bicycles, after that side had been sold off to Raleigh.

Wilf's responsibilities were in two parts: a commercial repair operation, mainly for accident damage; and work done under warranty. Peter Glover was in charge of the repair work. What were the troubles with the Group's two-wheeled products? 'We'd already had problems with the Sunbeam S7 and S8, both the rear drive bevel set-up, and camshaft chain tensioner problems. The tensioner was originally a very simple spring, which broke and was then hard to replace. That was changed to a plunger-type tensioner with a screw-in knob, which worked well – but then the camshafts themselves wore. With the early, long-stroke A7 twins, the Star Twin version with two carburettors had a reputation for catching fire – the movement of air was too low – so whenever we had one of them in, we'd get out the fire extinguishers!

'The main range in the fifties, however, the A7/A10, B31/B33, M20/M21, the C11 and Bantam, were mostly reliable, and lasted a long time. The only exception was when they put the side-valve 250 engine into Bantam cycle parts to form the C10L. The service lads used to call it The Pogo Stick!'

It was lightweights which were consistently troublesome. 'The prototype Beeza scooter had no power, and in the end it was never produced. The Dandy step-through 70cc two-stroke with its two-speed pre-selector gearbox was ahead of its time. However, it suffered from frame and fork breakages, but principally from oil not getting to the main bearings – in the end, a grease nipple had to be fitted for them! We serviced both the BSA and Triumph versions of the Sunbeam/Tigress scooters; the Bantam-engined ones had electrical problems. The twin cylinder 250 engine on them was good, but there was a major problem with the oil pump's timing; in the end we had to have the first full recall of a model on that, to strip down the pumps and modify every one ...'

The scooters, of course, had been designed by Triumph's Edward Turner, and after he took over as automotive division chief in 1957 they were not the only problem which he threw service's way. There was a Turner-designed industrial engine with unsuitably high-revving characteristics, and the Tina automatic scooter with its problem-prone transmission. 'We had one in for repair which had succumbed to the two-stroke problem of running backwards; a girl was sitting on it at the traffic lights, the engine coughed, and then when she opened up she ran into the bloke behind her!' But for BSA the worst machine was the 250 C15 unit single, derived directly from Turner's Tiger Cub, and, on his orders, rushed into production without proper development. 'The clutch, the kickstart, the plain main bearings – you probably know that the first thousand machines which left the line weren't really runners.'

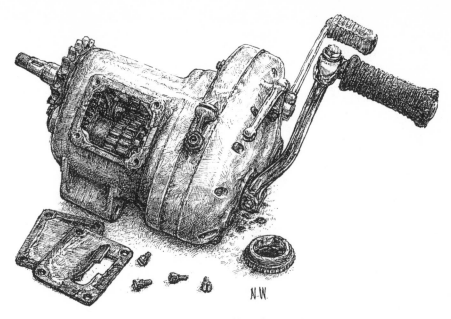

'They're still all in there ...'

Electrical problems were also a consistent theme from then on, and in Wilf's view these arose in part 'because the designers weren't used to asking questions, and Lucas weren't very good at suggesting the questions they should ask. For instance, in the sixties Lucas supplied us with Zener diodes, a good replacement for the fiddly mechanical rectifiers – but Lucas didn't say that the diodes needed a heat sink. They gave us the alternator, and told the designers the stator/rotor clearances – but nobody asked the question, do the clearances vary when you start the engine? And they did, with crankshafts flexing, but no one had said, and stators got chewed up before we found out.' Edward Turner favoured alternators not just for economy but for their tidiness, and Wilf confirmed that, while the detail work on the twin to replace the A7/A10 was done by BSA development man Len Crisp, Edward Turner did have a large hand in the original design of the A50/A65 unit construction twins, with their alternator electrics.

The unit twins came at a lean time for the motorcycle industry. 'After 1960 we thought the end had come, with the Mini and so on,' Wilf recalled. Service was moved into the Small Heath works, and in 1964, when John Balder became manufacturing director, Wilf was made general service manager, and for the next two years would be in charge of a department now jointly serving BSA and Triumph, which had been integrated into a single division. While BSA rivalry with Triumph may have been increasingly fierce at shop-floor and dealer level, Wilf said that he had been co-operating with his Triumph opposite number John Nelson for years, and that it was Nelson, rather than the generally credited American Pete Colman, who discovered the solution to the 'rogue' idle spark which had been dogging the high performance A50/A65 models.

Wilf had also been having more to do with export, as 'suddenly, around 1963, we could see the US market potential – every kid there wanted a motorcycle. Honda had stimulated this, appearing in places like launderettes where they'd never seen a motorcycle before.' In 1964, Harry Sturgeon, BSA/Triumph's dynamic new managing and marketing director, asked Wilf to visit Triumph's East Coast HQ at Baltimore, the first of several such visits providing service with valuable feedback on US market needs and product problems.

In 1966 Wilf got another call from Sturgeon, who had a problem: West Coast-based Pete Colman, then BSA's technical director in the USA, wouldn't take any A65 Spitfires, the newly-introduced tuned sports roadster version of the unit twin, due to problems with seizure and with the Mk II Spitfire's racing GP2 carbs, which had never been designed for road use. 'Pete Colman was a pre-war Pasadena speedway ace. He was self-opinionated, and he made some decisions on technical matters which were not always correct,' Wilf observed. This was a crucial call for Wilf, as Sturgeon told him that if he sold the Spitfires to Colman, there would be a new job for him – and Wilf knew that Bill Rawson, BSA's export sales manager, was soon to retire.

Wilf had already written two clearly laid-out service booklets on the Spitfire's problems, *The Amal GP2 as fitted to BSA*, and *Timing the Spark on 500/650 Unit Twins* – and concluded that 'if it needs a book as thick as this about it, we're fitting the wrong kit!' Once in the States he soon knew, because BSA East Coast man Ted Hodgson emphatically told him so, that the Spitfire's main problem was the GP2's inability to idle. So Wilf drew up a positive-stop mechanism within the throttle cable, allowing the throttle to be shut off without killing the engine. He sent the design's details back to Small Heath by telex, and Al Cave had the equipment made up and flown back to Wilf in the States in a week. 'If you had friends in the factory, you could get things like that done,' said Wilf. To emphasise Spitfire reliability, he and Peter Glover, whom Bert Hopwood had decided would be Wilf's assistant, rode a pair of export Mk IIs the 1,200 miles from BSA's East Coast centre at Nutley, New Jersey, to South Carolina. Colman relented and took the bikes, and Wilf got the export manager's job. Next year's Mk III Spitfires, however, fitted conventional Concentric carbs. 'It had been a good exercise,' said Wilf, 'in making me think hard about selling.'

The new job was not to be all plain sailing, though, for the smoothly contoured A65 was known disparagingly in America as 'the water melon engine', and 'we were in trouble in the States with technical problems. I was sent back to Nutley – very woodsy it was – for a 200-dealer meeting. I'd been told it was no good going without answers, and decided that attack was the best form of defence. I got the service department technical artists, who did the spares lists and so on, to do illustrations of some solutions to the problems.' It worked, and Wilf then had to repeat the performance on the West Coast. Wealthy veteran Hap Alzina still owned the BSA distributorship there, and had told Harry Sturgeon: 'Don't send Harrison here to meet the dealers, they'll kill him!' But Wilf got away with it, 'though for the first and last time in my life, I had to be on my feet speaking for seven hours! Never again!'

Next time he took slides rather than drawings for his presentations. But the crux was whether the dealers' specific complaints would be met with effective remedial action back at Small Heath. 'There, Bert Hopwood was a gem. I would go to January/February dealer meetings on the East Coast – I was away from home a lot, which was not always pleasant for our young children, John and Judy. When I got back, Hopwood would call a meeting of key personnel, Al Cave, Ken Whistance, and designer Ernie Webster. The meetings would continue until solutions were found which could be implemented, and Bert had made sure that I was happy with them – because I had to go back out to Nutley the following month, and later to the West Coast. As a result of the improvements, the A65 was a good engine by the end.

'So we were doing very well, and then early in 1967 Harry Sturgeon died from a brain tumour.' Who would succeed him? Wilf believed that 'Bert Hopwood could have been MD if he'd just got up and moved down to the office. Eric Turner [the Group's chairman] wanted him to stand up and be counted.' Hopwood always denied this, citing the chairman's 'firm non-acceptance of practising engineers.' Interestingly, Wilf can see that point of view. 'Bob Fearon was an engineer who became general manager, and while I was in service we had a case where a customer was complaining about a broken gear. The service department was not always perfect, and handling this we dug ourselves deeper and deeper in; it was indefensible really. Finally, after justifiable complaints from the customer, I was summoned to Fearon's office. I started to explain the situation, but within 30 seconds Bob had lost interest in the service problem, and anything else, except correcting the *technical* problem with the gear ...'

In Wilf's view the man who should have become MD was his old boss John Balder. 'He could motivate people, and he could analyse problems, and most importantly, draw conclusions – this comes up in service, as you fetch up against problems, and decide what ought to have been done. Jofeh, on the other hand, couldn't make a judgement.' For in the event Eric Turner appointed, from outside the industry, Lionel Jofeh. This was the crucial turning point, for Jofeh was the man who would steer the Group into disaster.

'My first meeting with Jofeh was at a gathering in the Small Heath showroom,' said Wilf. 'I'd been abroad and had just flown up from London to Birmingham. When we were introduced, Jofeh said "Well, Wilf, what have you been doing?" I replied "Flying round the world, selling motorcycles." "There won't be much need for that from now on," said the new MD. "We're going to *market* our motorcycles now, and soon the world will be queuing up at our door ..."' The faint sound of Loony Tunes could already be heard in the air.

Wilf gave another example of Jofeh's disastrous influence relating to the infamous 1971 restyled range. 'The '71 bikes weren't even on show in most US salesrooms – the dealers were too ashamed of them. I believe they were styled that way following a US market survey which said that 68 per cent of those who bought a BSA there, did so because of its appearance. Now anyone else would conclude that was pretty good, and that major restyling would not be necessary. But Jofeh said that if that's so, and if the most popular bike in America is a Honda, if we make our bikes look like it, then we'll sell even more ...'

The man's personal style was also unfortunate. 'With Sturgeon, he might bawl you out in the morning, but by the end of the day he'd call you in for a drink – he never let anyone go home ruffled, and people would have gone through hell and high water for him. Jofeh was the opposite. He would get you into his office after a day's work, and keep you there – I held the record, he had me there till 12.30 one night, and there was never any question of a drink or anything to eat.' Yet despite these exhausting consultations, the many ideas Wilf and others offered about what to do in the three or four years' breathing space before a genuinely new range would be necessary, Jofeh always ignored. 'I wrote to him that we could sell 600cc and 750cc versions of the A65 twin, with minimum engineering input and the styling intact. But no ...' In the end only a couple of hundred 750 versions would be released late in the A65's oil-in-frame swansong.

Quite soon after he arrived, Jofeh told Wilf that the USA was just too big a market for export sales to handle, and that he would look after it personally. (The result would be the wholly-owned subsidiary organisation, BSA Inc, whose costs and extravagance contributed much to the final crash.) Wilf was told to handle the rest of the world, with the brief that in four years, orders in its stagnant markets should be increased to equal those in North America, which at that time was taking 85 per cent of export sales. 'In fact we did it in less,' Wilf smiled. By 1970, only £2.75 million of the £10 million export sales total would derive from the USA/Canada.

'Peter Glover and I developed a philosophy. Up till then, no one travelled – when Bill Rawson had once gone to Australia, it was such a big deal they made a film about it. We liked flying, and our thinking was to visit markets in person, and once we'd arrived, if we could then go on to somewhere else on the same trip, we'd do it. They were often amazed when we turned up, and we picked up a lot of business. We divided up the globe, with Peter as the African specialist – and West Africa was very much the Wild West; we used to say Peter started civil wars wherever he went! He was in Nigeria when the Biafra war broke out, and he nearly got locked up in Egypt. Our bikes were on their way to Libya when the king was deposed. And I went through Beirut airport the day after the Israelis had attacked it. We valued South African business enough to send Pickrell and Smart down there to race on the works triples.

'Peter developed the B25 Fleetstar, and we sold it to police and government departments all over the place. The Malaysian and the Australian armies took WD B40s. The Burmese Army had A50s; the Jordanian forces took Thunderbolts, and so did the Nigerians, but you had to be very careful with them to get the money. For civilian sales, once again we had a philosophy. There were the Western countries where practically everyone could afford a motorcycle (and the UK home market finally came good again around 1969–70). And then there were markets where only the "haves" could afford one, and these we targeted – South Africa, Malaysia, Mexico. Those markets would take mostly twins. We got in with a lot of machines in Mexico, but in 1970 we had to keep them waiting because there were no bikes being produced due to the chaotic reorganisation for the 1971 range. Then the next year they were overwhelmed with too many bikes, which swamped their financial set-up; but we were covered by export credit guarantees, and we got paid in the end. Another string to our bow was personal export, where US tourists could come over and buy motorcycles free of all UK duties, spend a summer touring Europe and then ship them home. The big dealers like Slocombes would even meet them in vans at Heathrow.'

'Tell me the name of your bike again, grandad ...'

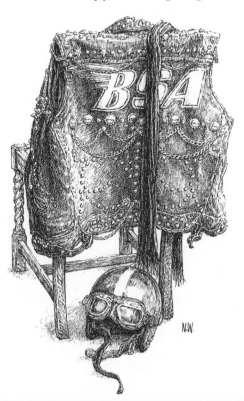

All too soon, however, the Group's chaotic situation intruded. In April 1971 Eric Turner sent for Wilf and said he wanted him to go back to the USA. What about Jofeh? Turner said that 'he hadn't yet told him, but that Jofeh wouldn't be around any more in June, when I was to go. This was very awkward, because I then had to live with that knowledge for months. In the end I only stayed in the States for six months, the deciding point being a 50-mile car journey with a consultant, during which I asked him what BSA's prospects were in America and he answered, effectively, that we didn't have a chance.'

Back in England late in 1971, Wilf discussed setting up the Harglo company with Peter Glover, but meanwhile he was given the job of general sales manager for the Group, operating out of a Portakabin at Meriden Triumph, as Small Heath was being run down. For the next few months he was often off round the world again, but it was 'a very unhappy time', with whispers of the Poore take-over circulating towards the end. In the summer of 1972 he phoned Dolly from New Zealand, and told her 'I'm weary. But I'm going on to Fiji.' 'No you're not,' he was told, 'you're to fly back to Amsterdam to meet Peter and the people from Batavus.' Glover had already resigned, and Harglo was launched, importing Batavus mopeds. After 23 years Wilf left BSA/Triumph, with no golden handshake of any kind. 'But at least we didn't get depressed at the fall of BSA; we never had time to be unhappy, because we'd created Harglo, we were our own bosses, and there was too much going on.'

So the 'young man interested in motorcycles' who answered that BSA advertisement in 1949, did indeed prove versatile.

CHAPTER SEVEN

My journeys IV: To Provence with Anneka

It was the best of times, it was the worst of times. It was the year I was to turn 50, the one which had started with the death of a beloved elder relative. And a couple of months after that, my partner had announced a radical new direction for her affections.

Since she, I and her 12-year-old daughter had recently moved into a beautiful 400-year-old country house where I had fully expected to pass the rest of my days, this was rather a body blow. With two failed marriages behind me and the big Five Oh looming, things looked a bit grim. Oh yes, and a couple of months after that, my 850 Commando, a stab at recapturing the good times I'd enjoyed on my previous 750, blew up big-style at speed on the M25.

At junctures like that you either get flattened or you bounce back. I sometimes felt that it went the latter way because something or someone was looking after me, but what I can say for sure is that I wouldn't have made it without the extraordinary kindness of friends like my best mate Carey in Ireland, like the Noble family who, as you will read, shared their holiday in Provence with my sorry self, and like Tony Miller, the mechanic who pulled out all the stops to make the trip down there a Go. It was Tony who had christened my moribund BSA A10 'Anneka' – because she had been a bit of a challenge, even for him, to rebuild into the sweet machine with which he eventually presented me.

And most of all I wouldn't have made it without my new girlfriend, Molly. What the piece doesn't say is that in Provence, during the evening out at a neighbouring village, I proposed to her, and was accepted – so no wonder Anneka then threw a wobbly!

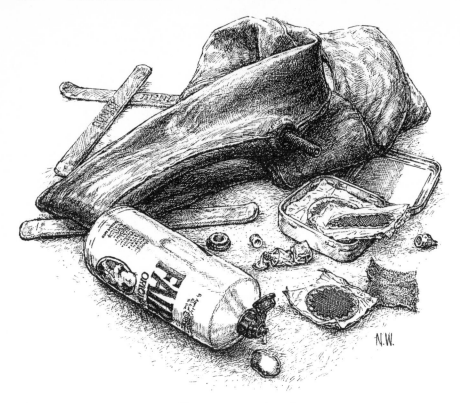

'Here we go again ...'

Well, the trip started with a bang. Even though the bang came a couple of months before I was due to leave for three-and-a-half week go-round in France. It was a dramatic concussion too, because when a rod lets go on your 850 Commando at 80mph in the fast lane of the M25 during the rush hour – you don't forget it in a hurry.

It meant that I was short of a mount for France, and by the time that became clear, there was less than a fortnight to go before the off. And I was particularly determined to make this trip. Firstly, France has always been my magic land. But I had not returned for some years, as my girlfriend hadn't liked the place. So I did wonder if, as some said, the country had changed.

Secondly, then came 1993, my personal *annus horribilis*, where a death in the family was followed by a painful break-up with the girlfriend and an enforced change of address. More than ever I felt I needed the revitalising French trip. Further, as the months went by, a new and very wonderful lady called Molly hove over the horizon, and after a while she agreed to fly out and join me for a long weekend in Provence. So this trip was definitely going to go ahead!

But on what? There was, of course, always my 1956 BSA A10, Anneka ... but though her cycle parts were sorted and she was a sweet ride round the local lanes, could the old girl really handle a couple of thousand miles to the sun and back? Tony Miller at Miller Motorcycles in Hastings, who had refurbished her so far, certainly thought so. With the days running short, I turned Anneka over to him to check the engine.

And the news went from predictably dire to potentially disastrous. The rear chain needed replacing, threads were clapped and one of the cylinder base studs missing. Then the barrels were lifted. The first cylinder liner proved to have large bite-size chunks missing from its lower edge. But when the second one came out – it revealed the fact that the thin-flange pre-'58 barrels themselves were cracked at the base on that side; not uncommon with high-mileage A10s.

If we hadn't known, she might have managed the trip like that anyway, but now we did … With a week and a bit to go, I got on the phone to the BSA twin specialists, SRM. Securicor delivered a new set of thick-flange barrels and pistons the next day. At a cost of a little under £250, these were unused but reject barrels; sound, but needing some work by Tony trimming rough lower edges and aligning stud holes. They were, of course, like the cylinder head, of iron, not alloy – and an all-iron engine is not the best formula for cool running.

This quickly became a matter of concern when, just two days later, Tony had the bike ready and I tried to rack up some running-in miles. The weather was warm, and soon, every ten or twelve miles, despite holding speed down to 50mph or less, the A10's engine would falter ominously until I had shut it down, and the boiling hot oil tank cooled a bit. On return to Millers, the GTX oil we had favoured for convenience was replaced by straight Castrol GP50. And re-reading the Pitmans manual, I now held the throttle opening to one-third, and speed to 45mph.

By the Saturday before the Monday on which I was leaving, I'd put in 200 steady miles, and there had been no recurrence of the severe overheating. So I was feeling a bit more optimistic when I stopped to fill the tank with English four-star (I had heard that in France, the price had topped £3 a gallon) – only to then notice petrol dripping down over the hot engine.

I drained a bit out, as it seemed to be coming from the top of the tank, and drove home carefully. Tony had always said that the original tank had been poorly re-welded and was liable to split. Millers had in stock one solitary can of Petseal, the stuff that secures tanks internally. I fetched it; and was also handed by Tony the correct socket head for the four bolts on the qd rear wheel, in case it would need to come off. The Petseal instructions spoke of trying the stuff out on a small area first, but since I only had 24 hours for it to work or not, I just plugged the tank's tap holes and filler orifice, mixed the tin of guck with the catalyst, poured it into the tank, and sloshed it around very thoroughly as recommended; then left for a 300-mile round trip by car, a last lightning rendezvous with Molly.

When I got back to Sussex on the Sunday afternoon, the Petseal hadn't hardened … and the thought of it mingling with the fuel and getting into the engine was not a pleasant one. On the phone again, Tony Miller proved himself a real friend. Within three hours he had borrowed a black replacement tank from a fellow A10 owner, and when I went to pick it up, Tony and his wife laid on a meal and hospitality so generous that I wasn't worrying about anything very much any more as I tottered away from their home. Of course, I still had to fit the tank, complete a last piece for *CBG*, finish packing, etc.

The run to Portsmouth the next morning was slow, and Anneka's power band was narrow, between lugging too slowly, labouring too fast, and pinking whenever the engine was under load. But though she did run hot, there was no recurrence of the faltering, and the weather was nice, and the P&O ferry folk their usual friendly selves.

It was 7pm local time when we finally docked in Cherbourg, and we were then kept waiting too long in the noisy, smelly upper car deck. I only had about 60 miles to go, as I was booked in at Le Grand Moulin Le Comte at Bacally outside Avranches, a rural B&B run by Brits Alan and Gwen Harvey. But all too soon rain began to fall, and it was dark, with the six-volt headlight fading and flaring on the throttle, by the time I spotted the large BSA sign fortuitously painted on the side of a furniture factory, which marked the turn-off for the Harveys' lane. Alan and Gwen were as hospitable as ever at the rambling mill, and Anneka was tucked away safely in a barn, out of the wet.

However, that Breton rain is penetrating stuff, and soon after setting off the next morning I realised that the throttle was sticking. The exact same thing had happened for the same reason to the cable on a mate's Triumph in Brittany, ten years previous. So stopping for petrol, I borrowed an oil can from the garage's workshop and spent an uncomfortably sweaty, messy, tense half-hour (oops, dropped the cable spacer again) dismantling the twist grip and attempting to force oil down the throttle cable. No-one was more surprised than moi when finally it worked, and the throttle freed off.

That day I rode across Normandy to the Loire. I had a week before joining friends in Provence, so I was giving myself a leisurely three or four days to cover the 800-odd miles to the South. It was harvest time, and in this rich arable country, patches of maize and sunflowers were interspersed with the grain fields. Enjoying the sights and smells as the day warmed up, we passed giant bailers, combines and tractors with trailers full of produce, all carrying orange flashing warning lights stuck up high on poles. Some fields were irrigated by long-necked watering devices that pumped spurts of water which the slanting light sometimes turned into rainbows. In the heat of the late afternoon, bum-sore from hours at a steady 45mph, Anneka and I were both glad to ride through the occasional arc of spray.

It was getting on for seven by the time we reached the little town of Châteauneuf sur Loire. I pushed on down to the river, and tottered stiffly off the bike. There was a small hotel overlooking the narrow suspension bridge and the dusty triangle where men were playing boules. Miraculously, the nice man running the hotel was glad to rent me a room, and there was a shed for Anneka.

The place was everything I had hoped for, and that evening, through the arched windows of its restaurant, France unfolded – the river and the trees on the other side, the deftness of the big lorries swinging on to the bridge, the many mopeds and bicyclists, one with a spectacular moustache (that funky French chic). And the meal. I had to check a nearby family to see what you did with the peppery fish soup and its attendant grated cheese, crumbly white toast and – mayonnaise? (Basically, you dumped it all in.) Not all the food was first rate, but the ambience was so fine, and for around £15 for four courses including a beer and a jug of wine, I wasn't complaining. My gluttony was rewarded by the traditional severe indigestion all night.

Next day was less interesting. I followed the river Loire south, but some of it was depressingly industrial, culminating in a nuclear power station. I missed my way out of Nevers and soon stopped deliberately in the shade for 20 minutes, topping up with a pint of oil, as the bike felt jaded and the oil tank was very hot indeed. By the evening we had covered over 300 miles, the country had changed to pleasant hills full of pale Charollais cattle, and after an extended, frustrating hunt for a hotel, I was lucky to find a nice one off a bypass south of Roanne, the last big town before Lyons. The proprietor cleared his own garage, where he had been tinkering with a collection of tiny old Fiat Cinquecentos, to get Anneka under cover – just as well, as it rained in the night.

Next day, the third, was the big challenge – over 250 miles round Lyons, up to Grenoble, and through the French Alps down the Route Napoleon, the N75, to Haute Provence and Riez, my intended first destination. Would Anneka manage the climbs? She seemed OK on the quite steep pull on the way from Roanne to Lyons, though plodding up in third with little in reserve rather than flying up in top as a good twin should. At town lights, once the engine was hot she was spontaneously over-revving at tickover in neutral, so that changing into first meant a fearful clang. Compensations were that then, and for the whole trip, a well-sorted magneto meant she started first or second kick every time; the riding position was comfortable; and she was returning around 65 miles to the expensive gallon, to which I was adding a drop of Redex. Our lack of the legally required daytime lights did not prove to be a live issue, as although some motorists flashed, plenty of other bikers weren't bothering and neither were the police.

The Lyons suburbs were successfully skirted, largely thanks to the excellent continuous *Flèche Verte* (Green Arrow) signs, which were already indicating a non-motorway route to Grenoble. As we approached that city, the weather ahead was menacing, visibly blowing sheets of rain over the mountain tops, but it opened out almost miraculously, as an unavoidable motorway led us around Grenoble and up to the start of the Route Napoleon.

This road proved to be less of a challenge than anticipated. True, there were some climbs to start with, but none of the sheer drops and hairy hairpins I remembered from before, just a fine mountain backdrop – and plenty of traffic. I ended up, all too emblematically, stuck behind a Harley being trailered down to the coast (though later, on a day out along the Côte d'Azur when I saw the Harley pilots risk life, limb, and £10–£20,000 of brute metal to play contrapuntal chicken with the traffic while dressed in just shorts and tank tops, I had to grudgingly admire their crazed pursuit of the proper style at whatever cost).

As the afternoon wore on and the N75/N85 dropped down out of the mountains, it also started to get seriously hot. I began a progressive striptease which lasted several days: scarf off, then shirt off, just a tee-shirt under the Barbour jacket, which got unfastened at neck and cuffs, then the anti-chafe cravat off, heavy gloves replaced by light, jacket replaced by just shirt, and so on. (But never down to shorts!) Through Sisteron and Digne it got hotter and hotter, and the August traffic to the coast thickened up.

This included many small packs of bikes, mostly big trailies, Honda Dominators or Transalps and GS boxer BMWs, usually with at least one ridden by a girl. On the winding roads I would occasionally find myself ahead of some of these dudes; Anneka handled herself unfailingly well round the swervery, even loaded up. Soon, though, the packs would become understandably impatient with our 45–50mph speed on the straights and zip by, always with friendly waves, but it got a little depressing to be the oldest and the slowest every time. Increasingly Anneka and I harked back to her Scandinavian origins: ve vanted to be aloone.

This came to pass around 6.30, when with great relief we turned off the busy N85, with less than 30 miles to go to Riez. Instantly it was a different world, the quiet, bumpy back-roads climbing and dipping through forested slopes in the evening light. We were climbing one such, savouring the smell of pine needles and the knowledge that after a hard day there were less than ten miles to go – when the clutch cable snapped.

'It could be worse,' I thought, standing by the bike pulled over at a beautiful wooded spot, shaking with tiredness. I fetched out the spare cable Tony Miller had made up (the lengths are unconventional because of Anneka's high bars). As carefully as I could, I began to fit it. The casing of the old cable was broken open – I had pinched it when fitting the replacement tank, which explained the cable snapping. Oh no, oh no, the replacement cable inner seemed too short – but once I had undone the lever pivot bolt on the handlebar, it proved to fit just perfectly.

I left the cable looping loose under the rubber tank bag straps, and, perspiring but with a flush of shaky self-satisfaction, proceeded gently, you can believe, in the evening light up the hill, across a plateau, through a nice-looking little town which I clocked for future reference, and down a twisting hill road to Riez. No sweat.

But it was not to be. The town turned out to be touristic bedlam which had me turning round and riding straight out again. The clutch was also proving harder and harder to operate. I returned to the nice little town, Puimoisson. But its only restaurant with rooms was full.

This was the downside of the free-form approach to accommodation – the dark was coming on, I was in fashionable Provence (thank you, Peter Mayles) at the height of the hols with no room at the inn, fierce signs prohibiting *Camping Sauvage* (dossing down), and both bike and rider knackered. In desperation, I took a side road with a sign announcing camping and caravanning at a village 7km away. In the clear twilight we droned across an empty plateau towards the silhouette of mountains with the

Communing with nature.

lights of the village, St Jurs, set in the foothills. The place itself yielded nothing, so I returned to the campsite I had passed on the way in.

A pleasant, soft-spoken guy regretted they had nothing to rent, but when I pleaded, thought he'd better ask his wife, since as he explained he was principally a farmer, growing lavender (*la*-veng-*dre*, in the strong Provençal twang, and indeed its fragrance came from the arid fields all around). His wife, sitting on their porch finishing a supper of melons, was a tough, quizzical blonde, but turned out to have just the thing, a solo caravan to rent for two nights at around £3.50 a night. Yes! Soon I was parked up, showered, and enjoying a supper of melted Toblerone, duty-free cognac, and Evian water, looking up at a clear sky full of stars.

First thing next morning I did my best to fettle the clutch, oiling the cable, carefully re-routing it under the tank and fastening it with cable ties, before walking into the village for breakfast. The views of the mountains ahead were spectacular, with the first glider being towed by light plane towards the thermals over the peaks. Soon I counted up to seven circling at one time, wheeling like white gulls in the silence against a peerless blue sky.

Next I rode back to Puimoisson and booked a room at the restaurant. The clutch was soon a depressingly stiff pull again. In Riez, after bank, postcards and phoning friends, I sat in the shade sipping a cold one and deciding the town wasn't so bad, when I noticed that Anneka's horn was dangling, where its bracket had broken.

But it was too hot to worry about that, other than taping it up. The grindingly stiff clutch action was more bothersome, though, since it felt as if the cable might snap, and I had no replacement now. So riding in the warm wind to an artificial lake nearby for a swim, I tried clutchless changes – and the lovely winding roads, some now with melted tar on their bends, needed quite a lot of changes. I had only read about the clutchless technique in old road tests, and I proved uneven at it – changes were sometimes smooth and silent, but often a fearful jerking clang. The swimming too proved a mixed blessing, for though the water was warm and refreshing, it was a shade awkward to be a single middle-aged foreigner arriving in trunks and motorcycle boots (I'd changed in the woods) on a small beach full of topless young couples.

In the afternoon, back at the hot campsite, I went to work on the bike again, attempting to ease the stiffness by adjustment at the clutch end. Nothing doing, and eventually, to gain more play, I even carefully cut an inch off the cable's outer casing. Still no joy; I reckoned the clutch pushrod was the problem. It was a worry, but one which the cooler evening sky, and supper in St Jurs with rose wine, helped to dissipate. But walking back under the starry sky, I was missing Molly. Still, I'd arranged to meet some other friends the following day.

The next morning, a Saturday, I had the bike loaded and was riding off across the campsite grass, when I noticed something funny about the rear end handling. The surface? The luggage? Nope – the rear wheel puncture …

I knew I had to get to Puimoisson, both for the meet with my friends and because there was a car garage there which might help. So after a desperate struggle to lean the bike against a post-box, I fished out the Finilec puncture foam aerosol and inflated the tyre (at which point, as the cover swelled, the loaded bike dislodged itself from the post-box and tried to fall over). Then with an initial fish-tail, I set off quickly to whirl the foam around the inner tube as recommended, and at a steady 30 with a semi-inflated rear tyre, rode the seven anxious kilometres into town.

The car garage felt they couldn't help, and in fact, it wouldn't have been any good if they had, since the culprit would prove to be a four inch long splinter of hard wood which had ripped open the inner tube beyond hope of repair. And in the interests of lightening Anneka's load, for the first long trip in years, I had come away without spare inner tubes. But the garage boss was friendly and rang a bike place 30 miles away. Yes, if I could get the wheel to them they had an inner tube (*chambre*). With the tyre inflated on the air line and apparently holding, I rode to the hotel, parked up and walked off for a long lunch with my friends.

Bad move. When I got back the tyre was completely flat, oozing white Finilec round the edges, and couldn't be re-inflated. I would have to remove the wheel and get it over there some other way. And it was too late in the afternoon to do that, so I was stuck in Puimoisson till Monday (Tuesday, as it turned out, because like many French places, the bike shops were closed the day after the weekend).

Still, there were a lot worse places to be stuck. The Auberge La Michade, named after Micha Schons, the proprietor's wife and chef, provided a pleasant bedroom and *cuisine soignée* (elegant grub) in a cool tile-floored restaurant with good wine, nice linen, and a stylish atmosphere; it was never less than a pleasure, a peculiarly French one, to hear the way the talk rose in the room as the guests got into their meal. And over the days, several of them would be touring motorcyclists.

Then there was a garage for Anneka. And in there I could remove the rear wheel with no-one to observe my difficulties with the brake torque arm (one nut wouldn't budge, so I just bent the arm out of place), my uncertainties disconnecting the cable, and my struggle with tight bolts; I would have been lost without the socket head which Tony Miller had provided. Also the fun of tilting the bike and easing the wheel out without toppling the BSA off its centre stand. Luckily the unflappable M Schons readily provided me with the right size plank to put under the centre stand while replacing the wheel, which made the job comparatively easy.

And there was the telephone at the auberge; a chat with Molly perked me right up, and I also rang Tony Miller. He quickly and calmly diagnosed the clutch trouble as primarily overheating, and we arranged for him to send a couple of spare cables and a clutch pushrod and adjuster to my next and main destination.

This was real reassurance. I slept well, and so evidently did Anneka in the cool garage, for when I tried the clutch on Tuesday morning, it was working fine. The village taxi-driver had departed with the wheel, and I fretted as the hours passed from the time he'd said he would be back, as I had 60 miles to do to the hill town where I was joining up with my friends that evening. But at 4.30 the taxi returned; the guy had had to try three different places to locate the necessary 19-inch inner tube, not a regular size in France. In an hour I had the wheel on, the bike loaded and was waving goodbye to the Schons – I can still taste Micha's Poulet Provençale.

It was quite a long run down to Draguignan and up into the hills to Bargemon, and the A10 still had to be coaxed up the steeper slopes, some of which were smouldering from a recent forest fire. But we made it, and from then on, as I rendezvoused with the Noble family and we enjoyed a hilarious dinner together by the fountain in Bargemon's main square, with the Noble's kindness and back-up, the pressure was off, and the real holiday began. Bargemon is so good I'm not even going to talk about it much; we were staying in a rented house built into the walls of the old chateau, with the use of a large and idyllic pool set above terraces of olive trees and looking off down the valley. Paradise.

After a couple of illicit days parked in the chateau courtyard (no vehicles permitted, but Anneka was more than a vehicle), once again the bike got garage parking; just as well, as she had begun to weep oil rather embarrassingly. I took her out to change the oil in a lay-by, filling up with the fresh GP50 which the Nobles had brought down for me. And Anneka got her portrait painted by Amelia Noble, an artist like her parents.

There was also a longer trip, starting in the cool of the morning which the engine really appreciated, back into the hills and round the side of the spectacular canyon, the Gorge de Verdon. We enjoyed cool shadows and near-empty roads riding along to that artificial Lac de Sainte Croix, where at lunch with some other friends I watched the lumbering *Canardes d'Air* propeller planes swooping down on the lake to scoop up water for fire-fighting; tough bananas for any swimmers and wind surfers who didn't know what the three-blast warning on the klaxon had meant – you've all heard the story of the flippers and aqualung found where a fire had been? The trip back along the southern edge of the gorge provided even more dramatic views, but by then the winding road was clogged with traffic.

Anneka had performed well enough on that hundred-mile day to make me risk using her to collect Molly from Nice airport the following weekend. Anneka obviously got jealous about this in advance, for as I was putting a little air in the tyres, her hot exhaust pipe nipped me viciously on the elbow. But she ran well in the early morning down from the hills and along the motorway to the airport, and carried Molly and her luggage (four pairs of shoes for two-and-a-half days?) safely back to Bargemon, though the motorway climbs got the engine a little hot and bothered. It was Molly's first time ever on a motorbike, and she really liked it, even saying she was glad the bike wasn't too fast while she was getting used to it. Well that was true.

On our final evening we rode out to eat at a village only some 5km away, but the whole five wound down to a valley and then steeply up again.

Leaving Bargemon, we fell in behind a modern bike with a lightly dressed *pillioniste* who kept looking back coolly over her shoulder at us in a provocative manner. No way were we going to be left behind! Unfortunately the A10's rather tired suspension units were only set to the middle position, and the combination of a passenger plus bumpy downhill roads meant that on a couple of left-handers we noisily grounded the centre-stand extension, forcefully enough to put a ding in the silencer. Molly, quite correctly, yelled at me to stop showing off.

The dinner outdoors as night fell was as romantic as you could wish for, and with Anneka parked safely within view, Molly and I made some plans for the future. However the jealous cow (Anneka) must have overheard us, since on the way back, about halfway down the winding hill, all the lights went out. This was, ah, disconcerting, a Blues Brothers moment as it was a dark night, we were both wearing sunglasses and even the rear reflector had dropped off by then. I somehow kept the bike between the ditches until we reached the bridge at the bottom – when the lights came on again. We crept up the hill and home. Back in Blighty Tony Miller would tell me: 'I know what happened – Anneka told me. You and Molly were bouncing up and down on her, weren't you?' The base of the non-standard seat had made contact with the top of the battery and partially shorted out the fuse …

Molly left safely, and then it was time to head for home. I was so thoroughly restored by then that though I knew the journey was not likely to be trouble-free, I felt quite serene about the return haul. Leaving really early, we traversed the great sweeps of inland Provence and by early afternoon had crossed the Rhone. Junking my worked-out route, we then followed 'Green Arrow' signs towards Dijon, even though they led us up a 6,000-foot mountain climb, and then down again to Clermont-Ferrand.

After 300 miles I stopped the night at the same friendly place at Roanne, and with the Provençal weather just a memory, set out in wind and misty rain the next morning, the lack of headlights being rather a disadvantage. The oil weep was now becoming a bit serious, too. It was from the right hand side below the oil tank, and I couldn't decide if it was a loose oil-line connection, a split in the tank (dread), or the breather pipe (it proved to be the last, aggravated by the heat, and the pipe is now routed to the rear mudguard).

The oil level in the tank was low, and at a filling station I topped up with 20/50, while whingeing about the weather to the rider of a chopped 650 Yamaha who replied coolly '*Non, non, c'est agréable*'. Halfway through the day, almost imperceptibly, the gearchange intermittently stopped working unless, as I soon discovered, you nudged it gently from underneath. The spring had broken (weakened by those clutchless changes?) and this, plus the furious over-revving tickover, didn't help when we finally got caught up in a two-mile traffic jam caused by 'road improvements' in Orleans. But we snaked and slithered through, the clutch performing particularly impressively under all demands, and put in another 300-mile day.

Worth it, because 180 miles later, by 2pm the next day, to avoid a night run in England, we were at Calais, not Cherbourg, where the nice P&O people swapped our ticket with no problem, and got us on a ferry which pulled out 15 minutes later! Not before time, as despite bandages of paper napkin, oil was now finding its way onto the side-wall of the back tyre. That afternoon, 2,122 miles after departure, we were home.

Anneka had done well, but in honesty I had enjoyed the trip in spite of rather than because of her. Even when run in, the engine had pinked badly at any hint of a gradient or even a head-wind, and this plus restricted speeds had been tedious on the long straights; while the lack of reliable power hadn't allowed much enjoyment of the twisting hill roads, which really needed a ready motor to ride round them. Apparently there had been complaints about pinking on French four-star from a number of bikers that summer. With a tank full of Jet, some adjustments to the carburation, and the timing backed off very slightly, Tony Miller has now virtually cured the problem.

And I have no fundamental complaints. Under rushed circumstances, Anneka got me down there and got me back; even when she was sidelined, it turned out for the best. And the long slow journey had let me absorb a sense of France's abundance. The majestic or clever meals, different wine, the chic in so many little things, village squares, fountains, shady trees, organic architecture, the sights and smells – I could go on. France is still there.

'Right then, running weak – er ...'

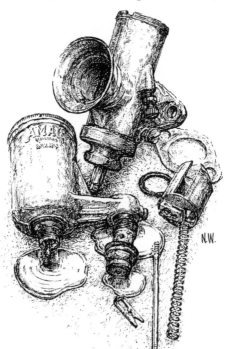

Conclusion

I still have Anneka the A10. In fact I believe that she will be the last bike that I'll let go, if I ever do at all. But though I'm old enough now to know better, and thanks to Molly a father as well, in the past few years I also seem to have had an unabated obsession with unit BSA twins. In fairly short order I've owned a '72 oil-in-frame 650, beautifully done up for me by marque specialists SRM, and, though an electrical glitch let me down on the way home from another French trip, a good runner – so naturally I sold it on, to Cyril Ayton, ex-editor of *Motor Cycle Sport*. That was to finance work on another oil-in-frame A65, one with a 750 big bore conversion by Devimead, the former specialists. A flaw in the bores meant that it had to be re-sleeved, and when it had been, and was pulling like a train – I sold it on, so I could get the 'modern'.

Before dealing with the current follies, there are some instructive contradictions to consider about these unit twins with 'the water-melon engines'. In their day, as already mentioned, they were very much the low men on the Norton/Triumph/BSA totem pole of parallel twins. And in the late seventies, when the classic movement was just starting up and old motorcycles were still cheap, they were consequently very cheap indeed.

There remained the question of why one bothered with the unit twins at all, when, for not a lot more money, you could have a pre-unit sweetie like Anneka. Especially when a seasoned rider like the late Ken Craven (he of the excellent Craven panniers), after a troubled trip in the sixties on an A65 outfit across the burning lands of Texas and Mexico, observed crossly that

'the egg-shaped engine mass is a highly efficient heat storage unit – a point against unit construction.' But an oil cooler can help there, and the real-world point of the short-stroke unit twins is that, in my experience, on the road they're about 10mph faster throughout the range than the admittedly more congenial pre-units.

It had also soon dawned on a few of us that the unit twin's original major problems (a trouble-prone timing side main bearing, and electrical difficulties causing erratic ignition timing), could be remedied by, respectively, conversions from the specialist companies Devimead or SRM, and electronic ignition. Conventional wisdom also said that twin carburettors were fiddly to adjust and brought little performance gain, so that single carb versions were the ones to go for; and that high compression models like the Spitfire were to be avoided due to their equally high levels of vibration.

But ... the hardest thing to nail down, in this game, as in so many others, is a solid fact. My first oil-in-frame A65, with single carb and compression reduced to a modest 7.5:1, was as flat as a fart. My next, the '62 Star Twin featured in chapters 1 and 3, covered the 10,000 miles during my ownership with no timing side conversion at all, just a new bush, and gave no trouble in that department whatsoever. (In fact it has been suggested that the real value of the end-fed crank conversion is its use on crankshafts which are badly worn.) And the best unit twins I ever rode on test were an SRM '65 twin carburettor Lightning with their 750 conversion and X-65 body kit; and an export '68 Spitfire Mk IV, twin carb again, that had once belonged to Robert Plant of Led Zeppelin – and which felt to be the smoothest runner of them all, something that had also been written of the even higher compression Mk III, in US road tests at the time. Strange but true.

Perhaps the bottom line with them all, however, goes back to the original low-man-on-the-totem judgement. In practice none have proved very reliable, and that also goes for the reimported-from-America desert sled '66 Hornet, plus the '70 A50 Royal Star 500, both currently languishing in my shed. Of course, I know it's unreasonable to expect that a range where the youngest machine is now over 25 years old, *could* be completely reliable, and they are probably no worse than their Norton or Triumph equivalents from the sixties. The Nortons handle better and Triumphs are livelier, though the core BSA virtue of durability means that they do well over the years. But fifties bikes like Anneka and the M21 tend to do even better, with magneto ignition, separate gearboxes and engines in lower states of tune, though it's swings and roundabouts because they are also heavier and slower. And the sixties as a decade was the Time of my Time.

In the end, the real question remains the one posed in the introduction: why keep doing it? That neurotic inability to learn from experience, perhaps? Or is it something more fundamental, like the percentage of birds recorded in the natural history classic *The Life of the Robin*, who would fly into a baited trap again and again, even after they had been caught in it and released several times? Sometimes I think it's just that 'low man' status about these BSAs that attracts me – they're losers' bikes. 'Loser' in the film *The Wild Angels* was always my favourite name for a fictional character, apart from the gambler in *Guys and Dolls* called 'Regret'.

I keep a record of expenses on all my machines, and those little notebooks make pretty gruesome reading. I've hardly ever made any money on an old bike, and the cheapest to buy have usually ended up costing the most. Classics are rarely going to be worth what you pay to get them even into decent running order, let alone fully restored. So why do it? Are we back where we started, with Mavis and 'too stupid to ride anything else'?

Maybe. We certainly don't do it for the money, so I guess we do it just to do it. And I for one certainly can't help it. Why? Because I feel at home on a British bike. And it's been a life, a sort of a life, and, despite all, not a bad one – the long, lonely roads, and the people you meet on the way. Such as the ones you've read about in this book.

Nick Ward:
A portrait of the artist

Nick Ward lives out on the edge. The first time I met him, driving up before Christmas to the Norfolk coast above Great Yarmouth, I was reminded just how bleak the eastern county is, and just how long the distances can be.

Passing a field full of vast white wind-turbine windmills like children's beach toys stuck upright in the mud, I absorbed the Quixote-like echo while recalling that the county's motto was 'Do Different'. Would this prove to be appropriate for an artist much of whose work celebrated the ragged glory of machinery in dereliction?

But any attempt to type-cast Nicholas Ward RE as a demented genius was doomed to failure, even if his garden was littered with half a dozen derelict British cars, and his numerous sheds ('I'm a "seven-shed" man …') were stuffed with side-valve motorcycles, lightweights and cyclemotors – he's an active member of the National Autocycle and Cyclemotor Club, or 'Sad Persons Club' as he jokingly referred to it. Among the many lightweights was a scarlet and cream Excelsior Autobyk. 'One of those, in 1967, was my first ever bike. I had it for ten years; it was already well-worn, and it was on that I learned how to do roadside repairs. And now I've got another – you never learn, do you?'

There was not much of the Sad Person about Nick. There was no morbidity and precious little sentimentality about his choice of subject matter, either. Nick grew up in East Anglia, and salvaging unwanted machinery from rubbish tips as a kid, or hauling it from bushes and ponds, seemed a natural thing to do. His grandfather was a farmer who kept his tractor as highly polished as a saloon car, while his uncle rode a Bantam (there's a great photo of a very young Nick being taken for a ride on its tank), and ran a hot A10 in the fifties. He was a local legend for achieving a particular run on A roads from Great Yarmouth without once dropping below 90mph.

The cars in the garden were not just junk, but a response to Nick realising that his subject matter was drying up. 'I started doing this, derelict vehicles in natural settings, around 1980 – previously it had gone no further than landscapes with tractors and so on. But soon I realised that the old vehicles were going, fast. Some had gone between one visit and the next, I'd come back to find they'd been dragged away or cut up. That's why I started putting them in the garden, where they could rust in peace, as it were.'

At that period Nick was still using a BSA M21-powered sidecar outfit as his only transport. Already a graduate of St Martin's School of Art, a post-graduate at the Royal Academy and the winner of awards and medals for landscape drawing, Nick's sidecar in its way was an equally impressive achievement. Now 'resting' in the garden, the massive 2x6½ft plywood box in its heyday sported rails along its edges, and big chrome saloon car bumpers with over-riders plus a horn at the front. Nick had built it large enough to transport an entire exhibition of framed pictures. And once, when he and his wife Liz moved house, he carried a three-piece suite on it. Painted funereal black, people tended to give the outfit a wide berth …

'One night I took a mate home in it after he'd got dead drunk. He'd laid down in the box and closed the lid, and despite the M21's motor thudding along beside his head, when I got him home and lifted the lid, he was fast asleep. When the neighbours saw this figure finally emerge from the box in the middle of the night, they thought he was a vampire …'

Despite being used as his only transport for so long, that original M21 never let him down. 'I was the thirteenth owner, including one in Northern Ireland, and the bike is still going, as far as I know. During the petrol shortages in the late seventies I ran it on 30 per cent paraffin mix; it went OK, though the engine joints used to ooze a little oil and it made a funny smell.'

He also ran an ex W.D. M20 solo, but found the 500cc was never as free-running as the 600cc. 'With a sidecar attached you really notice the extra 100cc. I like side-valves – low tech, low maintenance, and nothing in them goes round too quickly.'

Nick's biking-only days came to an end after 14 years, returning home one Christmastime at night on the M20. He had checked for black ice, but had forgotten about the frozen sea spray on the promenade at Yarmouth. He came off abruptly, ending up still in The Position, with his hands on the bars, but now horizontal, and with his head inches from the kerb. 'I thought, 'I'm getting too old for this', so I took my first driving lesson the following week, and became a softie.' But Nick still liked his side-valves. His current star machine was a rare 1955 rigid 600cc Ariel VB. 'It's more sporting, and you can tell when you work on one that they were designed by people who cared.'

Nick did the running repairs on his own bikes, but, not unnaturally for an artist, really enjoyed the painting and finishing. 'After a day's artwork, when you're not sure if you've done it right or wrong, because there is no right and wrong, it's really nice to line a tank where there's only one way to do it properly.' He lines freehand, saying the secret is in the consistency of the paint. He favours humble Humbrol and a nice new half-inch brush; 'someone once swore a tank I'd hand-painted must have been sprayed.' In fact Nick may be a bit of an eccentric, but everything he does is done competently. This is certainly true of his press, which he's mounted on a tramway in the floor of shed No 1 so he can push it around. He uses the press to produce the limited editions of prints from his etchings; 'an intaglio method of print making, which means that ink is retained in grooves that have been bitten into a metal surface with acid, the top surface remaining clean. Under pressure, the paper is forced into the grooves to pick up the

'… very eager to get it stripped down …'

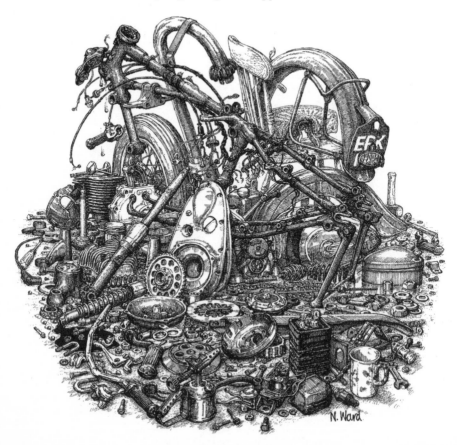

'… this year's present was a complete mystery …'

ink.' The pressure is supplied by the large press, with its maker's plate from 'Harry F. Rochat Ltd, Moxon Street, Barnet, England'. But despite its antique air, the press is 'fairly new. He still makes them as they were in Victorian times,' said Nick, who compares the simplicity of the press to side-valve technology.

Nick Ward's own words, written to accompany an exhibition, explain why he favoured the relatively complex technique of etching:

'At 17 I enrolled on a pre-diploma course at Art School and also purchased my first motorbike. For the next 25 years, motorcycles played an indirect part in subsequent endeavours: much of my preferred subject matter was first seen from a motorbike saddle: gasometers, abandoned junk in the landscape, corroding farm implements, derelict industrial machinery. But once any (motorcycle) drawings were initiated, pencils would soon be dropped in favour of spanners as the bikes' mechanical shortcomings became apparent.

'By the time a test ride was completed, artwork would be long-abandoned or covered with oil spatters and tyre tracks.

'It was not until 1993 that I first drew a motorcycle without distraction or interruption. The immaculate Brough Superior had belonged to a friend who died tragically in an accident. Being familiar with the subject, I now had the opportunity to observe it at leisure without the temptation to tinker. Despite the sad circumstances, this study proved immensely absorbing and resulted in an etching which helped to raise money for a memorial fund.

'Later, I treated my BSA Bantam to a bout of maintenance. Anyone who has owned a Bantam will know that the amount of time and temper involved in making it run properly is out of all proportion to the net result. So, taking a break from repeated, futile kick-starting, I looked at the clutter of grubby parts, tools, and empty mugs – and realised what I saw was actually a still-

'… and a quick wipe over with an oily rag before the MOT …'

life telling the whole sorry story. This time, artistic desire overcame the drive for mechanical perfection and the ensuing etching caused me to embark on a series of motorcycle prints: etchings on zinc plate.

'The enthusiasm with which these images were received surprised me. (It seems there are lots of ex-tearaways masquerading as respectable citizens!) With funding from sales I was able to buy derelict machines specifically for drawing, and fellow enthusiasts have been particularly generous – loaning their vehicles.

'However, it is the choice of surroundings that sometimes causes consternation – a specially assembled environment is always in danger of appearing contrived.

'Recently I purchased an Ariel which had been exported to India, when new, 40 years ago – and deserved a typically British scene to depict its homecoming. Deciding that a big puddle might be appropriate, I constructed a dam so that the backyard could be flooded. I chopped logs to build a woodpile; and added dustbins, flower pots and a bucket of coal, before the bike was finally wheeled into a setting which, I hoped, contrasted with its former location.

'Incidentally, the original Bantam, perhaps realising that life as an artist's

'… apparently it had only failed the MOT on a bald tyre …'

model was preferable to being thrashed along muddy lanes, refused to start and was sold the following week …'

The question remained, particularly after seeing his wonderful preliminary drawings – why choose the relatively diminutive 6 x 4-inch etchings as the medium? Nick explained that he was careful to 'produce escape routes for the viewer's eye, to allow the vision to wander off the plate. You must allow people to travel off around walls and into reflections. With images this small it is vitally important to avoid claustrophobia. You have to avoid the temptation to overwork the plate and fill everything in.' But why so small in the first place? 'The images have to be small to match their importance,' Nick had said bluntly. 'A scrap car is not an earth-shattering image, after all.' To me he added, 'I like the etchings because you can take in a composition at a glance, yet closer up, see all the detail, which on a larger drawing or painting might get lost.'

Nick might have been modest enough not to consider his automotive imagery 'earth-shattering', but it did please people. At the Art in Action exhibitions in which he participated, he enjoyed watching dads and sons being dragged in to look at pictures by their art-loving ladies, then registering the old cars and bikes, and eventually having to be dragged away themselves as they pored over the details and enjoyed the memories these images evoked.

A selection of Nick Ward's current etchings is on permanent display at the Royal Society of Painter-Printmakers, Bankside Gallery, 48 Hopton Street, London SE1 9JH (next to Tate Modern), tel: 0207 928 7521, fax: 0207 928 2820.

'... you never learn, do you?'

Index